ESSAYS ON
THE NEW WORKING CLASS

by Serge Mallet

Edited and Translated
by Dick Howard and Dean Savage

Preface by Dick Howard

TELOS PRESS • ST. LOUIS

TABLE OF CONTENTS

Editors' Introduction

Serge Mallet often wondered why his writings were never translated into English. Several hypotheses could be offered. His best known volume, *The New Working Class* (1963) contained a lengthy theoretical-historical essay, followed by three sociological case studies. The method applied in these latter as well as the political conclusions drawn were not up to the demanded Anglo-Saxon empirical level; and the subject matter—specific French firms—was unknown to the general English-speaking reader. It appeared, moreover, that it was the Anglo-Saxons, not the French, who were the "advanced" capitalist countries (with the most advanced internal contradictions). The same is even more true of Mallet's important studies in *The Peasants Against the Past* (1962). His work as a political and sociological journalist was centered on France, again limiting its appeal. One could add that his political engagement which affected his style, subject-matter and conclusions could not find appeal in a society which thought it had reached the "end of ideology." When the theme of the "new working class" was spoken of in the Anglo-Saxon world, it was either empiricized and purified or labelled and criticized.

From the practical standpoint (of commercial publishers, or even a then-growing movement), one understands the neglect of Mallet—yet it seems erroneous. In discussing with him the project for this book, we agreed that its title would tell the story. On the one hand, the theme of the new working class; but from the socialist perspective. It is this latter which colors Mallet's analyses, gives them their coherence and defines their validity. Mallet does not present a firm, fixed and repeatable analysis; not a series of facts, a representation of the world. His views change with their object, as he himself underlines in the "Preface" to the 1971 collection of his writings in *Le pouvoir ouvrier* (printed here). The analysis aims at influencing its object, and must remain a step ahead of it. As with his model, Marx, this character opens him to the cavelling of the academic critic — was the Paris Commune "really" what Marx said it was? — ; but such is Mallet's option. It is through reading his work with an eye to this option and the way it affects his analyses that the reader will gain from this book.

Serge Mallet died prematurely, before seeing this volume in print. He had contributed greatly to its realization. He discussed the choice of articles; helped with the textual apparatus (footnotes, glossary, technical terms, and the map of the locations of the firms dealt with). A lengthy interview over two days with Dick Howard was to have provided the Preface to the volume — in its place, we are printing as a Preface Howard's commemorative essay, first published in *Telos*, Summer, 1974.

The translations of the "Preface" to *Le pouvoir ouvrier* and "Workers' Control, Party and Union," were done by Dick Howard. The others are the work of Dean Savage. Each of us checked the work of the other. Each added materials to the footnotes and glossary. Materials listed in the glossary are those which appear more often in the various essays; other information is provided in editorial footnotes to each essay. Since the number of these latter was greater than that of Mallet's notes, we have left our editorial footnotes unmarked, and added the initials SM following those of Mallet.

It is no use to again express the feeling of loss and grief evoked by Mallet's death. His work was a project, ongoing and incomplete. It is to be taken up.

Preface

The work of Serge Mallet — brutally interrupted as it was entering a new phase — was not well known in the United States. Many of us knew the name, associated with the label "new working class," which he coined. Few had read his work, and fewer knew the man and the movement behind it. His sudden death in a car accident stops the work and makes it into a theoretical *corpus*. The turning point in his work is May 1968. Untypical of the Parisian politico-intellectual, Mallet was a fish-in-the-water: he lived May '68 from the inside, not simply as a member of the Political Bureau of the PSU. May seemed to him at once the confirmation of the tendencies discovered and analyzed in his work, and the impetus to a new stage of struggle and of theory. The abstract notion of workers' control began to take on a concrete form; the question of the party-union relation was posed in a practical form; new strata entered the struggle, and new modes of political relations developed. The post-May period has been in large part marked by a recrudescence of class struggle, sparked now by the unskilled and immigrant laborers. While this might seem to contradict the "new working class" analysis, for Mallet — a political militant far more than an abstract theorist — it in fact shows a different strategy of the same capitalism which, in its period of forced modernization under De Gaulle, created the "new working class" and structured it as a political vanguard. The contradiction is not between two theories, but rather in the different responses of one, self-contradictory, system to the class struggle. For Mallet, as for Marx, the point is not simply to understand it but to change it.

Mallet's sociological work is situated within the context of a reorientation in France during the 1950s which recognized that, under the influence of what it is not unfair to call the "Stalinist Metaphysics of the Working Class," the proletariat had been reified and theorized as a kind of philosophical Thing-In-Itself, fixed once and for all by the Doctrine. The real, living and struggling working class, had to be rediscovered. The "metaphysical" view, insisted

Mallet, characterized not only the Communist Party, but also "left" groups such as the Trotskyists, for whom the class is monolithic, revolutionary in its heart of hearts, but duped by the bad leaders, and still constantly ready to recreate scenes from 1871, 1917, and the other Holy Days of the Revolutionary Calendar. Sociologists like Alain Touraine (in *L'evolution du travail ouvrier aux usines Renault*) and Georges Friedmann (in *Le travail en miettes*), along with their teams of co-workers, took it upon themselves to study the concrete changes introduced by the changing structures of capitalist industry. The work of these sociologists was, however, situated in an academic milieu, and read mainly by specialists. Moreover, the industrial sociology they founded concerned itself only secondarily with day-to-day political and tactical implications. In this sense, Mallet's writing is related to theirs but stands apart in a crucial sense: it is the reflection of a militant on his own experiences and those of the workers, and it stands rather with the work of two other militants, published at the same time: Pierre Belleville (*Une nouvelle classe ouvriere*), and Daniel Mothe (*Militant chez Revault*, and *Journal d'un ouvrier*).[1]

Discussing the relation of his work to the kind of studies done in the world of Anglo-American sociology, Mallet noted that a major difference concerns their respective attitudes towards change. French theory is profoundly influenced by French history. Its milieu is a history marked not simply by the Great Revolution of 1789, but by the continual threat of social upheaval which concretized itself not only in the years immediately following the Bourgeois Revolution (in a way that cannot be brushed aside, as we in the U.S. do, for example, with Shay's Rebellion), but again and again, a priori fixed and functional. Any analysis—whether leftist, rightist, or 'neutral-academic'—must take into account the potential and immanence of social upheaval. This orientation towards openness and revolution is not ideological, the result—as some Americans have erroneously argued—of the strength of Marxist culture in France. It is rooted in the presence of French history in its present.

One can take the threat of change into account in several ways. Mallet's two poles of reference are Marxian theory, and his own empathetic understanding of the culture, desires and lived

---

1. Cf., also the use that Marcuse makes of Mallet's work, for example in *One-Dimensional Man*. Mallet and Marcuse were in regular contact during Marcuse's year of teaching in Paris (before the publication of *One-Dimensional Man*), and therefore at various meetings, such as those of the *Praxis*-group.

experience of French workers. Particularly this latter pole was crucial to this theoretical and political work. His Marxism became what Marx had always claimed for his theory, but which had been dissipated in the *Realpolitik* of the Social Democratic and Communist Parties: the theory "of" the workers (not the instrumental knowledge "for" it); the theoretical expression of the situation, experience, evolution, hope and possibilities that each lives daily.

Mallet was born into a working class family in the Gironde, near Bordeaux. He recalled with great pleasure his grandfather, a socialist militant who, as did skilled craftsmen of the time, made his "tour de France" and ended up working on the leather interiors at the automobile works in the Paris suburb of Puteaux. There, he was befriended by an older socialist, Paul Lafargue—the son-in-law of Karl Marx. Grandfather Mallet was among those who voted to adhere to the newly founded Third International, splitting with it only when the Party attempted to exercise control over the union in a heavy-handed way which went against the anarcho-syndicalist leanings of this skilled worker. Too young to be affected by the Popular Front of 1936, Mallet's first political experience came during the Occupation by the Nazis. He belonged to a small group, some of whose members were caught distributing anti-Nazi leaflets. He was expelled from the high school, and joined the *maquis*, spending the rest of the war in the Resistance.

Mallet joined the Communist Party after the war, working as a journalist for its local paper in the Gironde before going to Paris to study cinema for a year, during which he made two documentary films on the working class. He was then hired full-time by the Party, and worked in the cultural affairs section of the CGT (the Communist-controlled trade union). It was there that his first quarrels with the Party occurred. He was struck, first of all, by the fact that the "culture" to which the Party wanted the workers to accede was "bourgeois culture," the theater, art and literature of the classics. Moreover, the mode of acquisition of culture had always to pass through Party channels. It began to appear to Mallet that perhaps the Party's relation to the mass of workers was not what the Theory said it should be. He was further marked by the fact that, as he travelled throughout the country, visiting factories in each locality, he would be greeted by the local Party or CGT representative, whose first words seemed always to be: "Comrade, you know that the situation here is particular..."

Before his doubts could grow to disagreements, Mallet was elected to the Executive Committee of the International Federation of Youth, and spent much of the next few years living and travelling in Eastern Europe. There, he got to know "socialism" from the inside, and found his doubts about the party-mass relation nourished by the passivity of the working class and the omnipresence of the Party. It was not the purges—whose real grounds he strongly suspected, due to his sufficiently high position in the hierarchy; these he could accept within a logic not unlike that of Koestler's Rubashov in *Darkness at Noon*, admitting that those purged were certainly not Gestapo or CIA agents, but arguing that political mistakes in a situation of all-out Cold- or Class-War had to be punished. Nor was it Krushchev's "secret report," or the risings of 1956 in Poland and Hungary, that led him to leave the Party. Rather, it was those growing doubts about the Party's relation to its base, about the structure of the working class itself, in which each situation was said to be "particular" while the Theory claimed that the class was unified and homogenous, and the tactical decisions that followed from this. Mallet was led into a series of disagreements with the Party, which reacted by demoting him from his official positions (leaving him without a job as well). He remained a member of his local cell, continued to argue his positions, claiming support from developments within the (slightly) more liberal Italian Party. He even learned Italian in order to read Gramsci—who had not been translated into French: Mallet says that the Party publishing house had the rights since 1945, but published only a small, insignificant volume of selections. For this latter step, he was again accused of deviating!

It was the inability of the Party to pose any coherent resistance and alternatives to the advent of De Gaulle's Fifth Republic that led Mallet to quit the Party and begin publishing the theories and strategic analyses that he had been developing from hand-to-mouth since his demotion, working on odd jobs, hitch-hiking to the different factories he was studying, supported somewhat by a small grant from Jean-Paul Sartre. The theory of the "new working class," and Mallet's political analyses of Gaullism (the latter contained especially in three lengthy articles, later published in the volume *Le Gallisme et la Gauche*), appeared at a time of despair on the Left. In this climate of uncertainty, Mallet suddenly became a star. His articles appeared in journal after journal, unleashing a debate and a renewal. In *L'Express*, the mass-circulation left-liberal (at the time!)

French weekly, there was a regular two-page spread, featuring on the left an article by Mallet, and on the right a contribution by the Gaullist technocrat Albin Chalandon. This was also the time of the formation of the PSU, with which many of Mallet's theories came to be identified. The Chemical Union of the CFDT, and its leader Edmond Maire (presently head of the whole CFDT), were only the best known of the union and leaders who recognized themselves in the "new working class" theories of Mallet and his realistic analysis of Gaullism as representing a radical change in the face of the French capitalism: the victory of the technocrats of organized capitalism over the familial and colonial form which had held the balance of power in the Fourth Republic.

It was at the same time that Mallet began the research that led to the volume of essays, *Les paysans contre le passe*, a journalistic masterpiece of sociological and political insight into the problems, contradictions and future possibilities opening up to France's rapidly changing agricultural sector. Once again, Mallet attempted to identify the differentiations within a social formation which had been "philosophized" to death by the tradition, treated as monolithic and unchanging, shorn from the living evolution of the social dynamic. As with the "new working class," it is a question of showing, on the one hand, what the direction of neo-capitalism portends and the effects this will have at a human level of daily experience; and on the other hand, of pointing out the intuitive forms of struggle that have developed out of that situation and are signs of a future clash whose contradictions will not be so easily resolved. In the case of the French peasantry, the contradictions are not simply local or regional; nor are they specific to France's individualistic and archaic agricultural forms. Their roots, rather, lie in the contradictions engendered by France's entry as a nation into the world of organized capitalist competition in its modern phase, and the specific problems that this engenders on a structural level between—in a formula—the need to modernize in order to increase relative surplus-value production through technological innovation, and the social possibilities that the new, larger scale, more mechanized, more productively efficient techniques engender on a social level. Mallet chronicles, for example, the "artichoke war" in which the peasants of Brittany learn not only the role of the middleman and the advantages of cooperation, but adopt new forms of struggle, new methods of disposing of their crops, new types of self-reliance. He shows the internal logic that drives small-scale cheese producers towards cooperative ventures, how livestock raisers discover the relation of their problems to those of society as a whole. The peasants begin to lose that proprietary individualism that made Marxists consider them a reactionary class—for now, objectively, mechanization is necessary, bringing with it forms of cooperation, new attitudes towards one's neighbors, and one's form of life. Mallet's empathetic description of the lived contradictions and stammering attempts to resolve them is most striking in his ability to paint a portrait in which the subject recognizes the implications of its own action.

Mallet has been reproached for his impressionistic portraiture, and the "vogue" and journalistic nature of his work. In partial reply, he talked about two lessons that he learned in the *maquis*, both of which Mao Tse-tung had articulated years before on the basis of analogous experience. The first insight is that the peasantry is not a monolithic and eternally static class; its interests have to be understood in their dynamic specificity and historical context. This, of course, applies to all social classes. More important, he learned the "fish-in-the-water" lesson: that a vanguard which cuts itself off from the masses, by theoretical excesses, terrorism or elitist theorizing, is doomed to failure. His experience as "cultural mentor" with the CGT also taught Mallet to pay attention to the capacity of the workers to manage their own autonomy, to integrate new forms of struggle and social relations. The theoretical translation of this experience is a dialectical theory as the reflexion of the implications of the already-present autonomous class activity in which the reader recognizes him- or herself as an actor whose actions have implications on an overall social plane, implications that may not have been apparent when the actions were undertaken. Thus, for example, Mallet spoke of peasant "Kolkhozes" in France—those collective farms that were ideological anathema to the traditional peasantry—and crystallized a split in the peasant movement around these issues, leading Bernard Lambert, the peasant leader of the Loire-Atlantique, to bring his entire federation into the PSU.

Mallet is not a "heavy" theoretician. His citations from the classics are usually from memory, and his theoretical remarks are frustratingly vague. He described his method as a "genetic structuralism," a term borrowed from his friend, the late Lucien Goldmann. Society is seen as a continual process of structuration and destructuration. Theory has to describe the combination and interaction of these structures within the horizon of a social totality.

The structures are historical, dynamic and changing; a stress at one point calls for an intervention that only weakens another, letting loose new contradictions. This is almost common sense. Yet its implications are seen if we note that a non-genetic-structuralist politics would be one which, in an *opportunist* fashion, attacks a single hot-point, trying to make political capital out of it without recognizing that if there is, say, a housing problem this is because of the structure of the banking sector, construction industry, as well as the urban politics of the society, etc. It is not possible to strike at only one hot-point; if one doesn't see the interconnections, a mass, articulated socialist movement can never be developed. But at the same time, one's structuralism must avoid the dangers of an a-historical approach which, perhaps citing the sacred texts of *Capital*, sees the structural contradictions as fixed once and for all. In fact, there is a continual dance, a de- and re-structuration which must be taken into account. The genetic structuralist approach, then, will not provide eternal Theory, Truth with a capital "T." It is for this reason that, when pushed, Mallet would admit that, for example, one cannot say once and for all that this or that sector of the working class constitutes the "new working class," or that such-and-such a sector performs necessary productive labor where another doesn't. The shifts which take place due to historical change and the play of contradictions within the capitalist society call for continual re-evaluation.

Theory and praxis are thus intimately related to one another in Mallet's work. That is, not simply are the theories formulated with an eye to their political utilization—it is not a question of a theory *for* praxis, one which tells the reader "See, here is the problem; here is how you should act to set it right." Rather, the theory is at once a theory *of* an already ongoing praxis; and as theory it intervenes in that praxis insofar as the participants understand their praxis in the theorization of it. Class consciousness, insists Mallet, is not something that every worker "has," in the same way that one "has" a job, wage rate, car, television, etc. Class consciousness comes out of political struggle; it is the articulation of the implications of that struggle. It has a negative and a positive pre-condition: recognition of the impossibility of continuing to function in a system that is based on expropriation of surplus-value so as to continue to accumulate dead labor on the backs of the living; and, on the other hand, the self-understanding of the working class that it can run the society without the aid of bureaucrats, managers and capitalists.

There is a tendency to accuse those who hold to a "new working class line" of being the new technocrats or aristocracy of labor. Although this was never Mallet's position, it is worth noting here the shift in his attitudes since May 1968. Mallet insisted that the change was not in his theory—that it was never his view that the "new working class" *alone* would make the revolution in the name of and for the rest of the class—but rather than the structuration-destructuration process in France demanded a theoretical reformulation. During the mid-1960s, i.e., after the formulation of the notion of the "new working class," Gaullist policy consciously aimed at adopting the energy that these strata had revealed at the beginning of the Fifth Republic. Indeed, it succeeded to some degree in this—only to see the developments of May 68 throw its politics into question from another vantage point, and recreate the conditions for new working class action. Nonetheless, since 1970, Gaullism again tried to use new mechanisms such as union participation and no-strike "progressive contracts" to integrate this stratum. The result, however, is a disequilibrium elsewhere, manifested now in the more traditional sectors of the working population, as well as in the radicalization of the struggles of immigrant labor. The "new working class" is thus—for the time being—no longer in the vanguard. The development of the struggle is presently moving through the incorporation of its demands for control, now at the level of the traditional working class as well. The task of the theorist becomes the thematization of the implicit dialectic which underlies these developments and the articulation of self-management type demands which are beginning to emerge.

Mallet insisted that his genetic-structuralist approach, stressing both the historical aspect of structural interaction and interrelation, and the fact that the structures are interwoven in a totality such that the attempt to correct a disbalance at one point creates a problem elsewhere, permits him to account for the evolution that led to May 1968, and to understand the forms that were taken by the student, peasant and worker struggles then and since. Immediately after May, he began a research project, studying the attitudes and reactions of the medical students, traditionally a passive and a-political (or rightist) bunch, who were drawn into the action of May at first by simple solidarity and by the need of medical personnel at the barricades. Once the barricade stage had passed and the occupations of the schools, with the accompanying series of strategic, programmatic and theoretical discussion, had begun, their involvement took the interesting form of a challenge to the medical profession in general, both as concerns the role of the physician, and as concerns the hospital, para-medical personnel, etc. Mallet's research found in their reaction a confirmation of the tendency to throw into question the bureaucratic forms of social control, which increasingly and in all sectors, reduces individual and collective autonomy, and calls forth a reaction in demands for social control.[2]

During May itself, Mallet was able to witness this process from within, having been actively involved in perhaps the most advanced experiment in workers' control during that period: the "Commune of Nantes."[3] There the workers, farmers and students effectively took control of the situation, arranging for farmers to provide food for the strikers in exchange for which the strikers put some of their factories to work, policing the city and preventing merchants from raising their prices, and generally setting up the embryonic forms of a workers' council government. Mallet's strategic perspective at the time, which was adopted but not carried through by the SPU, was to attempt to set up such situations of dual power wherever possible (including the use of force: e.g., Mallet was involved in the elaboration of a plan to seize control of a regional radio station — the plan, however, failed). The idea was to gnaw away at the legitimacy of the central power, establishing perhaps in the person of Pierre Mendès-France, a provisional government in order to grant the councils time to develop their self-understanding and confidence (remember: from February to October, 1917, was an eight-month gestation period!), and generally to move forward on the basis of mass self-management.

Mallet's theoretical and political position does not tend toward the looseness implied by the neologism — that is part of the problem, for in insisting on his rootedness in the Marxian analysis, Mallet often tends towards a kind of determinist reading of the genetically

---

2. At least three major studies by Mallet are not yet published. One is written, but due to French libel laws which are structured in such a way as to make it difficult for political criticism to emerge, it has not found a publisher. The book concerns the financial scandals in the Gaullist regime conerning the building of a new commercial and diplomatic sector outside of Paris, called "La Defense." The second study was not completed in a publishable form. The third is an analysis of French working class struggles in the past few years, and was to be part of an European attempt to understand the present stage of struggles and the different forms it takes in different countries. Partial reports of the latter two can be obtained from the CORDES, 30 rue Las Cases, Paris 7e, France.

3. On this cf. Hannick Guin, *La Commune de Nantes* (Paris, 1969) — which incidentally does not mention Mallet's role.

evolving structures. The argument for the existence of a "new working class" is posed in terms of Marx's discussion of the changing organic compositions of capital. But there is a crucial ambiguity, both in Marx and in Mallet. At times it appears as if it were capital, and its iron laws, which is the independent variable and working class behavior and consciousness which depend on it. In this sense, accusations of technocratism and even crude materialism which have been levelled against Mallet (and Marx) would make sense: the "new working class" would simply be the changed face of the servant of the machine, and would not be capable of making a socialism which implies the changing of the machine from master to servant. One would thereby be omitting from the fabric of the theory precisely that active element of praxis which makes it different from an empirical-descriptive analysis. At the same time, the objections to Mallet (and to Marx), that his analyses are based only on a specific phase or structure of capitalist development which has now passed, would hit the nail on the head. Replying to such criticism (made, among others, by A. Touraine), Mallet insists that there is a grain of truth to this, inherent in the genetic-structural account, yet it is more important to see the other side and its implications. Mallet stressed the "fluidity" of his categories. Such fluidity can lead to the accusation of vagueness, as for instance when Mallet called the young unskilled workers (the *OS*) who have temporarily been the vanguard of struggle in France a "new category of workers," or indeed, when he is unwilling, or unable, to specify which social categories do and do not belong to the "new working class." Whatever the difficulties of such a position, Mallet would no doubt argue that this is not his vagueness, that the weakness is a strength, since the reality that he is attempting to theorize is itself fluid and criss-crossed with ambiguity, contradiction and struggle.

   In the U.S., one particular usage of the "new working class" notion stands out within the Left, where it was introduced as the radical counterpart to the soporifics of sociological pluralism with its status, stratification and psychological orientation which tends to make a blur of class theory, replacing it with a vague notion of "middle class" and then playing grantsmanship and publish-or-perish embroidery on statistical scales in what is literally a fugue. The usage I am referring to is that embodied in the "Port Authority Statement" of SDS, developed by Gilbert, Gottlieb and Tenny, and popularized by Greg Calbert during his term as national president of SDS. The notion was, unfortunately, put forward in a vague political context, without the sociological underpinnings that were really needed.[4] In the context (1966-67), SDS was in the throes of moving from a moralistic student movement to a conscious revolutionary organization. This basically student movement felt itself forced to justify itself in the eyes of a History it was only just learning about, and a Theory which only a few of its leaders knew. The question everyone was asking themselves was: who are we? If we are but students, and hence petty-bourgeois future-exploiters, how can we claim to be revolutionaries? The reply suggested was a variant of the "new working class" notion, arguing that the conditions of neo-capitalism brought with them a proletarianization of students and academics at the same time that the knowledge industry became an essential cog in the machine producing surplus-value. Unfortunately, events moved more rapidly than self-understanding, and the acceleration of the war against Vietnam coupled with the growth of a militant Third World movement, pushed SDS toward a series of identifications with other "revolutionary" movements that ended in the disaster of the Weatherpeople, while many of those who did not take that route fell back on the old metaphysics of the working class—or fell out, period.

Very little of the research that has been done in the U.S. on the notion of the "new working class" bears any resemblance to Mallet's theorization, partially because of its quantitative character, partially because of a lack of understanding of the interrelation of the Marxian categories within a dynamic understanding of the capitalist totality based on class struggle, and partially because it is abstracted from the immediate political considerations of a revolutionary change which is already implied in the daily practice of individuals—the category has been adulterated, and its usage vulgarized and-or treated as a straw man. It is true that Mallet's "genetic-structuralism" lends itself to the criticisms that the "hard" social scientists love to throw at it. It refuses to pin down the category, not just quantitatively but qualitatively as well, because it insists that the changing structures of capitalism which are its response to the class struggle can lead to the incorporation of different forms of labor into the productive mechanism while excluding others whose functioning formerly was central to the mechanism. Mallet's is a theory *of* praxis, based on actions and deriving its justification from the struggles in process. Mallet's

---

4.   It is somewhat more developed in *A Disreputed History: The New Left and the New Capitalism,* by Greg Calvert and Carol Neiman (New York, 1971).

arguments that May 1968 was a "new working class" phenomenon, and his discussion of the strikes after May, are not empirically convincing in the abstract. That was never his goal. Mallet pounced on trends, tendencies, intuitions; and there is certainly an element of wishfulness in his choices. This was his vice, and his virtue.

The character of his work, infected by his life and that of the workers' struggle, makes Mallet's loss irreplaceable. He was a singular, unique human being who combined in his theoretical and practical work the best of his class and its history. The class and its struggle will continue, in new and creative forms, as long as the capitalist exploitation and domination continue. They will produce other theorists, each as unique and forceful, as independent in their practice and as dependent in their relation to the class as was Mallet. It is this interaction, so strongly imbedded in Mallet's person, which must be remembered: the worst monument for a revolutionary is one that preserves the form while losing the spirit. The friend, the comrade, the teacher is gone. Present still is the legacy: the legacy of the movement which he carried in his person, and the legacy of a forward-looking creativity never too old to learn.

Dick Howard
SUNY at Stony Brook

PART I:
Evolution of the Working Class

Industrial Labor[1]

Industrial labor—that of the worker—is in a way 'privileged' in our eyes, as if it were the pre-eminent contemporary form of labor. And in fact, it was in the working class that labor problems were born in the modern consciousness. But the problems which generally confront workers, and particularly that of their relation to society as a whole, are rapidly evolving. Because of automation, for example, the nature of labor, its mode of remuneration, the possibilities of organization available to workers, the power they have, the attitudes they are led to adopt, change from day to day. One will see here examples drawn from the situation in France. Elsewhere the problems may present themselves in other terms without, however, modifying the general sense of an evolution which makes organized labor weigh more and more heavily on the productive apparatus and thereby on the whole of industrial society. Owing to this fact, the working class is emerging little by little from the ghetto in which the nineteenth century had confined it.

Industrial labor made its appearance in Western Europe during the eighteenth century and its first sociological descriptions are found in the work of the creators of modern political economy, Adam Smith and then Ricardo. As opposed to artisanal or agricultural labor which exists, under different forms to be sure, at all levels of human civilization, industrial labor was born with a specific technology, the machine, and a particular social system, the capitalist system.

When one wishes to oppose it to preceding systems of labor, the current definition of industrial labor presents it as labor executed in a group. And this perception is so widespread that popular usage readily defines by the term 'factory' any place where a considerable number of men gather to work—even if this work has nothing to do with industry, or even with production.

---

1. This article originally appeared in the *Encyclopédie Kister*, Geneva, 1965.

In fact, if the grouping of a more or less considerable number of workers at the same place of production indeed constitutes one of the necessary characteristics of industrial labor, it is not for all that a sufficient definition. Sociological students of classical civilization (notably G. Glotz[2] and G. Thompson) have been able to establish the existence of large workshops for pottery, weaponry, and tanning counting up to several dozen workers in the Greek commercial cities of the fourth or fifth century.

It seems, according to administrative documents, that the situation in Pharaonic Egypt was the same. Closer to us, the worksites of the Medieval cathedrals grouped together, in addition to manual laborers, a certain number of artisans harnessed to the same overall task. What fundamentally differentiates industrial from artisanal labor is that the former can only be realized collectively. The potters of Exydias worked for an employer under a roof furnished by him and in his workshop, but the pot produced by their hands remained the individual work of a creator (in the productive, if not artistic, sense of the term).

Industrial labor truly exists only when the creation of the product entails the simultaneous combination of several operations which can not be accomplished by an isolated individual. For the force of simple labor—that produced by the human hand prolonged by a tool—is substituted the force of complex labor accomplished by the machine. The entire evolution of industrial labor is summed up in the perfecting of machines accomplishing the breaking down and then the recombination of the different productive operations.

The transformation of autonomous labor into collectivized 'socialized' labor could not fail to exert a profound influence on the status of the worker. During the entire artisanal period—that which the American sociologist Lewis Mumford calls the "eotechnic phase"[3]—the worker's occupational qualification, the *métier*, i.e., the acquisition of the psycho-physical reflexes and servo-sensory mechanisms adequate to the chosen function (the Italians use the term *idoneità*—in the sense of the old French word *idoine*—to designate this strictly professional skill), is very much like an 'initiation,' from which it borrowed, moreover, its ritual forms. Once

---

2.   Gustave Glotz, *Ancient Greece at Work: An Economic History of Greece from the Homeric Period to the Roman Conquest*, New York: Knopf, 1926. George D. Thompson, *Studies in Ancient Greek Society*, two Vols., London: Lawrence and Wishart, 1949-1955.

3.   Lewis Mumford, *Technics and Civilization*, New York: Harcourt, Brace & Co., 1934.

a worker had become a day laborer [*manouvrier*] or a journeyman [*compagnon*] he acquired a durable clearly-defined social status which tended to replace the geographical bonds of the peasant community. Even when he moved, he transported with him his essential property, his *métier*, which sufficed to locate him quickly among his peers and in relation to other social strata in a particular human group. The guilds or corporations, and later on the *compagnonnage*,[4] were basic social units more than simple professional associations. It was in terms of this social role, moreover, that they carried out the functions of mutual aid and training, delimited the reciprocal rights and duties of members, and made rules about the organization of the religious and cultural forms proper to the corporation.

Labor and Levels of Skill

From this point of view, the first phase of industrial labor—what is called 'phase A' in French industrial sociology, and 'paleotechnical' by the Anglo-Saxons[5]—is not yet fundamentally different from the medieval phase. To be sure, as early as the eighteenth century, Adam Smith distinguished three categories of industrial labor:

1) Traditional, highly skilled *métiers*, the only ones to which the English economist accorded the term "qualified" (the corporations, he said, must train "properly qualified masters"):[6] the workshops of cabinet-makers and watchmakers belonged to this category, in which the artisan, if he ceased to own his means of production, nevertheless retained the autonomy and power of decision which were the mark of the medieval artisan.

2) The first primitive factories [*manufactures*] based on the increasingly developed division of labor in the workshop and on the use of mechanical energy which simplified tasks: from this time on textile and weaving shops belong to this category, the forerunner of the modern factory.

---

4. On *compagnonnages*, see Emile Coornaert, *Les compagnonnages en France du moyen age à nos jours*. Paris: Les éditions ouvrières, 1966.
5. The three phase classification of forms of labor is borrowed from Alain Touraine's classic work, *L'évolution du travail ouvrier aux usines Renault*, Paris: CNRS, 1955. Excerpts from this volume have been published in English in Charles R. Walker, ed., *Labor and Working Conditions in Modern Europe*, London & New York: Macmillan, 1967, pp. 122-134; and most recently in Edward Shorter, ed., *Work and Community in the West*, New York: Harper & Row, 1973, pp. 80-100.
6. Adam Smith, *An Inquiry into the Nature and Causes of the Wealth of Nations*, New York: Modern Library, 1973, p. 120.

3) Workshops or rather 'primary' work sites devoted to the extraction of primary materials or to their initial transformations (mines, foundries, forges) which used common labor, the ordinary unskilled labor which could be learned in a few days by an irregular work force without any industrial training.

It was to the second category, the only one truly characteristic of modern industry, that Adam Smith devoted his attention: the British economist observed that occupational skill (in the sense of the rapidity and precision of work motions) was due here to the simplicity of the task, which had been broken down prior to the action of the worker. This type of skilled labor appeared in the eighteenth century as the harbinger of fragmented labor ('*le travail en miettes*' which Georges Friedmann has so brilliantly analyzed.)[7] Next to the two traditional types of labor, skilled labor linked to the fabrication of a whole product, and common labor reserved to manual laborers, a form of labor now appeared which, with the development of large industry, became by far the most important. The journeyman-manual laborer pair was replaced by the *OS* [*ouvrier spécialisé sur machines*, or semi-skilled worker], the representative type of the working class of the first half of the twentieth century.

Smith did not, however, consider the spread of semi-skilled labor as a regression: he saw a considerable social progress in the fact that it announced the abolition of the technical secrets characteristic of the guilds: the magic qualities of work gave way to the rational utilization of skills; the organization of work soon appeared in its turn in the prophetic texts of the economist.

Marx in his turn celebrated in *Capital* the liberation of work from the magic rites of the medieval period: "Modern Industry rent the veil that concealed from men their own social process of production, and that turned the various, spontaneously divided branches of production into so many riddles, not only to outsiders, but even to the initiated. The principle which it pursued, of resolving each process into its constituent movements, without any regard to their possible execution by the hand of man, created the new modern science of technology.[8]

---

7. "Le travail en miettes:" literally, "work in bits and pieces." See Georges Friedmann, *Le travail en miettes*, Paris: Gallimard, 1956 (English translation: *The Anatomy of Work: Labor, Leisure and the Implications of Automation,* New York: Free Press, 1961).

8. Karl Marx, *Capital*, New York: Modern Library, Vol. I, p. 532.

The Notion of Work Skill is an Historical Notion

But two hundred years were needed for large-scale industry to drive out the demiurge, to break "this bond between hand and tool born of a progressive possession, of deft and coordinated movements, of habit, and even of a certain wear and tear..."9 Cast out of the mechanized sweatshops, kept away from the assembly lines of large-scale industry, professional skill, the consciousness of 'fine work,' took refuge in particular sectors of modern industry. The detached mechanical part, a fragment to be sure, but a complete fragment lending itself to the hand which adjusts, smooths scoops, and palpably evaluates the resistance of the material, preserved for a long time the illusion of the unfragmented form [of labor.] In evolving, technological language has itself retraced this long history of the resistance of 'whole production' to the invasion of work decomposition which broke the personal relationship of man and object.

The term used by Adam Smith, skilled labor, applies today in the Anglo-Saxon countries to the *ouvrier professionnel* [*OP*]: in fact, the use of new machines is re-creating a new stratum of polyvalent workers whose training, more technical than corporative, more intellectual than physical, will nevertheless take on again a part of the old attributes of 'properly qualified masters;' [the old type of] skilled labor, on the other hand, will degenerate more and more into mechanized work where even specialized manual skill will tend to become useless. The history of industrial labor is not linear. Pierre Naville, one of the most penetrating analysts of work skills [*qualification du travail*] was quite right to remark:10

1) that the notion of work skills appears to be entirely relative;

2) that its forms depend on those of the productive forces, and at the same time on those of the economic structure of society;

3) and that, finally, to the extent that the criteria of skill are closely dependent on the productive forces and the economic structure, they appear as social more than individual criteria. In a word, there have always been 'aristocrats' in the working class who took on, under the best conditions possible, the functions required by production, and thereby received a larger part of total wages; there have always been 'expert workers,' but each industrial phase has had

---

9.   Henri Focillon, "Eloge de la main," in *Vie des formes,* Paris: Presses Universitaires de France, 1955, Fourth edition, p. 106.

10.   Pierre Naville, *Essai sur la qualification du travail,* Paris: Rivière, 1956, p. 27.

its own—and they were not the same ones. The skilled *métier* of times past disappeared or degenerated into a marginal artisan class or into maintenance functions, and new skills based on different aptitudes emerged but these, in their turn, were disqualified with the introduction of new machine tools which performed tasks more efficiently and steadily than the human hand or eye.

It is this perpetual questioning of established situations, not only from the material point of view, but from that of social standing, which gives such a dramatic character to the problems of reconversion. Miners, who were common laborers in 1830, a time when women and children were still used for this work, conquered an incontestable occupational dignity in the first half of the twentieth century. The introduction of better cutting procedures and improved tools (the jack hammer), the improvement of removal procedures requiring a new organization of mine shafts and recourse to more developed timbering and support techniques, made miners into genuine specialists. The legislation of wages and the institutionalization of the "task-price" (individual output) had even restored to a certain extent the illusion of an autonomous labor to the deep pit miner.

In 1850, miners were recruited preferentially among convicts, vagabonds, and unemployed agricultural workers. In 1900 and until 1940, they constituted one of the proudest and most esteemed strata of the workers' aristocracy. In 1960, the miners' young sons massively abandoned the pits where a mechanization of tasks pushed to the extreme had deprived the work of all material as well as moral interest. And it is from the proletarian countries of southern Europe, Africa, and western Asia that the French, the Belgians, and the Germans must recruit deep pit miners, while the English depopulate their last colonies to this end. The desperate side of certain workers' revolts—the violence of the Borinage strikes[11] recalls those of the English weavers of the eighteenth century—is not at all accounted for by the sharpness of wage demands. More than greater or lesser purchasing power, the occupational categories condemned by technological evolution are defending their social dignity. The error is unquestionably to believe that it may be safeguarded by the maintenance of archaic structures rather than by the profound modification of the nature of labor which, however skilled it may be,

---

11. The reference is to strikes by Belgian miners in the Borinage region during 1960-61 which took on an insurrectional character.

remains a commodity, subjected like other commodities to the pitiless law of the market and of competition.

Adam Smith, we have seen, pointed out already in his time the continuous existence of three forms of industrial labor in the eighteenth century. The sociologist doing a monograph today on the department of the Basse-Pyrenées alone could observe within a distance of a few kilometers the automated complex of Lacq-Mourenx [a natural gas refinery, power plant, and chemical by-products factory] staffed by a technician working class, the steel-working group of Boucau where skilled modern labor and the semi-skilled labor of the first half of the twentieth century rub elbows, the tanneries and leather-working shops of Oloron, whose conditions of production and tools have scarcely changed since the manufactories of the eighteenth century, and the artisan cabinet-makers of Nay, who practice their *métier* in conditions almost identical to those of their ancestors of the medieval epoch.

In these circumstances, is it possible to classify 'historically' the stages of work organization? Can one speak of the age of the skilled worker, of the semi-skilled worker, and of the technician as one speaks of the age of stone, of bronze, or of iron? We have seen that even if one could 'date' the appearance of the semi-skilled worker as one could date that of the technician, multiple transfers in diverse directions take place among the types themselves and that in each period the different types of work organization co-exist.

Legitimacy of a Periodization of the History of Work: The Model Sectors

Proudhon spoke already of 'working classes.' Nevertheless, each industrial period, each age of work organization tends to create a relatively homogeneous structure in the class which operates the means of production. The totality of social-psychological factors tending toward cohesion which every society secretes acts in favor of this homogenization. The State, which is by nature centralizing, and the labor movement, in its desire to do away with differentiations [among workers], weigh in the same direction. Thus the social images, the vision which the working class has of itself and which others have of it, take on a totalizing character which does not reflect the complexity of real phenomena but which is nevertheless truer than the photographic or statistical reality. When we imagine a worker of 1848, one of those who brandished the first red flags, the image of a journeyman-cabinetmaker or glassmaker of the *faubourg*

Saint Antoine comes to mind. The memory of the great struggles for the eight hour day calls forth the miners and railwaymen; Basly, 'the indomitable miner,' and 'the heroic strikers of Vierzon' [a railway center] form a part of the folklore of the labor movement. Nineteen thirty-six was dominated by the Parisian metal-workers; Billancourt [Renault plant] and Javel [Citroën plant] were then high places of labor history.

In practice, one is thus led to note in each period the existence within the working class of a *structural kernel* around which the concepts, forms of organization, and action of the labor movement are organized. But such observations only reflect the *model* role played by certain sectors of production, whose determining influence on social relations accelerates the process of change in other sectors. The strata of the working class not belonging to these 'leading sectors' which express the economic reality of their period, find themselves rejected in practice from the leadership of the labor movement.

Constant, fundamental change is the defining characteristic of the capitalist mode of production. Unceasingly, the introduction of new techniques, the discovery of new primary materials or of new sources of traditional raw materials, the invention of new products, come along to upset the established division of labor. Masses of capital or workers are constantly thrown from one sector to another, old industries decline or disappear. The modifications which intervene ceaselessly in the apparatus of production cannot fail to remodel the face of the social strata which are engaged there. And the ineluctable consequence of these changes is precisely to bring to the fore within the working class and its organized movement this or that fraction of the working class, while the leading sectors of the past lose their influence.

Thus analysis may elucidate the models of organization of the labor movement of this or that period and establish correspondences and relationships between them and the economic, technical, and technological relations of production which determine them. Analyses of the 'phases' of work organization always rediscover, no matter who the writers are, this notion of 'dominant poles.' And it is for this reason that it is legitimate to speak, with all the necessary reservations, of the 'age of the skilled worker, of the semi-skilled worker, and of the technician,' or, if one prefers to refer to the organization of industry rather than to that of workers, to the age of the manufactory, of the mechanized factory, and of automation.

Phase A: The Beginnings of the Industrial Era

At its beginnings, industrial organization scarcely went beyond the phase of familial or group capitalism. Juridically, it was the time when partnerships dominated. Each enterprise, geographically delimited by the proximity of a source of raw materials or of a market, undertook an entire production process, i.e., the integral production of a certain product. This led, within an entirely competitive market, to a relative fragility compensated by the existence of localized monopolistic situations and the scant fluidity of commercial currents.

The division of labor within the factory was itself a division of a simple form and called upon a single category of specialists or technicians particular to an industrial branch. Nor are these industrial branches as exhaustively developed as they will be later on: they still have *métiers* in the sense of the old corporations. Within the process of fabrication, the specialization of labor remained little developed. Of course, production was already diversified among different workshops. But these constituted autonomous units: each worker had his own work, his personal rhythm, and was paid by the piece. He continued, like the artisan or journeyman of old, to produce a concrete object, be it only a detached part. He knew the peculiarities of his machine, his 'crutch,' which he repaired himself. In a word, the only difference between the skilled worker of this period and the individual artisan is that the ownership of his means of production and of his labor have escaped him. Socially the difference is fundamental; psychologically it is less so, because the jobbing artisan had already been subjected for some time to the law of the supervisor [*maître d'oeuvre*] who divided the orders. The reaction of the polyvalent skilled worker dispossessed of his instruments of production remains a proprietary reaction; he defense as his most valuable possession the sole property which is left him, his *métier*.

This structure of the enterprise is linked to that of the economy as a whole. Alain Touraine was correct to observe that "as long as the economic conditions and techniques of production prevented forecasts of the exact nature and quantity of manufactured products, the organization of the workshop was reduced to the division of labor among workers and teams able to adapt themselves to varied tasks, able above all to organize their labor themselves, i.e., to choose the tools, the methods, the appropriate motions. In these conditions, the enterprise had no real unity, it was only the coexistence of two worlds: that of production, where the skilled worker possessed great autonomy of decision and that of management, entirely reserved to the employer's initiative."[12]

Apparently, the entrepreneur therefore found himself in a dominant position *vis-à-vis* his employees. But only apparently: the paleocapitalist enterprise is, we have seen, narrowly determined by its family structure. The familial proprietorship is tied to the possession of the plant and the land—in a period when land and other real estate capital had more value than capital equipment. The location of the latter, we have also seen, was determined by specific local conditions: deposits of raw materials (iron mines, quarries, forests), agricultural production, geographical potentialities used by the production technique (the characteristics of certain running waters for tempering steel or curing leather) or, more rarely, by the presence of a specific local market. Let technical modifications come to transform the conditions of production, let a better equipped new competitor enter the market, and the factory will be in trouble.

The worker, on the contrary, moved about at will. In a set of circumstances in which, owing to the low degree of urbanization, the housing problem was less serious than later, he easily transported with him his only property, his occupational skill, which allowed him to find work easily. Until the beginning of the twentieth century, the geographic mobility of the skilled worker remained very great.

The equipment of this industrial phase reinforced this worker's autonomy: the 'universal machines' used at this time were not specialized, not inserted in a fixed schema of production. Their 'correct use' depended essentially on the occupational ability of the worker who used them. And the worker found the same machines from one end of this 'Tour of France' to the other. At Denain or Moulins, at Nantes or Saint-Etienne, the skilled worker who entered a new workshop felt at home; he found there a known world which he understood. His essential relationships were with his peers. The importance of human relationships was even greater insofar as the worker hierarchy—an interior hierarchy which the employers had nothing to do with—was very strong: apprentice, journeyman, foreman formed the rungs of a stable professional hierarchy accepted

---

12.   Alain Touraine, "L'organisation professionnelle," in Georges Friedmann and Pierre Naville, *Traté de sociologie du Travail*, Paris: A. Colin, 1964, Second edition, Vol. I, p. 387.

by all because it was the internal law of the working group and not the fact of external decisions. Thus work discipline itself was independent of the ownership of the enterprise.

The Craft Union

The existence of this upper stratum of skilled workers, still very close to the journeymen of the eighteenth century and the Middle Ages, gave birth to the first phase of unionism: *the craft union.*

Owing to labor mobility, the living place was not the preferred ground for workers' solidarity. Rather, this solidarity exerted itself very strongly on the level of the occupation. Occupational relationships were, in effect, favored by the constant exchange of workers between centers of production. And this exchange often went beyond national boundaries. The conditions of the exercise of an occupation were as homogeneous as the instruments of labor. To be sure, craft unionism was traversed by different ideologies: among Proudhonistes, Bakuninists, and French socialists, political rivalries were very lively.

But socialism, for all of them, was the reappropriation of the means of production of which the artisan had been despoiled. Whether this demand expressed itself through the development of Proudhonist producers' cooperatives or through strikes for control by the anarchists, the objective remained very precise, very concrete: to reconquer, through possession of the means of labor, the liberty of the Jacobin artisan of 1791. This homogeneity of goals expressed itself with the greatest clarity in the anti-centralizing character of the entire labor movement before and after the Commune. The notion of a planned economy is on the other hand very rare in the union literature of the time; pre-Marxist socialism expected the harmony of the golden ages from the free communities of labor.

This unionism of skilled workers was organized by craft rather than by industrial branches; the automobile upholsterers belonged—like the saddlers and shoemakers—to the leather and skins union, and this situation was all the more easily accepted as these polyvalent workers passed indifferently from one branch to another. The coordination of actions (strikes for example) was rarely done at the level of the enterprise or locality, and almost always at that of the branch. But the degree of unionization was very high, the union meetings very well attended, and unions such as the molders or founders, book printers, mechanics, and teamsters practically imposed the union label: every journeyman had to be a union member if he wanted to join the work crew. Union actions were truly the work of all the unions. And it was moreover only because they were the work of a very large majority that the strikers were so firm in the use of physical violence toward strikebreakers. The 'scab hunt,' a permanent practice of the labor movement in a strike period, is possible only because of an extraordinary cohesion of the mass of strikers: the strikebreaker is a traitor, and he is rejected by the closed community. Moreover, the craft union is not only a defensive organism; the labor Exchanges [Bourses du Travail] where the different guild associations gathered (and which, originally simple meeting places, gave birth later to the administrative organisms known as departmental and local unions)[13] were also centers for the elaboration of an autonomous workers' culture, it too organized around the notion of the *métier*. Occupational training courses were given there to the young. The Labor Exchanges were true centers for vocational guidance and employment.

This initial phase of unionism gave it a powerful impulse. Through the different guild associations, an interoccupational solidarity leading to a collective consciousness was established. But this organized working class, a small minority in the nation (all the more so as it grouped only a fraction of the class: tens of thousands of worker-peasants utilized by the iron, textile, extractive, and similar industries remained apart from union organizations for a long time, as did seasonal manual labor and agricultural workers), fiercely jealous of its autonomy, cut the bonds which linked it in 1848 to the republican petty bourgeoisie. Fragile bonds moreover: under the Restoration, the attempts of the *Charbonnerie* to enter into the *sectes* of the *Compagnons* were desgined to fail most of the time.[14] And the alliance established in 1848, symbolized by the presence in the provisional government of *'l'ouvrier Albert'*—the only member of the

13. The Labor Exchanges (Bourses du Travail) played an ambiguous function in French labor history. From hiring halls, they expanded into meeting places, educational centers, self-insurance organizations and the like. In this function, they received a modest state subsidy, and were perceived as a rival to the growing trade union organizations. Mallet's interpretation here gets away from the schematic interpretation of good and bad in order to stress the development of a workers' culture and autonomy.

14. The *Charbonnerie* was a republican political organization composed largely of petit-bourgeois elements given to cloak-and-dagger methods of installing a republican constitution especially in Italy at first. The artisanal *Compagnons* of the time were, as Mallet indicates, socially militant but thoroughly apolitical and hardly tempted by the programs and promises of the *Charbonnerie*. An alliance of the two was thus impossible.

provisional govenment whose social origins were emphasized—did not survive the June days. The failure of the Commune further hardened the union movement in its skepticism regarding political action.

Anarcho-syndicalism, which became the dominant ideological current of the union movement in France, made clear its rejection of parliamentarianism, its refusal to compromise with the republican petty bourgeoisie. Griffuelhes, one of the principal founders of the Confederation General du Travail [CGT], wrote in his *Voyages révolutionnaire*: "Everywhere where the union movement participates in political action, in elections, it weakens its own action in the workplace."[15]

Phase B: The Organization of Work

Thus the conditions of production and especially the technical relations of the first phase of the industrial period did not differ fundamentally from those of the preindustrial phase. This occupational situation was modified to the extent that the technical and economic conditions of production became foreseeable and that it was possible to establish a plan for production on a certain scale. Certain industrial sociologists (notably Georges Friedmann and Alain Touraine) consider that this shift to the primacy of problems of output [*production*] over those of workmanship [*fabrication*] fundamentally separates one system of work, which they call the 'professional system,' founded on the autonomy of workmanship and decision, from the other, which they call 'technical,' in which the technical apparatus of production is independent of the workers who make it function. The appearance of phase B began, we have seen, in English industry about 1840 and was technologically linked to the capacity to foresee and organize work. On the technical side, this can mean respecting specific norms and the standardization of raw materials and products. Nevertheless, even products produced to order or in small batches—machine tools, for example, and capital goods in general—may also entail the disappearance of worker autonomy to the extent that there has been a separation—through the intervention of the Methods Department—between the conception and the fabrication of the product.

---

15. Victor Griffuelhes (revolutionary syndicalist leader of the C.G.T. from 1902-1909), *Voyage révolutionnaire, impressions d'un propagandiste*, Paris: Rivière, 1910.

What is essential is thus not technical evolution in itself, but the economic feasibility of this evolution: mass production or other analytically organized work requires, for the firm which sets it up, a long term production schedule and the possibility, indeed the guarantee, that the large output can be distributed on the market. Big firms and mass production, characteristic of phase B, resulted from the enlargement of the market and the accelerated development of capitalist concentration. The evolution of French industry, somewhat behind its British sister, was indicative of this process.

The development of French industrial capitalism was extraordinarily rapid. In 1856, the population employed in the secondary sector (industry and transports) numbered 4,384,000 persons. But, except for certain large centers like Paris and Lyon, it was disseminated in countless small provincial towns. In 1881, a date considered to be the beginning of the period of massive industrialization, it was still only 4,444,000. In 1906, following a constant increase, it reaches 6,338,000. In order to appreciate the significance of this figure, one must be aware that the contemporary working class (plus technicians in industry) groups 6,862,000 active persons. In twenty-five years (1881-1906) the secondary sector was thus inflated by nearly two million individuals, while it had only absorbed 60,000 in the twenty-five years preceding. And since this date—that is, during fifty years of almost uninterrupted technical progress—the figure has only increased by 700,000. The massive growth of industrialization provoked an extensive development of production, while the next period saw, with the increase in labor productivity, a primarily intensive development.

As the mechanization of labor developed, the large enterprises had less and less need for a stable workforce. The labor market was all the more widely open insofar as anyone could be trained on the job for elementary and fragmented tasks in a few days. The enterprises' policy on labor was adapted to the uncertainties of the market: in a period of economic expansion, the factories hired massively. As soon as problems appeared, they fired just as massively. The power relations were thus exactly inverted: the worker not indispensable to the firm was obliged to find another job in the very place to which he had been attracted by the factory. The industrial *faubourgs* became the barracks of the reserve army of labor. Capitalist industry had definitively gone beyond the stage of the manufactory.

The upper stratum of the proletariat saw, in the preceding period, its standard of living grow appreciably. But it no longer comprised more than a minority in the labor army. Paralleling the entry into the industrial world of the greater part of the agrarian countries which furnished cheap manual labor, the further development of the process of work decomposition provided precisely the utilization for these unskilled masses. For the old primary division of labor — skilled workers carrying out a complete task and unskilled labor assigned to simple work requiring only an expenditure of physical force — a more complex category, born with the introduction of semi-automatic machine tools in the twentieth century, was substituted. Pierre Naville described this change in the organic composition of the working class as follows: "Workers quickly brought up to date served this equipment in growing numbers (in particular in the machine goods industry) and it was they who made up the mass of 'specialized' workers, i.e., specialized in such and such a machine, at such and such a post, rather than in a particular product. Above them a decreasingly important stratum of workers held out, those to whom a methodical appreticeship of several years had given a complete professional competence. These were the professionals, strictly speaking. Finally, beneath the specialized [semi-skilled] workers were the unskilled laborers, suited to simple handling and rarely in contact with complex equipment. This new division of labor led to a decrease in the proportion of skilled workers and to elaborate mechanized specialization which brought about an extreme lowering of the skill level required for each job."[16]

The decomposition of the manufacturing process was pushed toward a total analysis. Already assembly line work and its socio-psychological corollaries, developed by Henry Ford and Frederick Winslow Taylor, appear at the end of this evolving elimination of complete tasks.

Taylorism: The Hour of Tame Gorillas

Mass production as we know it today appeared in the United States of America at the end of the nineteenth century with the experiment of F.W. Taylor in the railroad car shops of the Bethlehem Steel Company; but its real career dates from the day in 1910 when Henry Ford launched the Model T Ford from his Detroit factories. Since that time, mass production has developed the world over, reaching the agricultural sector (American cotton plantations or Soviet

---

16. Naville, *Essai sur la qualification du travail*, p. 41.

kolkhozes) as well as the tertiary sector (widespread mechanization of office work.)

The fundamental principle of 'scientific management' is the concentration of production decisions in the hands of a central authority. The workers no longer represent a highly skilled, diversely utilizable potentiality, but men assigned to work posts. Task analysis does not concern itself with the individual potential of this or that worker, but with stages of the production process. Training on the job increasingly replaces traditional occupational training. The occupational hierarchy reflects these changes: for the old names of *métiers*, heavy with socio-cultural baggage, is substituted an abstract categorization based on a simple appraisal of the rapidity of movements. The goal of the training was moreover to obtain from the workers a genuine conditioning of physiological reflexes, calling for no reflection, initiative, or knowledge. With the exception of a few privileged workshops, of some sectors preserved from industry where 'whole labor' persisted, occupational skill was driven out of large-scale industry. Moreover, most of the old workers proved incapable of adapting to this new 'work;' on the other hand, many elements without a working-class tradition—among which women comprised an increasingly large part—entered into production.

Large masses, until now kept apart from the problems of capitalist society, were thrown in, often in dramatic conditions. The semi-skilled worker is the proletarian in the pure state: even the consciousness of participating individually in social activity has been wrested from his. Depersonalized abstract [*abstractisé*] labor was no longer the means of insertion in the world that it remained for the skilled worker. In the plant itself, a vast hierarchicalized agglomeration, work relations ceased to be human relations: the more numerous the working group, the greater the isolation of each worker at his machine.

Industrial sociologists have pointed to the phenomenon of 'de-skilling' for a long time. From observations made in 1945 in the principal American factories, Georges Friedmann noted that training on the job, so widely-practiced in modern enterprises, could in no case be compared to a genuine occupational training. Nevertheless, after two or three days of training, the new arrivals were put on the production line and at the end of about sixty days their productivity could rival that of their most experienced comrades.

Contrary to the fallacious hopes which most union militants, themselves issued from the old stratum of skilled workers, continued to entertain, occupational training is no longer indispensable, given the progress of technology. Most of the specialists of the Methods Departments even think that it is more harmful than helpful to productivity.

In 1911, F.W. Taylor estimated that it would be possible to carry out production with tame gorillas.[17] This cynical naiveté is no longer fashionable in organizing work. But the end in mind has not changed; it is still very much a question of developing to a maximum in the worker machine-like and automatic aptitudes, of breaking the old physical and psychic concept of skilled occupational labor which demands a certain active participation of the intelligence, initiative, and taste of the worker, and of reducing operations solely to their mechanical aspects.

In France as in Italy, the weight of artisanal tradition, the cultural heritage of the working class, the scorn for 'mass' production, weighed for a long time on production operations. Social legislation, the fruit of long battles of the labor movement, protected the *'metier'* longer than elsewhere. But this situation could not prolong itself when it was a question of European industry resisting the invasion of the market by American mass production. The laws of the economy swept away the resistances.

To be sure, the frequent conflicts provoked by the spread of 'fragmented work' very quickly brought about a reaction to the mechanistic current of industrial relations developed by Taylor, Ford, and their European emulators (among whom one can not fail to make a special place for the engineer Bédaux who inaugurated, with the adaptation of wages to 'points' of production determined as a function of each work post, a whole new practice of wage relations free of all 'personalization').

Industrial Social Psychology: The Reaction to Taylorism

Starting in 1924, the psychologist Elton May established on the basis of a multi-year study made at the Hawthorne plant of Western Electric that industrial relations in the mechanized factory remained humanist relations and that the 'hedonist' incitations alone, allied

---

17. As Taylor puts it: This work [pig iron handling] is so crude and elementary in its nature that this writer firmly believes that it would be possible to train an intelligent gorilla so as to become a more efficient pig iron handler than any man can be." F.W. Taylor, *The Principles of Scientific Management*, New York: Norton, 1967 (first published in 1911), p. 40.

to physiological research on the material conditions of work, did not suffice to compensate for the 'lack of interest' that the robotized worker brought to his work.[18] The analysis of Mayo, and following him all the researches on the social psychology of work—the work of Moreno, or the Bethel school, or Lewin[19]—have incontestably helped to demystify an atomistic theory of *homo oeconomicus* which justified, through the unpolished physiology of the nineteenth century, the enslavement of man to the machine; they rediscovered the importance of social structures in the productive group.

Yet in reality the intervention of social psychological methods in the conduct of interindustrial relations rapidly ran into an insurmountable obstacle: it is that 'scientific management' appeared more as a transitional phase, a compromise between the structure of interindustrial relations of phase A (manufactory) and that of the socialized organization of production announced by the whole development of industrial society, than as a final phase. "The semi-skilled worker," said Georges Friedmann, "is the stopgap substitute for automation."

The industrial organization of phase B already exhibited strongly its tendency to integration. In this direction, the subjection of workmanship to the production system, of technique to organization, represented a fundamental break with the old system of production. The enterprise, as a homogeneous production unit, had integrated both its shops and its producers. But the persistence of productive activity by men, the assignment of men to machines, maintained the appearance of the traditional type of occupational activity: the illusion of 'individual productivity,' of an 'individual labor,' or an 'individual production.' This anachronistic persistence of a notion of 'individual productivity' that Mayo, like most industrial social psychologists after him, did not criticize, was not the pure product of a lag in awareness.

We have seen that in phase A, fabrication is so to speak separated from management. Although he is located in the employer's enterprise, the worker conducts himself toward the employer somewhat as a subcontracting artisan. The employer's profit appears

---

18.   The standard reference on the Hawthorne studies is F.J. Roethlisberger and William J. Dixon, *Management and the Worker*, Cambridge: Harvard University Press, 1939.

19.   J.L. Moreno was an innovator in many fields, including sociometry and psychodrama; the National Training laboratories at Bethel, Maine, have been instrumental in the spread of sensitivity training; and Kurt Lewin's writings on group dynamics have influenced a large number of social psychologists.

to him as the remuneration for capital invested in the fixed equipment of the factory and the stocks of raw materials, and above all for the commercial risk assumed by the entrepreneur. This is the source of the continuance, so protracted despite the diffusion of Marxist theses on surplus value, of the notion of the 'just price of labor.' Moreover, in piecework, the predominant form of payment for the skilled categories, the worker himself adds up his own output.

Along with occupational autonomy, 'scientific management' destroyed the justification for wages based on individual output. In the integrated factory, individual output no longer existed: it was a direct outcome of the soundness of the organization itself as a whole, i.e., of a production system from whose decisions the worker is by definition excluded. Social psychologists today are beginning to formulate this in explicit terms when they observe that if it is logically consistent, industrial social psychology research must go, as far as questioning the decision-making powers in the enterprise.

Besides its economic advantages—a greater flexibility of the productive organization, a less important immobilization of fixed capital—the 'fragmentation' of work has the great advantage for management of preserving the illusion of an individual contract between the hirer and the hired, and therefore of eliminating the latter from the organic life of the enterprise. In fact, the semiskilled worker, stripped of individual advantages, of the real autonomy which his capital of skill used to assure him, and excluded from the management of the productive whole in which he participates, cannot but feel sentiments of hostility and indifference toward the enterprise.

Class Consciousness and the Fragmented Worker

Taken as a whole, this situation led the workers to experience more strongly the feeling of belonging to a 'specific class'—opposed by nature to other social classes. This class feeling was not, to be sure, a new phenomenon: what was new was, on the one hand, its extension to very large masses, including the worker's family, and on the other hand, the alienation of a part of its content. For the skilled worker, 'class consciousness' was characterized by the double consciousness of being exploited and being the producer of wealth. "Producers, let us save ourselves," wrote Eugène Pottier.[20] And the exploitation was

---

20. In the verse that became *l'Internationale*.

principally felt in terms of just this quality of producer. The worker's family, especially the women and girls, stayed apart from class activities, as it was apart from productive activities. In the workers' suburbs filled with semi-skilled workers, it went quite differently. Class consciousness was grounded essentially in the feeling of exploitation, and this was felt as the expression of an inequality in the distribution of wealth. Class consciousness thereby ceased to be directly linked to productive activity and became the expression of a social condition. There too, the terminology indicates the change undergone: the term 'proletariat,' charged with an entire symbolics of misery, replaced 'the world of work' or 'working class,' and even 'producers.'

The expression of labor's social demands thus moved from the place of production to the living place and therefore from direct conflict in production toward political and notably electoral struggle. Furthermore, several 'technical' conditions favored this sideslip: the insecure status of the semi-skilled workers made the organization of movements in the factory very difficult. On the other hand, the grouping of workers' living places made geography a stronger coordinating element. From this came the importance taken in the union movement by the local and departmental unions alongside the federations of industry, and by the same token the closer tie between union and political struggles. What the semi-skilled worker was incapable of obtainng as a producer, he sought to gain as a consumer; the role of the working class municipality as an organ for the redistribution of wealth became larger.

The very nature of labor demands changed. Superficially, one may say that, conscious of clashing with capitalism as a whole and not with an individual and isolated employers' group, the working class became conscious of the political dimensions of its action. The considerable progression of Socialist, then Communist votes in the legislative elections seems to confirm this thesis. Nevertheless, this view is only partial.

For parallel to the extension of the electoral influence of workers' parties, one witnessed a progressive deterioration of union power. The percentage of organized members fell: outside a few periods of intense activity (1935-37, 1945-46), the union movement no longer succeeded in organizing the majority of workers. Moreover, the overall rates of unionization were falsified by the permanence of old structures. The shop steward ceased to be the direct representative of the group: with the introduction of the election of stewards (starting in 1936 with their official recognition), the gap between the rank and file and the union militant was accentuated. The latter was obliged to take into account in his activity this redoubtable unknown, the reaction of what the *C.F.D.T.* today calls '*la basse base*' [the lower base] and the *C.G.T.* 'the unorganized.' [These were] unforeseeable reactions, which gave birth to the collective psychological notion known as 'the climate.'

A double evolution thus appeared within the French union movement, which followed a tradition already rooted in the English and German union movements where the passage of the economy to the stage of industrial capitalism had been more rapid.

On the one hand, unionism evolved toward a systematic search for free bargaining with employers. The dialogue became the principal element of union action, struggle and conflict being no more than a secondary element.

On the other hand, in order to obtain overall protection for its constitutents, the union movement relied more and more on the political parties and Parliament, and this protection was no longer accorded without cost: political rivalries penetrated the union apparatus, breaking union solidarity in decisive fashion.

This evolution was clearly favored by the changes taking place in the nature of the State. As capitalist concentration developed, as the economy became integrated (in a country where until 1914 autarchic agrarian structures continued to make up the vast majority), the State penetrated the workings of the economy more and more deeply. The very importance of its role forbade its being exlusively on the side of the employers, at least in too visible a manner. It tended more and more to intervene in their favor only to the extent that their interests went in the direction of the overall development of capitalism.

Toward the authorities, the confederations and federations of industry followed a standing policy of a relatively passive presence, trying mainly to obtain by and from the law advantages of a general nature which reinforced their influence and their instruments of representation with the workers. Collective agreements at the industrial branch level dispossessed the local or enterprise unions in favor of central organisms, the only ones recognized as 'valid negotiators' by the State as well as by the employers' organizations. Bargaining focused on narrowly technical criteria of general applicability—such as the *S.M.I.G.* [minimum wage], the wage hierarchy and, in the civil service, the notorious indexes, instruments which by their abstract and methematical nature totally escaped the comprehension of the rank and file.

The institutionalization of unionism, the importance it was led to acquire in macro-economic types of decisions, ought to have opened for it the path to a true *de facto* participation in power. In reality this did not happen; not only did union organizations prove impotent, except for conjunctural exceptions, to establish an organic liaison between the propositions which they formulated at the state level and the actions which they controlled or organized at the base, but they showed themselves to be just as incapable of linking together the demands of a general nature formulated by their industrial branch federations.

Instead of an economic program, the unions elaborated catalogs of demands. For the old unionism's hostility toward the State, it substituted an integration into the State without, for all that, elaborating an overall policy which alone would permit it to play a true role in [the exercise of] power.

Nevertheless, in transcribing into legislative terms, into acquired rights, the conquests which the workers wrested free when the economic conjuncture was favorable to them, it had a share in modifying the outlook of the authorities themselves. It aided in the development of new economic notions: expansion, greater market stability, full employment. In a word, unionism, transformed into a pressure group, helped to create the conditions of development of technocratic capitalism.

Phase C: Automation

It was only since the great crisis of 1927-1931 that the introduction of assembly line work and the standardization of mass production definitively eliminated 'quality' production. Moreover, the war of 1939-1945 completely checked the modernization process. Thus one could still, in 1959—while taking into account the gap which always persists between the appearance of phenomena and the awareness of their reality—consider the phenomena typical of 'fragmented work'—massive de-skilling, acceleration of work rhythms, decomposition of tasks—as the essential aspects of the evolution of industrial labor in France. In fact, behind the spread of mass production, an absolutely revolutionary technology was making its appearance: automation, a truly dialectical negation of the fragmentation of work, developed at full speed in the advanced industries, those whose object was the treatment of new materials: oil and petrochemicals, synthetic chemistry, electrical energy, telecomunications. During the years of economic expansion, (1950-56) it reached new sectors: *Renault*, with its automatic transfer machines [for machining engine blocks without human intervention] led the way in the automobile industry. The *SNCF* [French national railways] automated some of its installations, the *EDF* [French national electric utility] did the same, and the coal mines followed; the prolonged crisis in textiles, which precipitated concentrations, introduced into spinning and weaving in the north of France. The new steel complexes — *Sollac, Sidelor, Usinor* — progressively replaced their conventional rolling mills with automated ones and the new Dunkirk complex will only use 800 workers to accomplish a production identical with that of the 18,000 workers of Denain.[21] It reached a certain number of old industries, such as wood, class, and food products where it completely upset the existing mode of production. Finally, and it is even a sector where progress has been particularly rapid, office work itself has been very rapidly transformed by the introduction of computers, calculators, and the like. This widespread penetration of new techniques into sectors as differentiated as production, distribution, transports, and services renews in decisive fashion the very idea of the working class. Up to and including [the period of] specialization, the distinction between productive and unproductive labor remained relatively easy. To be sure it tended more and more to part company with the old distinction between manual and intellectual work upon which it had a tendency to superimpose itself at the beginnings of the industrial era, and took a more theoretical, more economic character.

In industry itself, the stockroom clerk performing an essentially manual task was classified in the 'white collar' category and as such was paid by the month, the notion of payment according to productivity being strictly linked to a process of creation of material worth, of object production. The semi-skilled worker, on the contrary, however fragmented his task, participated in this production of material worth and as such received an hourly wage plus a productivity bonus, a complex form of the traditional piece work wage. In automated industry, the nature of industrial labor is totally changed: one speaks more readily of 'supervisor' or 'operator' than of producer. It appears that the final logic of automation eliminates men from the stage of object-production. Objects are produced by other objects which are capable of self-adjustment, of correcting their own imperfections, even of producing themselves. In

---

21.   A study has since been done on this complex; see Jean-Daniel Reynaud et al., "Le personnel de l'usine de Dunkerque: attitudes, perspectives, et relations," *Studi di Sociologia* (Milano) 7 (1-2), 1969, pp. 157-188.

this self-regulated whole, man is no more than the distant demiurge which invents the mechanisms of production.

As André Barjonet has noted, the 'first industrial revolution,' most often linked to the discovery of the steam engine, was above all marked by the invention of the machine-tool: i.e., to the fact of fitting a tool to a motor replacing the human hand. In this sense, the gigantic progress accomplished by industrial technology since the eighteenth century is all situated in the same line of development (internal combustion engine and electricity included.) These advances did not constitute a qualitative change in production technique. Down to this day, most of the technical discoveries applied in classical industry still belong to this series: automatically powered machines eternally redo the same operation once the motive force is provided. True automation, which was able to develop only with the discovery of electronics, ensures not only the totality of operations formerly effected by the human hand, but also certain functions reserved until now to the human brain. Feed-back processes, the self-regulation of operations and errors, the synthesis of certain economic data, and the computerization of conventional production operations are all entirely normal today.

In these conditions, the intervention of men is increasingly exiled to the 'before' and 'after' of the production process strictly defined. Its domain is found on the level of intellectual creation, of invention, on the one hand, and of supervision on the other.

The essential element of production having become its equipment, the essential concern of the capitalist will be to amortize exceedingly costly machinery in the minimum time period, and he will naturally seek to adjust his labor and investment policies. The problem which presents itself for him will no longer be, as in 1925 or 1935, to have at hand a flexible and easily 'condensable' reservoir of labor, but on the contrary to assure himself a permanent labor force trained in the particular techniques of the company.

The Demands of the Workers

Technical evolution thus gives to the 'new working class' means of pressure much more effective than those which the semi-skilled workers, replaceable on the line from one day to the next, could possess.

Automated industry creates a new type of skill highly remote from the knowledge of the traditional *métier*, but which requires a much greater cultural and technological knowledge: it begins the progressive elimination of the distinction between manual and intellectual labor. In the same way, the gap which separated workers and *cadres*[22] is filled: between the operator of a cracking unit who, in a white collar, watches over the continuous flow of oil and the diverse pressures to which it is subjected and the engineer or higher level technician who supervises him, there is no longer a difference in kind, simply a difference of hierarchical situation—just as the relations between the pilot of a plane and the technicians of his crew are fundamentally different from those existing between the infantry commander and the mass of his soldiers. Modern industry tends to 'technicize' the entire working class at the same time that it reduces the number of persons used in production.

These tendencies have brought about a certain number of new orientations in the union movements of these firms: to the extent that the production unit is more homogeneous, where the workers know each other and where mingling between workers and technicians takes place more easily, setting up the union organization is easier and union membership more sought after.

The technical characteristics of the enterprise give, we have seen, the working class more effective means of pressure than in the past: the security of militants is better assured: one does not replace an electronics techician overnight as one replaces a semi-skilled worker. This reinforces the confidence of workers and technicians, leads them to organize without fear of employers' sanctions. The rate of unionization in the productive sectors of the electronics, electro-mechanics, oil and chemical industries very often exceeds fifty per cent of the workers; in metallurgy the rate of unionization according to the different unions scarcely exceeds fourteen to eighteen percent; even this figure is distorted because workers in small firms, very often unionized in a purely formal way, are often included.[23]

We also observe an important change in the nature of demands. The immediate demands appear more and more linked with the totality of the technico-economic organization of the firm, with the form of work organization, with production rhythms. Demands then show a trend toward demands for control over the direction of the enterprise itself. They sometimes take forms unexpected from a

---

22. *cadres*: middle and lower echelon management
23. In evaluating these percentages, it should be remembered that the check-off system does not exist in France and all dues must be collected each month by the union steward.

union movement: thus in February, 1960, the Massey-Harris workers at Lille (a company in which the percentage of technicians is on the order of sixty-five per cent) went on strike to obtain the departure of their director!

The technician working class, strongly integrated into the production process, is led to demand, beyond its immediate needs, the possession of certain instruments of control over the economic activity which makes it live. At the beginning, this trend appeared principally at the level of the enterprise: the recent development of firm-level contracts shows how, in certain cases, it can come to an actual institutionalization of elements of workers' control over production.

The firm-level contracts are formulas for contractual accords between employers and wage earners begun on a narrowly paternalistic basis. For the former, it was a question of concluding with more or less consenting unions an ideological accord in which the employers pledged practically nothing at all, but through which, on the other hand, the union forbade itself all action at the work place. But it very quickly went beyond this character to appear as the new form of the negotiated accord between unionism and the employers in the framework of an economy where the concept of the enterprise tends to take an increasingly large place. It thus replaces the old round table agreements concluded at the level of an industrial branch. The disparity between enterprises in France is in effect such that the advantages acquired by modern industrial workers cannot be extended to less developed enterprises without serious resistance by the small and middle sized employers, which would block negotiations. In the course of the recent period, the renewing of firm-level agreements took place in the context and under the pressure of powerful strike movements, which introduced the maximum of advantages for the working class into the accord. The development of mass actions with a view to including in the enterprise accords not only immediate demands but also clauses assuring the unions of control over a certain number of elements of management probably marks a decisive turning point in the strategy of the French labor movement, and the first attempt of the working class to adapt its forms of struggle to the new structures of capitalism.

But this evolution had been possible only because of the greater and greater autonomy of the large enterprise sublocals with respect to the confederal leadership, and because of the development of a new type of labor unionism, founded on the objective notion of the integration of the workers into production. Other evolutions also came to spur the development of these new union orientations.

A New Conception of the Strike

In the unionism of the semi-skilled workers, the limits to the demands of a movement were always determined by what is called 'the climate' which established itself at a certain moment in a factory. Spontaneity thus played a greater role than the organization and leadership of the union. Because of this fact, movements in no way took into account objective criteria which could have ensured success. One has very often seen a company's management, facing a production surplus, push their workers to go on strike, so as to obtain the desired slowing of their productive capacity without assuming the financial burden.

In most large and medium sized modern enterprises, on the contrary, where the higher rate of unionization and more elaborate technical training of the personnel permit a greater cohesion and confer greater authority on the unions, the notion of climate disappears almost totally from the basic facts of the action, and one arrives at a true scientific organization of strikes. Instead of launching unlimited strikes which cut heavily into the buying power of strikers, the union, relying on a deepened knowledge of the production system of the enterprise, organizes the systematic disorganization of production by limited work stoppages, spread out along the production posts at the most sensitive places. The slogan of the *Thomson-Houston* strikers in 1959—"three days of production lost by the employer, one hour of wages lost by the worker"—succeeded in paralyzing the production of the most important French electronics factory for a month and a half, without the workers having to notice it in their family budgets. In other cases, the union launched actions at certain delicate moments in the life of the enterprise, confronting it with difficulties which threatened to have repercussions on its competitive position. When prestigious companies are involved seeking psychological effects which are then exploited by the large daily press can also play a decisive role.

The Union Organization in the
Era of Automation

But it is not sufficient, one fears, that the [necessary] objective conditions exist in order to bring off such actions: it is also necessary that the union organizations be up to organizing and supervising them, and this involves several conditions:

1) As a general rule, interunion unity comes about fairly easily on the question of demands, but the morning after a strike or a day of action, it disintegrates again; worse yet, if the movement drags on, the practical modes and techniques of action always give rise to controversies which turn into 'ideological' debates. Now what is peculiar to the new forms of action is that they require long term *continuous action*, in which the technical conditions for the fulfillment of the movement must be *constantly modified*. They leave no room for interunion competition: they require, more than coordination, the unity of leadership. Thus all the companies where actions of this type have been possible have seen permanent interunion committees form on the model of the one formed at *Thomson-Houston*, which assure an actual organic unity among the rank and file.

2) But union cohesiveness settles nothing if it does not rely on an adaptation to the particular conditions of the enterprise: bypassing the old union rules, [the unions in] several enterprises of the Paris region have, within the last two years, adopted a unified union structure, regrouping the different sublocals of geographically dispersed companies on the basis of trust. This new structure, made necessary by a recognition of the determinisms of the modern enterprise, is spreading. In the same way, the old occupational classifications gave way before industrial realities.

3) Finally, at the basis for the movement's demands is the productive organization of the enterprise itself, an understanding by militant workers of the market mechanism and of financial management of the firm is indispensable. This knowledge—which has begun to revalidate the role of the plant committee [*comité d'entreprise*][24]—thus leads the unions themselves to ask about the problems of company management. More and more often, it is the validity of the policies conducted by the managers which are called into question.

Thus, new conceptions of demands and conflict have been progressively elaborated in the union movement which, beginning with the fitting of the forms of conflict to the conditions of

---

24. Since 1945, a *comité d'entreprise* is supposed to exist in all firms with fifty or more workers. Elected by all workers, it is intended to have a measure of responsibility in directing the firm's *oeuvre sociale*, which can include restaurants, recreation programs, and certain social welfare arrangements. For a careful study of their functioning, see Maurice Montuclard, *La Dynamique des comités d'entreprise*, Paris: CNRS, 1963.

production, lead toward the control of the organization of production itself.

Enterprise-based unionism shares, on an organizational basis, certain traits with craft unionism: a high rate of participation in union activity, de-bureaucratization through the enhanced role of the sublocals of each company, an orientation toward control. They have another trait in common: mistrust toward traditional forms of political conflict, and the belief in the validity of organized union action. Some have spoken of the renaissance of a 'modern anarchosyndicalism.' It nevertheless differs fundamentally on two counts:

a) the emphasis placed on [macro-] economic phenomena;

b) the narrowness of 'company spirit' serves, more seriously than in the corporatism of the *métier*, to isolate the elements of the working class in advanced sectors of industry from the other strata of the population. From this point of view, class solidarity, which in the craft union was expressed in the form of corporative solidarity, is absent from the enterprise-based union.

The Future of Union Action

The problem posed by the future evolution of unionism is found entirely in the contradiction existing between these last two attitudes:

a) given the overall integration of the economy, and the osmosis of economy and politics in industrial society, in order to be effective, all orientations toward control in an enterprise necessarily lead toward general position-taking at the level of the entire economy. Economic choices can no longer be made within the limits of one firm, no matter how important.

b) 'Company spirit,' not in the classic sense of submission to the company's management, but in the sense of a particularistic conception of the needs and aspirations of the company's wage-earners, could bring union leaderships to enter into conflict—on grounds of group interests—with other fractions of the union movement, and [to act] in the same direction as the management of their companies. The problem of 'particularism' is not, moreover, specific to the capitalist form of relations of production. It exists in the Soviet Union and it comes up in Yugoslavia where workers' self-management exists.

It is the total character of the economy in our time which is the best protection of enterprise-based unionism against the particularistic tendencies or narrow corporatist retrogression; this same character helps to diffuse the tendencies toward a control orientation into sectors where the objective conditions for these tendencies do not yet exist.

We could thus be led to say that the new consumption trends, founded on credit, correspond essentially to the situation created for wage-earners of the most advanced branches of the economy. Now we know that credit, institutionalized by the State itself, notably in the case of construction, has been rapidly extended to all strata of the population, including that fraction of the working class population, the largest, which does not benefit from the job security which workers in the advanced industries enjoy.

In reality, the economic effects of the credit system could not have played their role if they were limited to the small fraction of the population enjoying job security (civil servants, technicians, workers in advanced industries).

The result is that at the present time, in the industries where traditionally the labor movement accepted job insecurity as a given and organized its material life with this situation in mind, the demand for job security has become the principal demand of the French working class, while the demands for wage increases have passed to a secondary level. The demand has led it to be preoccupied with the economic situation of the companies and sectors in which it works and to pose the problem of a structural reform guaranteeing economic stability to the entire economy and not just to a few privileged branches.

Thus, beginning with the effects that certain sectors have on the entire economy, we see a growing consciousness which, starting from economic demands particular to a certain sector, a certain firm, a certain region, brings the totality of the economic system into question and leads union organizations to go beyond the level of struggles for particular categories of workers and to move toward the demand for worker control over production, on the level of the company as on that of the entire society.

Alongside the traditional political front held by the parties and the social front held by the unions, we are therefore witnessing the opening of a third front in the secular struggle of capital and labor: the economic front, on which the labor movement contests the existing system, starting neither from ideological options nor from social demands, but from the practical observation of the impotence of this system to ensure the uninterrupted and harmonious development of productive forces.

The traditional distribution of roles among the union movement and the political movement of the working class thereby finds itself called anew into question and the unions find themselves led, as economic organisms, to politicize themselves in the true sense of the term, i.e., not to echo in a faded form the electoral slogans of this or that political party, but to intervene actively with the means and forms of action specifically theirs, in the political life of the country.

.

Socialism and the New Working Class [1]

Two tactics.

The analysis presented to this conference by Herbert Marcuse was, in many ways, similar to my own exposition of the situation of the working class movement in the advanced western countries. However, he differed fundamentally from me in his interpretation and his conclusions. There is no need for me to stress the importance of his contribution. There is no doubt that the theoretical theses which he put forward here are the most serious yet to have been developed by those Marxists who have come down on the side of Mao Tse-tung in the Sino-Soviet theoretical debate. In my opinion, it has been very salutary to have before us here a paper of such a kind, distinguished by its political and scientific honesty and free from the partisan and frequently hypocritical quibbles which mar the Chinese texts themselves.

Both Lucien Goldmann and Henri Lefebvre have made it clear that they do not believe that Marcuse's interpretation is correct as far as it applies to the European countries; but they felt it possible that his analysis might very well be true of America. Herbert Marcuse, however, defended his position on the grounds that, since the United States is economically more advanced than the European capitalist countries, it cannot be long before the phenomena which he denounces spread to western Europe. I feel bound to challenge this point of view of Marcuse's a second time, but on strictly methodological grounds, since I do not have the necessary knowledge of American society to do otherwise.

1. This article was first published in *Praxis* Nos. 2-3, 1965: the English translation included here first appeared in the *International Socialist Journal*, 1965, and is republished here with permission. We have cut the first 14 pages of this article, which are reproduced almost ver batim in "May-June, 1968," and which were cut by Mallet in the anthology *Le pouvoir ouvrier* where some minor changes are made in the text as well. The footnotes here are those which Serge Mallet added at the editors' request.

First, I would like to discuss the role of precursor which Marcuse attributes to the United States, basing my arguments on a series of lectures which he himself gave, two years ago, at the *Ecole des Hautes Etudes* in Paris. At that time, Marcuse held that although the American productive apparatus was immeasurably more developed than that of the western European countries, it was in those countries—and particularly in France—that what he aptly called 'organization capitalism' was furthest advanced and most institutionalized. Marcuse recalled Engels' celebrated remark about France, "the land where class struggles take the most sharply defined form and give rise to the most clear-cut political structures."

Indeed, any French observer is surprised to see the timidity with which "liberal" theoreticians such as Galbraith put forward arguments which are accepted in France by the most backward capitalist groups. The fascist tendencies which are developing today in the United States around the Goldwater phenomenon, which seem to be the product of an alliance between racists from the South, whose privileges are threatened by racial integration, and the most archaic elements of American capitalism, afraid of any advance towards state capitalism, do not seem to me to be a vanguard phenomenon but the re-appearance on a ten times vaster scale of conflicts which emerged in France at the time of the Algerian war and the Poujadist movement—that is to say, the desperate reaction of archaic elements in French society against the establishment of organization capitalism. The USA have just, after several years, set foot on the path that western Europe has been travelling down since 1945. If this hypothesis is true, and Marcuse at least seems to accept it, then we are definitely better placed than him to analyze the contradictions of organization capitalism.

Secondly, I am surprised that Marcuse should have based his conclusions about the voluntary integration of the American working class into organization capitalism on the findings of positivist and empiricist sociology. Even in France, our experience in this field has shown us time and again that a common type of inquiry, based on collecting questionnaires and interview of individual respondents, leads in the end to very coarse interpretations which are frequently refuted by more precise methods of analysis, based on group techniques and "non-directivism."[2] The respondents reply

---

2. A grotesque demonstration of the 'scientific' value of this methodology has been given in France by a survey carried out by the *Institut Français d'Opinion publique* under the direction of Prof. Jean Stoetzel in March, 1968. A very large sample of

automatically in the way the question indicates or seems to indicate, on account of extrinsic social conditioning. The majority of the replies are always slanted towards an acceptance of the dominant ideological themes, even though, very soon after the inquiry, the explosion of a particular social movement may prove that this conformism does not genuinely correspond with the respondent's real motivations. In the circumstances in which American sociology of work operates, it is not at all likely to give an accurate picture of the working class's degree of acceptance or non-acceptance of organization capitalism. America lacks a Marxist sociology even more than France. On the one hand, there are empiricist sociologists integrated into the system and participating, *bon gré mal gré*, in the fabrication of an appropriate ideology for organization capitalism; on the other hand, there are uncompromised academic sociologists, confined in their university ghettoes and cut off from the realities of American production. In between, there is scarcely anything; hence the difficulty we have in knowing anything conclusive about American society.

In my opinion, Marcuse also uses the concepts adopted by bourgeois economists in a non-critical way, although they correspond less and less to the facts as time goes on. For instance, Marcuse refers to the strengthening of the tertiary sector as against the weakening of the secondary sector. But we have found, and this must hold good for the United States even more than for France, that Colin Clark's terminology seems outmoded when applied to automatized industry. So, without making any judgments myself about the development of American society, I must protest against the grounds on which Marcuse bases his pessimistic interpretation. Furthermore, I would like to say something about one of his principal themes: the theme of the "principal revolutionary class." For Marcuse — and apparently for most American Marxists as well as Chinese Marxists — the only potentially revolutionary class in the advanced countries is the immigrant proletariat or the racial minorities. Evidently the situation is rather different in the USA, where the minorities have American citizenship, and in Western Europe, where they are aliens in the country where they are working. Marcuse's view was outlined, at another juncture, at the time of the Algerian war in France, by the group centered around Sartre and Francis Jeanson; these intellectuals held that the transition to socialism in France

---

workers was questioned on their attitudes toward the social policies of the Gaullist regime; a majority indicated that they were 'fairly satisfied.' A month later, ten million workers were on strike. — SM

could be implemented only through the aggravation of the Algerian conflict and its overspill into France itself through the large Algerian work-force in France. The armed Algerian proletariat was the substantial force, to which the left intellectuals would rally; it was the "only stratum which had escaped integration into neo-capitalism."

We know what happened to that dream. It is of course the case that the development of America has left an important part of the population to make their way outside the prosperity of the affluent society. But this "people of the abyss"—the phrase is Jack London's—is in fact nothing more than a minority, as such incapable of bringing about any total upheaval in social structure. Perhaps, in the last analysis, the negro question in the USA will be resolved by the creation of independent black states seceding from the central government, but this would be no more than a final phase of the colonial revolutions which have taken place throughout Africa and Asia.

As for the situation of the immigrant work-force in Western Europe, their position is quite different—indeed, all the more so for the success of the liberation struggles of the colonized nations. Until very recently, immigration into a developed country from an under-developed country, in Africa, Asia or Southern Europe, was a purely individual act. Immigrant workers, who on their arrival were completely isolated, tried to integrate themselves into the working class movements and trade unions of their new country, particularly because in countries like France and England most of these immigrants coming from colonial territories were, in any case, treated as full citizens.

However, during the last few years, organization capitalism has tended to organize the import of labor, in accordance with its new needs: quotas are fixed by arrangement at governmental level, as a quid-pro-quo for the development aid which the developed countries are giving their newly independent ex-colonies. Workers who are immigrants in this sense continue to depend on their own governments, even when they are in Europe, and they are organized in movements under governmental control. Newly independent governments, forced to rely on economic and technical aid, take good care, as their part of the bargain, that there is no collusion between the immigrant work-force and the domestic working class opposition. This new situation has grown up with ex-colonies, which are now effectively maintained by neo-colonialist methods. The agreements recently concluded between France and Algeria show that this situation holds good even when the ex-colony has a revolutionary side to it. What's more, two years ago a delegation of French employers opened negotiations with none other than the Chinese government, with a view to importing Chinese labor, which was to arrive organized and controlled by its own political institutions, in return for which China would be guaranteed the development of economic relations with France as a loophole in the economic blockade from which she suffered.[3]

Thus, the immigrant workers, far from being a potential revolutionary force in the advanced capitalist country, are in fact quite the reverse: a means of economic and political pressure on the domestic working class.

Moreover, for several years the growth of immigration has seemed to capitalism the easy answer to its contradictions. In Western Europe, as in the United States, it is the shortage of labor which forces capitalism to favor the introduction of automation. At this juncture, it is the state sector which for the most part carries the responsibility. Capitalism is able to make use of the economic difficulties of newly independent countries to procure the economically useful and politically inoffensive work-force for itself on the cheap; in this way, it can slow down the technical development of the productive forces and all the consequences which would follow, such as the fall in the rate of profit and the undermining of capitalism's independent structures. It is no exaggeration to say that the massive import of controlled immigrant labor as a result of intergovernmental agreements is, in fact, the principal source of weakness for the working class movement in the advanced countries of the western world.[4] So long as capitalism has this reservoir of available labor, there will be no spreading of automation, no reduction in working hours, no development of demands for a share in management. There are therefore direct contradictions between the interests of the

---

3. These discussions remain without a conclusion. On the other hand, agreements of the same type were negotiated with 'revolutionary' African governments, such as Mali, which was then led by Mobido Keita. [Added by SM for English edition.]

4. This thesis needs some correction. At the time of the May-June 1968 movement in France, as well as during certain 'wildcat strikes' in Hamburg and Schleswig-Holstein in Western Germany, the immigrant workers joined—for the first time—the actions of indigenous workers, and in highly combative fashion. But in no case were they the 'cutting edge.' On the contrary, it was only to the extent that the massive and radical character of the French (or German) workers' movement appeared to them as a sufficient protection that they were able to surmount the constraints that their immigrant status imposed on them. —SM

advanced working class and the prospects for socialism in the advanced western countries and the short-term interests and prospects of the newly independent nations. This contradiction can only be resolved at a higher level, at the time when the working class movement will be able to use its strength to grant a greater amount of technical aid to the newly independent nations, so that they can develop their productive potential with rapidity and thus absorb their own excess labor power. In contrast, their present policy of suing the excess work-force as if it were a bargaining counter to use to fill their coffers goes directly against the interests of the socialist movement in western Europe. In these circumstances, it is a complete hallucination, utterly without foundation, to see the immigrant working class as the vanguard of any movement to overthrow the established system.

No discussion of the prospects for the transition to socialism in the advanced countries can evade the issue which Henri Lefebvre discussed — that of the contradictions between the technocratic state sector and managers of private industry within organization capitalism itself and the connected issue of the relations between this state technocracy and the socialist movement, not only during the phase when organization capitalism is still pre-eminent, but also in the first phase of the construction of socialism. The papers presented to this conference by Yugoslav theoreticians — especially Vranicki, Milic and Supec — were of great interest precisely because they showed how, in the first phase of socialism, tehcnocratic and bureaucratic phenomena are inevitable and necessary, but how the working class movement must simultaneously set up nuclei of self-management as a counterpose to these technocratic trends: finally the strengthening of self-management must depend on the disappearance of these techno-bureaucratic structures linked with the very existence of the state itself. In the advanced capitalist countries, state technocracy and private organization capitalism both collaborate and combat each other. In practice, the state technocracy is constantly in an ambiguous position, caught between private capitalism and the socialist forces. Its fate is tied to the development of the productive forces and not to the ownership of the means of production and thus it is led into conflict with private capitalism each time it tries to slow down the development of the productive forces. On the other hand, it tends to re-ally itself with private capitalism each time that the working class movement threatens to challenge the hierarchic structure of the enterprises and economic system from which the technocracy draws its privileges and its power. The outcome of the conflict between capitalism and socialism in the advanced countries depends to a large extent on the possibility of forging a permanent alliance between the state technocracy and the working class movement. However, during this phase, the technocracy will tend to subordinate the working class movement to itself and hence the working class movement cannot wait until it has won full economic and political power before it sets up nuclei of self-management which will enable it, at a later stage, to counterbalance and finally to eliminate altogether the influence of the technocracy. Far from putting an end to its contradictions, as Marcuse supposes, organization capitalism engenders new contradictions, whose particular character is that they apply not only to the last stage of capitalism, but also to the first stage of socialism, though, of course, under different forms. Hence, on the basis of such an analysis, the working class movement must obviously reject the old notion of a minimum programme and a maximum programme. In fact, organization capitalism has already entered a stage of compromise, in which it is possible for the working class movement to grasp some of the economic power and I am fully in agreement with the comparison which Lucien Goldmann made when he recalled how, although the French bourgeoisie did not seize political power till 1789, it was by then already in command of economic power.

Not only will the phase of organization capitalism bring about a sharpening of its own internal contradictions but it will also bring about a sharpening of inter-imperialist contradictions. During the phase when finance capital reigned supreme over the economies of the great capitalist countries, contradictions tended to be neutralized by the interpenetration of capital. In contrast, the development of a state sector within organization capitalism tends to sharpen competition and increase the antagonisms between the various imperialist powers. It is clear, for example, that, probably because it is the country where organization capitalism is most developed, France had reached the point where it is leading resistance to American plans for world hegemony. At any rate, Germany and Italy, although their economic interests are just as antagonistic to America, are much more subservient and this may well be because of the much slighter role which the public sector and the state technocracy play in their economies. The development of inter-imperialist contradictions will give new opportunities to these countries which are subjugated by the most powerful capitalist power, particularly the countries of Latin America. Thus, both on the international level and in each country taken by itself, organization capitalism has been unable to overcome the classic contradictions of the capitalist system, as well as engendering new ones.

It is of the utmost importance to draw up a new strategy to solve the problems of the transition to socialism in the economically advanced countries; organization capitalism is engendering both new contradictions and new opportunities.

May-June 1968: First Strike for Control[1]

This is the fourth French edition of *La Nouvelle Class Ouvrière*, first published in 1963. Certain aspects of the descriptions contained in the book, some of the situations analyzed there, are today dated, even outmoded. This is even more true of the monographic part of the work, the outcome of studies done between 1958 and 1962.

But Alain Touraine is not wrong in considering that 1958 constitutes a break in the political and social history of France,[2] particularly with respect to the labor and union movement. Even if the economic conditions for it had been brought together during the long period of almost uninterrupted economic expansion from 1950 to 1958, it was only with the fall of the Fourth Republic that France, under the Gaullist scepter, entered — politically and institutionally — into the phase of 'organization capitalism,' to adopt the expression that Herbert Marcuse, then unknown to the French public, used during his course at the *Ecole pratique des Hautes Etudes* in 1962. May, 1968 is the first response to June, 1958, the first socialist struggle responding to modern capitalism.

Viewed from this perspective, the work remains, on the whole, entirely up-to-date. At least it seems so to me — and the reader will judge for himself. I have thus chosen not to subject him to any artificial 'rejuvenation,' any re-surfacing of the façade, contenting myself to indicate in footnotes the situational changes which have arisen since this time....

The reader must nevertheless be informed of certain modifications. He will not find here one of the three monographs on industrial firms from the first edition: the *Compagnie des Machines*

---

1. This essay appeared as the introduction to the fourth French edition of *La nouvelle classe ouvrière* (Paris: Seuil, 1969) and is reprinted here with the permission of the author.

2. *Le mouvement de mai ou le communisme utopique* (Paris: Seuil, 1968). SM [An English translation appeared in 1971: *The May Movement, Revolt and Reform* (New York: Random House).]

Bull.'[3]

The '*Compagnie des Machines Bull*' had been written in 1959. It was the oldest of the studies and consequently the one which had aged the most. [It was] also the one—and this was what determined its elimination—in which the analysis of the union activity of 'the new working class' was the least advanced—for the excellent reason that the new situation experienced by these young workers of the newly formed electronics industry had not yet found its expression in their social behavior.

This excision nevertheless entails a certain disequilibrium in the general picture of the industrial working class that I wished to present. While the two other monographs focussed upon two geographically united firms, two integrated production units, the study of the *Compagnie des Machines Bull* gave an account of observations made in three of the group's plants, each carrying out quite different activities and each one representative of the different 'phases' of industrial organization in this country.

Besides the Paris plant on the *avenue Gambetta*, the nerve center of the group where, with the research and development offices and the prototype construction shops, the essence of the technologically modern parts were concentrated, there were the provincial branches, decentralized shops of the main plant, having no initiative concerning the forms and rhythms of production. The Saint Quentin plant, formerly a specialized machine shop, 'rationalized' (i.e., robotized) a class of older skilled workers, while the Vendôme plant, using young girls of peasant origin almost exclusively, produced computer relays in the way cotton used to be woven fifty years ago around Armentières.

The Paris plant, rich in technicians and skilled workers, originator of a new type of job—for which the traditional criteria of classification (worker/technician, blue collar/white collar, second ary/tertiary) proved to be almost unusable—stood in opposition to the old 'reconverted' plants devoted to mechanical work, a hellish work pace, low wages, and insecure jobs.

---

3. In addition to a long theoretical chapter, a slightly different version of which is reprinted here ("Industrial Labor," pp. 17-47), *La nouvelle class ouvrière* contains three monographic studies, each one dealing with conditions and workers' responses in a technologically advanced firm. Besides his account of the ill-fated *Compagnie des Machines Bull*, which Mallet discusses here, the first edition included analyses of the electronics division of *Thomson-Houston* (now *Thomson-Houston-Hotchkiss-Brandt*) and of the Caltex oil refinery at Ambès. The latter study appears in English translation in Edward Shorter (ed.), *Work and Community in the West*, New York: Harper & Row, 1973, pp. 122-138.

[These were] transitional plants, stop-gaps against a coming automation whose generalization was retarded to the maximum by employers unsure of their financial and commercial situations, and whose introduction in France will always be slowed as long as internally or externally 'colonized workers,' Portuguese or Bretons, Algerians or Flemish, the rejects of technical education and peasants expelled by the concentration of agricultural lands, can be found to furnish a 'reserve' of unskilled slaves, always good enough for the assembly line, who have all the more difficulty defending their meager wages in that they know themselves to be permanently threatened by the danger of a 'modernization' for which they will foot the bill.

The subsequent fate of the *Compagnie des machines Bull*, taken over under conditions with which everyone is familiar by General Electric,[4] appeared as the bitter revenge of the 'colonialized workers' of Vendôme and Saint-Quentin and as the penalty for our capitalism's lobster-like fashion of advancing—backwards. The schema of structural dependence to which the former flower of French electronics was subjected by its new American master faithfully reproduced the one to which the *Compagnie des machines Bull* had subjected the personnel and *cadres* of the plants which it had taken over during its dynamic period. Here is an excellent subject of reflection for our centralizing planners, sincerely attached to French economic independence: the hierarchicalized industrial structures that they set up throughout the hexagon under the pompous title of 'concentration,' these bastard products of monarchical Colbertism and feudal capitalism, favor to the maximum the takeover of such units by more powerful groups disposing of markets, technological potency, and capital reserves ten times greater. American capital has only to flow into a world ready-made for it. Our capitalists, raised in the patriarchal tradition of a Michelin or a de Wendel, anxious to control their 'house' from the basement to the attic and their workers from the school to the cemetery, as well as our administration, which needs ministerial authorization to open a faucet to save the goldfish in the pond of the Rambouillet chateau, show themselves to be incapable of imagining

---

4. Subjected to increasingly severe competition by IBM, and suffering from internal managerial and technical problems, *Bull* was finally taken over by General Electric in 1964. The French government originally blocked the sale and sought to bail the company out, but subsequently abandoned its efforts in view of the firm's difficulties. General Electric eventually withdrew in its turn after having suffered heavy losses in its attempt to establish itself in the European computer market.

the truly 'supple' planning system which would assure the coordination of the activities of autonomous production units, each enjoying research and production initiative without isolating itself in a Malthusian stronghold. [These are] traits of our centralizing heritage, which leaves our suburbs only the choice between the promiscuity of barracks-like housing projects and the withering isolation of houses shut in by walls crenellated with shards of broken glass.

There is no chance of seeing French or even European industry escape the domination of American industrial and financial groups by copying administrative methods invented on a continental scale. We cannot permit ourselves the luxury of the waste constantly brought about by the obsolescence of these gigantic trusts—waste in the first place of human labor, intellectual and manual—waste of production too, a consequence of the famous 'erosion of morale' of which *Bull* was the victim. Moreover, it is necessary to know how far the world's greatest industrial power, incapable of giving regular work to one fourth of its active population, incapable at the same time of preventing its big cities from crumbling under the refuse of its permanent overproduction, will be able to go in this domain. The American J.K. Galbraith is less optimistic on this point than Jean-Jacques Servan-Schreiber.[5] The start of industrial democracy is in the self-regulation of advanced units of research and production. But it implies the destruction of the hierarchicalized administrative framework which, from top to bottom—and this is the story which this book tells—crushes initiative, blocks invention, rejects new democratic models of work organization toward which, the young industrial strata aspire wholeheartedly, though with a consciousness still obscured by the old authoritarian model.

The study on the *Compagnie des machines Bull* also illuminated the cohabitation within the most modern industry, within the same industrial groups, of a new type of working class, which by reason of its insertion in the most advanced sectors of production benefits from possibilities to think about its condition and to change it, and some more traditional strata, unskilled or de-skilled, who in a way carry on an outmoded phase of the industry to which they were attached. When added most of the time to an absence of a tradition of labor conflicts, this technological marginality naturally tends to make the

---

5. Jean-Jacques Servan-Schreiber, *The American Challenge* (New York: Atheaneum, 1968); John Kenneth Galbraith, *The Affluent Society* (Boston: Houghton Mifflin, 1958). —SM

semi-skilled workers of the 'decentralized' plants the sub-proletariat of the workd of work.

At the price of constantly increased physical and mental overwork, of a material distress not hidden by the precarious — and degraded — possession of consumer goods, symbols of our 'abundant society' — the second-hand car and the one-channel TV set — these obscure strata of our leading industries have largely compensated for the fall in profit rates imposed on the employers by their economic and technical development effort. The establishment — difficult to carry out — of separate balance sheets for each plant would probably show that Vendôme and Saint-Quentin for *Bull*, and Angers and Lesquin-les-Lille for *Thomson-Houston* have assured a good part of the initial financing of these industrial complexes. What a futile policy of vested interests [*politique de notables*] has called 'decentralization,' thus baptizing the scattering of production units stripped of all the real decision centers of the modern enterprise, showed itself in practice to be no more than a secondary form of the old 'primitive accumulation' of capital: the possibility of no longer grouping industrial plants on the production sites of primary materials has simply permitted capitalism to tap a cheap rural labor force on the spot — and thereby partially to palliate for a short time the necessities of a true enterprise modernization which would imply the installation of automated equipment with an infinitely longer amortization.

But as it is only a matter of a palliative, this labor force, which plays a non-negligible part in the development of key industries without really being integrated into them, creates, with the help of accelerated cadences and overtime, the conditions of its own elimination as an occupational group. The harder it works, the more it permits the big industrial firms to increase their self-financing and therefore their real modernization possibilities, and the more it hastens the hour of its eviction from the enterprise. At the time of the research on *Bull*, I noted the wide separation, the mutual ignorance of these two categories of workers in the same enterprise. In the research on *Thomson-Houston* in Bagneux, I witnessed the conflict between these two categories, this time within the same production unit. What happened in May, 1968 leads [me] to return to these misgivings.

The New Working Class in May, 1968

Surely, never as much as in May, 1968, has so clear a dichotomy appeared between the old and the new working class — all the clearer in that it appeared in a single, if not a unified, movement, in the context of a power vacuum which left the field open to deep antagonisms within the labor movement. It serves no purpose to regret it, even less to mask it: the absence of homogeneity of the labor movement was the sole life buoy to which, from the barricades of the Latin Quarter to the general elections, a faltering power clung. And it was this absence of a common will in the face of the political void opened in the decisive days of May 27-31 which made dizzy the mass of vacillating opinion and pushed it headlong into the arms of this specter of Banquo [De Gaulle], suddenly risen from among the dead.

I must emphasize: antagonisms within the labor movement, and not between workers and students, as many students, intimidated like blind kittens before a mythical 'working class' as little known to them in its diversity as it was to the grand masters of sociology who taught them, tend too much to believe. If the May conflict had split the labor movement and the student movement, the latter would not have had much weight and would have remained enclosed in its university ghettos, as in the United States or in West Germany. Nor should we repeat an inverse dogmatism: attempts to attribute to the *entire* working class the will to self-management which appeared massively in the most advanced sectors of industry are hardly serious — or consistent with the simple facts. But it is no truer to say that the working class fought only for its wages. An examination[6] of the factories on strike the day after the Grenelle accords[7] shows an almost perfect grouping (modified only by considerations of 'local climate') of the sectors which, entering the struggle late, in fact sought only the satisfaction of long outstanding quantitative demands and were ready to begin work the morning after May 27th — the powerful miners' union above all — and of those who

---

6. Such as, for example, the excellent study carried out by the National Center for Information on Firm Productivity — Josette Blancherie et al., *Les événements de mai-juin 1968 à travers cent entreprises*, Paris: *Centre national d'information pour la productivité des entreprises*, 1968. — SM [See also Gérard Adam, "Etude statistique des grèves de mai-juin 1968," *Revue française de la science politique*, Vol. XX, Feb., 1970, pp. 105-119.]

7. The Grenelle accords, a nation-wide protocol arrived at on May 27 by union leaders and the Employers' Association with the aid of governmental mediation, granted substantial wage increases to workers, especially those receiving only the minimum wage, but little else beyond some formal union rights which did not seem important at the time. When Georges Séguy, head of the *Confédération Générale du Travail*, presented the agreement to workers at Renault's Billancourt plant, they jeered him and refused to end the strike.

intended to give their action a much larger meaning, contesting the system of ownership and management of firms. This break corresponds partially to wage differences: the principal beneficiaries of the Grenelle accords were unquestionable the *smigards*,[8] the least well-paid workers, innumerable in the tiny provincial enterprises, in sectors such as construction, textiles, quarries and cement plants, and the food industries, who obtained from a general movement without precedent for thirty-two years what they would never have obtained through sectorial conflicts.

Most of these worried about giving up 'the substance for the shadow' and many probably voted *U.D.R.* [Gaullist]—the electoral results for the textile suburbs of Lille testify to this—in order to permit the established order to satisfy the accepted demands.

But this observation is only partial: in fact, the traditional sectors of advanced industries—the assembly lines of the automobile industry, the soldering and parts shops of the electronics industry, etc., in which wages are not much higher than those in similarly-skilled sectors of traditional industry—chose to continue the movement.

Even more, it is clearly established that the cutting edge of the movement, at *Sud-Aviation* as at *Renault's* Cleon plant, at *S.A.V.I.E.M.* in Caen as at Peugeot in Sochaux, at *Rhodiacéta* in Besançon as at *Thomson* in Lesquin, was made up of young workers, recently graduated from vocational schools, who had found at the factory neither the occupational rank corresponding to their training, nor the job and income security promised them, nor the professional autonomy or advancement possibilities which their school training entitled them (at least so they believed) to expect. They had thought they were entering the industry of tomorrow and they found the traditional sweatshop, the autocracy of foremen less qualified than they, the absurd strait jacket of stop watches and time clocks.

Not yet resigned to suffer 'industrial discipline,' the recriminations of watch-dog foremen, the ukases of the Methods Department deciding bureaucratically and abstractly the forms of work and its rhythm, knowing themselves to be the first threatened by lay-offs, these working youths has been strongly traumatized during the first months of 1968 by the repeated failure of traditional strikes. It was they who—well before the students—raised the first barricades and

---

8. *Smigards* are workers who receive the *salaire minimal interprofessionnel garanti* (*S.M.I.G.*) or minimum hourly wage.

attacked the *C.R.S.*[9] at Caen and Le Mans in January and February. The action of the students, who gained control of their universities in a few days and two nights of street fighting and forced the regime to accept it, was the signal for their revolt; [it was] the proof that more power could be obtained by action than by negotiation.

But if their movement was not limited to wildcat strikes, as was the case at Caen or Le Mans in January-February, 1968, it is because it was immediately picked up and advanced by the much larger stratum of technicians and skilled workers in modern industries. This conjunction—which Alain Touraine has perfectly described in what is up to now the only serious sociological analysis of the May movement[10]—was able to take place only because the industrial model to which both aspired was the same: that of modern industrial firms, democratically directed by the producers and using the capabilities of modern industrial technology to cut physical fatigue and fragmented work to the minimum. Touraine is correct in observing that "just as the skilled workers of the end of the nineteenth and the beginning of the twentieth centuries were the agents of a revolutionary movement only insofar as they brought about a union with the unskilled workers attracted in flocks by the development of heavy industry, metallurgy, railroads and docks, and whose wages and jobs were constantly menaced, so this new producers' aristocracy was able to advance the labor movement only when pushed by the revolt of those categoties least privileged, least integrated into the firm, and most directly threatened."[11]

But this is true only inside the modern sector of industry. What the evidence in May showed was that the criterion determining membership in such and such a group of the working class is less the individual status of each worker in the firm—skilled or unskilled, white collar or manual, young or less young, paid by the hour or by the month—than the position of his firm (taken here to mean the industrial group including all its organic liaisons) in the economy. The secretaries at the Atomic Energy Commission (at least those of Saclay, attached to the research and production centers) adopted a political and union behavior close to that of the research engineers and entirely unrelated to that of the secretaries in the administrative offices. In the same way there is a great distance between the Atomic

---

9.   *C.R.S.*, or *Compagnie républicaines de sécurité*, are special para-military riot police; the *C.R.S.* played a major and often brutal repressive role during the May events.
10.   *The May Movement, op.cit.*, pp. 207-218. —SM
11.   Touraine, *op.cit.*, p. 201. —SM

Energy Commission or petroleum engineer and one in the iron mines of Lorraine.

Of course, there is no question of pretending that the psychology of the young semi-skilled workers [in the *Renault* assembly plant] in Cléon exactly resembles that of the researchers of the R & D office of the firm, nor even that of the young ex-beet farmers of [the *Renault* plant at] Flins who perform the manual operations intended to serve the assembly line reason like the supervisors of the same assembly lines. The demand for control among the former groups takes the form of 'negativity' toward the firm and more broadly toward industrial society in general, while among the latter groups it is charged with 'positivity,' willingly adopts a 'rationalizing' language and, in ordinary periods (those in which the youhg semi-skilled workers shrug their shoulders and wait for the whistle to blow), a reformist strategy. The young semi-skilled workers of Cléon had not read Marcuse any more than had the students of Nanterre, but they would recognize themselves readily in "the substratum of outcasts and outsiders" who "exist outside the democratic process" and whose "life is the most immediate and the most real need for ending intolerable conditions and institutions."[12] But doesn't this sentiment of being 'outside the game,' to which they owe their ability to upset the established rules of 'organized' union contestation, find its positive issue—to recreate the enterprise through self-management and not to destroy it—only because it includes the rage of not having found in their work a real and concrete integration, of not having been able to reconcile their creative needs and the necessity of 'gaining their living as a consumer?'

In the language of activist students, the myth of 'the young workers' is replacing that of the working class in its entirety, which was going to "pick up again with [its] fragile hands the flag of revolution." Without at all misunderstanding the decisive role of youth in the movement, it must be admitted that their behavior was not homogeneous either. There were many young workers at the *Citroën* plant in Rennes who didn't budge. Although only the mass of workers at *Citroën* could make their town stir, the young workers, isolated from the modern sectors of industry, as yet felt only feebly the attraction of the modern industrial model glimpsed by the youth of Flins and Cléon, who were nevertheless of the same [social] origins.

The revolt of the young workers of modern industry must not be

12. Herbert Marcuse, *One Dimensional Man* (Boston: Beacon Press, 1964), p. 256.

misunderstood. Yet misunderstanding often does creep in between the students—who start from an often rather confused critical conception of 'consumer society'—and the young workers, who observe the unsuitability of the industrial structures to the possibilities of a richer life offered by new techniques. Marginal to the world of technicians and skilled labor, the student—especially in the humanities—has a ready tendency to place human liberation, 'instinctual' liberation, in the world of leisure, of 'a-production.' The revolt of those students most involved in steps toward cultural de-rei-fication—the Situationists[13] and the protesters of the Odeon Theater only reflected very widespread feelings—was principally directed a-gainst the *de facto* subjection of the previously free zone of the individual (but of the bourgeois individual) to the needs of organized production, in the loss of that ludic portion which archaic Christian society reserved for all and which the bourgeoisie has limited to the 'liberal' classes alone.

The revolt of young workers is situated, on the contrary, in the domain of production, and more generally within technical society. Daniel Mothé has described with emotion, in *Militant chez Renault*, the reaction of young semi-skilled workers [in the *Renault* plant] at Billancourt at the arrival of a 'new machine:' "Let him give us the manual (which explains how it works), let him put it on the table so that each may go through it, let him allow us to draw out, pick apart, know the details and together, yes, together, ignoring the prejudices of collar and rank, let us initiate ourselves into the mystery and functioning.... Let them leave us to plunge wholly into the dominating of the machine instead of letting us leave in the evening as we came, as deprived of knowledge, as ignorant of what crushes us..."[14]

This rage at suffering the technological process rather than dominating it is just as distant from the resigned attitude of the unskilled adult worker—who has accepted once and for all the curse of labor—as from that of the young intellectual who resigns himself with difficulty to seeing the institutionalization of cultural functions

13. The Situationists can be loosely classified as descendants of the Surrealists and the Lukács whose critique of reification as based on a contemplative relation to the world was fused to an activist cultural politics. The Situationists played a role in the outbreak of the student movement when in the face of apathy they won elected control of the student government in Strassbourg and published the booklet "On the Misery of Student Life." On their theory, cf. the pamphlet, "The Society of the Spectacle," published by *Radical America*, and Willener's chapter in *The Action-Image of Society* (New York: Random House, 1970).

14. Daniel Mothé, *Militant chez Renault* (Paris: Seuil, 1965), pp. 9-12.

which until now reserved a large part for play, for gratuitousness, for individual autonomy. It is equally foreign to the nostalgia for a 'liberal' epoch in which "a private as well as political dimension was present in which dissociation [between the individual and the established order of things] could develop into effective opposition."[15] The working class youth of 1968 do not contest industrial society, but plunge to the heart of its contradiction: "a trend toward consummation of technological rationality, and intensive efforts to contain this trend within the established institutions."[16]

From this point of view, nothing fundamentally differentiates the least qualified stratum of workers of the leading industries from those most skilled—unless it is the bitterness of their revolt. For the sentiment of alienation from the technological and technical universe is not peculiar to the young semi-skilled or skilled worker. It is not the absence of *knowledge* which prevents them from intervening as *subject* in the technological process: Daniel Mothé notes, in the passage I cited, that in fact, at the end of a few weeks the 'new machine' will have lost its mystery for those who serve it. The problem is the absence of *power*, and it exists just as much for the research engineer assigned to the fragmented production of a product alien to his creative function.

In each of these cases the contradiction between integration into an exalting technical universe—which man aspires naturally to know and dominate—and the structure of command based on the price and decision-making systems which exclude nearly all those who contribute to the functioning of this universe, is equally explosive. The model to which, consciously or unconsciously, the young unskilled worker in advanced industries aspires is not that of a life divided between meaningless and constraining work and a 'private' life provided with all the gadgets of a consumer society, but actually—just like the *cadre* of the same firms—that of a life reunified and disalienated in which productive work contributes to the 'erotic' self-realization of the individual.

And it is extremely significant that, far from demonstrating an easily understandable indifference toward an enterprise which refuses to integrate them effectively into modern industry, they have put forth the same type of demands for control as the technicians and *cadres* of these firms. It is not those who are "without hope"—to

---

15. Marcuse, *op.cit.,* p. 15. —SM. The phrase in brackets is Mallet's.
16. *Ibid.,* p. 17. —SM

borrow the formula of Walter Benjamin with which Herbert Marcuse concludes *One Dimensional Man*—who gave up hope in May.

On the contrary, it was [given us] by these workers, technicians and *cadres* profoundly 'integrated' into industrial society, in the most sensitive and crucial centers, so 'integrated' that they are in a position to express the possibilities for human liberation included in technological progress and to rebel against their misappropriation.

On the one hand, there are the sectors of large modern industry—chemicals, oil, aeronautics and aerospace, electronics and electromechanics, and (partially at least) automobiles. And there are the others—mines, traditional metallurgy, foodstuffs, construction, and still the essential part of steel. Despite its internal heterogeneity—technological and thereby occupational—modern industry tends to give all who participate in it a behavior based on their membership in the branches of the future. The behavior of those workers attached to sectors which haven't yet (construction, textiles) or will never (coal mines) pass to this advanced technological phase, whose existence underlies the new consciousness of the modern working class, is entirely different.

The discussion opened ten years ago in the important issue of the journal *Arguments*[17] on the political as well as trade unionist and cultural consequences of changes in the organic composition of the working class was in no way an abstract discussion of intellectuals. Nevertheless it was in May, 1968—nine years later—that it entered into that qualitatively superior phase where theory steps out of sociological works and trade union congresses to express the life of the masses in struggle. It was at the heart of the most violent confrontation occurring inside the French labor movement since the strikes of 1920 and the split at Tours:[18] behind the conflict over 'qualitative' and 'quantitative' demands, a divergence that was outlined in the conception of socialism in the developed countries, as well as of the respective role of the party, the union, and workers' initiative. Fundamentally, the conflict rests on the recognition or non-recognition of differentiations within the working class. It is

---

17. "Qu'est-ce que la class ouvrière française?" *Arguments*, Nos. 12-13 (Jan.-Mar., 1959). (Articles by B. Mottex, A. Touraine, S. Mallet, D. Mothé, P. Le Brun, A. Barjonet, A. Detraz, M. Collinet, J. Dofny, M. Crozier.)

18. The outcome of the 1920 Congress of the French Socialist Party at Tours consecrated the split of the French left. A 3-1 majority voted to accept the Twenty-one Conditions for joining the Third International, and became the French Communist Party. The minority continued as the French Socialist Party.

ultimately a question of knowing, not whether the working class still exists or not, but which forces within this class are the vanguard and have the capacity to formulate the workers' future clearly and which forces, because of their objective situation, cannot psychologically go beyond their present condition. So long as the technological division of labor persists, the working class will be unified only 'theoretically.' Its unity will never be accomplished on the basis of defensive battles — which on the contrary freeze each occupational group in its particular characteristics — but only by starting with a 'project' of transforming society. This project can be credible only if it represents a surpassing of the stage of economic and social development attained by the current technical level of society.

Only the strata of the active population involved in the most advanced processes of technical civilization are in a position to express its alienations and to envisage higher forms of development.

Just as the small peasantry as a whole, which was a revolutionary factor in 1789, was not able to understand the problems posed by the Commune [of 1871], the working class of archaic sectors of industry cannot formulate an alternative to neo-capitalist society in a positive way. Its struggle will necessarily take on reactionary, corporatist, Malthusian aspects, like that of the English weavers of 1840. This is not to say that it could not be drawn into a great social movement: but this will happen only if it surpasses its immediate situation. It can no longer express the vanguard themes of the movement.

I have been sufficiently reproached with 'do-gooder' shudderings unexpected among the tough-minded and pure Marxists who attacked me on this point, of 'privileging the leading sectors,' of being concerned only with the petroleum and electronics workers and of 'abandoning' the mass of workers in traditional industry, to refer my critics today, after May, 1968, to their qualms of five or six years ago. Yes, May, 1968 proved that the electronics and oil workers, the automobile workers (and at the automated Flins plant more than at the [older] plant at Billancourt), and the aeronautics and aerospace workers were the cutting edge of the labor movement. They were the ones who gave the movement its dimensions. It was the 'technical aristocracy,' the [*Peugeot*] 'model 404' workers, who won the increase in minimum wage which dozens of 'warning strikes' had not been able to advance even one point.

Differentiations within the Working Class
Whoever wishes to elaborate a strategy and tactics for the labor

movement must take into account the concrete character, the true face of the classes and groups which confront each other in social combat. Marx elaborated the philosophical concept of the proletariat as agent of history, as 'universal subject.' But in his political works, in those which deal with specific situations, he always refrained from reducing the societies he analyzed to the two great classes of *Capital*: he enumerated seven in *The Class Struggles in France*; Engels distinguished eight in *Revolution and Counter-revolution in Germany*.[19]

If all Marxist theorists have unreservedly admitted these distinctions within the bourgeoisie or the peasantry, a certain embarrassment has always marked their positions with respect to differentiations within the working class. Proudhon spoke of 'working classes,'[20] but he included in his analysis semi-artisanal strata who retained ownership of their means of production. Concerned to define the specific role of the working class, Marxists have often been led to deduce, from the philosophical concept of the proletariat, a sociological unity of the working class which in reality has never existed. This tendency became particularly marked with the development of Leninist ideas and the influence of Russian Marxism after the October Revolution. The Russian working class of the time when Lenin wrote *The Development of Capitalism in Russia* appeared singularly homogeneous in comparison with the diversity which already characterized the Western proletariat.[21] It reflected both the still primitive character of Russian industrial capitalism and the semi-feudal traits of Tsarist Russia where the persistence of servile institutions down into the nineteenth century, institutions within which industry itself had been born, checked the development of a class of industrial workers economically, technologically and sociologically distinct from the servile peasantry.

Setting itself up as the concrete consciousness of the still-forming working class and taking power in its name, the Party quite naturally tended to magify the concept of the working class, which was progressively divested of any relation with the sociological truth about industrial workers. The Stalinist period saw this situation spread to the Communist parties of the West. In certain countries

---

19. F. Engels (with the collaboration of K. Marx), *Germany; Revolution and Counter-revolution*, New York: International Publishers, 1969, pp. 11-17. —SM

20. *De la capacité politique des classes ouvrières* in *Oeuvres complètes* (Paris: M. Rivière, 1923-52). —SM

21. V.I. Lenin, *Development of Capitalism in Russia*, in Vol. 3. of *Collected Works* (Moscow: Foreign Languages Publishing House, 1960). First edition, 1899. —SM

like England or Belgium, where the Communist party never took root in the working class, this assimilation of the party to a mythical working class — the real working class being located outside the zone of influence of the Communist party — often led to caricatural situations. In fact, the movement of the working class developed there independently without the party playing the slighest part. In a country like France, where by historic heritage the Communist party enjoyed a working class audience which it was able to enlarge on several occasions, notably in 1936, the situation was more complex. The reality of its involvement in the working class protected the French Communist Party from the most flagrant excesses of this subjectivism. In the practice of class struggle, the French Communists never fell into the adventurism inevitably engendered by disdain of the concrete conditions in which the working class evolves. But they always experienced the most serious difficulties in concretely analyzing these conditions and in deriving lessons from them for the elaboration of an offensive strategy.

In the official theory of the French Communist Party, the only concession made to the complexity of the internal structures of the working class lay in the recognition of the existence of a certain 'workers' aristocracy' which, following Lenin, was considered as necessarily dedicated to reformism. The situation was all the more paradoxical in that it was precisely from this fringe of workers that, from 1936 on, the bulk of Communist working class *cadres* were recruited.

In the only work which French Communist theorists have published on social strata in France, Maurice Bouvier-Ajam and Gilbert Mury criticized the notion of 'workers' *poujadisme*'[22] used by certain writers, myself included, to characterize certain forms of labor action which led in practice to a defense of the economic positions of the most backward capitalist groups: "thus we see the absolutely original situation of the working class within the capitalist world develop itself and become specific: unlike the traditional middle classes, it has nothing to defend which is its own, its domain, its possession; it does not have the choice between a *poujadist* type of action, i.e., the illusory demand for a return to a better situation in the past, and an action of a truly revolutionary type which takes the necessities of the future into account. One party alone is open to it,

---

22. After Pierre Poujade, leader of the reactionary movement of small shopkeepers in France in the mid-1950s.

that of progress."[23]

Of course, any Marxist could only agree with the general formulation used by the authors to define the particular role played by the working class as a whole in the history of society. But it will be noted that this formulation leads the authors quite simply to conclude that there can be neither error nor deviation in any fraction of the labor movement in the course of episodes in the class struggle. The latter nevertheless constantly shows us examples of struggles led by a social group for interests not specifically its own. One comes here to the conclusion that the working class, or even a fraction of the working class, cannot, at any time or under any conditions, develop an action objectively contrary to its general interests.

We find here, eight years after the Twentieth Congress [of the C.P.-U.S.S.R.], a fine remnant of this 'party subjectivism' which has disfigured the face of Marxism and which must be continually denounced before the younger generations, who always have a tendency to confuse 'dogmatism' and 'ideological rigor.'

Towards a Marxist Sociology of Work

The dissolution of the Social-Democratic theoretical tradition, which became final after the destruction of the German and Austrian Social Democratic parties by Nazism, the triumph of Stalinist subjectivism in the Soviet Union and in a large fraction of the Western labor movement, left Marxism incapable of responding to the evolution of industrial society in Western countries. Just as Marxism ceased to be used as an instrument for understanding the societies where 'it had become the official ideology,' so it ceased to be used to study the class on which it based its emancipating will.

Marx and Engels had nevertheless always insisted on the fact that "the bourgeoisie cannot exist without constantly revolutionizing the instruments of production, and thereby the relations of production, and with them the whole relations of society,"[24] and that modifications in the organization of work like those of the technical relationships of production have repercussions on the behavior and characteristics of the working class itself.

---

23. Bouvier-Adam, Maurice and Mury, Gilbert, *Les classes sociales en France* (Paris: Editions sociales, 1964), p. 99. Gilbert Mury, whose personal researches are infinitely more nuanced than this dogmatic affirmation, quit the French Communist party in 1966 in order to join the 'Marxist-Leninist' (Maoist) party then being formed; he had to withdraw very quickly in the face of the attacks directed against him. — SM

24. *Communist Manifesto* in Marx & Engels, *Selected Works* (Moscow: Foreign Languages Publishing House, 1962), p. 37. — SM

Notwithstanding this warning, nor the fact that Marx had, notably in *Capital*, accorded the greatest importance to the organizational structures of industrial labor, and that he asserted himself there in a sense as 'the first sociologist of work,' Marxist theory between the wars took practically no further interest in the internal evolution of the world of work.

The texts of Antonio Gramsci, little known at the time, on 'Americanism and Fordism' [25] only confirm by their singularity this rule of indifference. And the ostracism from the French labor movement long endured by the works not only of Georges Friedmann but also of a Marxist like Pierre Naville [26] underlines this highly detrimental breach between the sociology of work and the labor and trade union movement.

If positivist and empiricist conceptions of American origin have been able to impose themselves in Western Europe despite the theoretical impregnation of the young social sciences by Marxism, it is in large part due to this deficiency of 'official' Marxism, to its incapacity to integrate the changes in the technical production processes and the new forms of work organization into [the theoretical treatment of] the conflicts inherent in the capitalist mode of production.

The positivist conception of the sociology of work, which gives technology primacy over the relations of production and dissolves social class into multiple groups of 'differentiated status' among which it avers itself incapable of establishing structural ties, has thus been able to appear to many Western researchers as the only method

---

25.   Antonio Gramsci, "Americanism and Fordism," in *Selections from the Prison Notebooks* (New York: International Publishers, 1971), pp. 277-318. —SM

26.   Georges Friedmann's major works in this field are *Problèmes humains du machinisme industriel,* Paris: Gallimard, 1946 (English trans., *Industrial Society, The Emergence of the Human Problems of Automation,* Glencoe, Ill.: Free Press, 1955); *Ou va le travail humain?,* Paris: Gallimard, 1950; and *Le travail en miettes,* Paris: Gallimard, 1956 (English trans.: *The Anatomy of Work; Labor, Leisure and the Implications of Automation,* New York: Free Press, 1961). Pierre Naville's numerous works, much less familiar to U.S. readers, include *Essai sur la qualification du travail,* Paris: Rivière, 1956; *Vers l'automatisme social? Problèmes du travail et de l'automation,* Paris: Gallimard, 1963; and a five-volume work titled *Le nouveau Leviathan*: Vol. I, *De l'aliénation à la jouissance, La genèse de la sociologie du travail chez Marx et Engels,* Paris: Rivière, 1957; Vol. II, *Le salaire socialiste: les rapports de production,* Paris: Anthropos, 1970; Vol. III, *Le salaire socialiste: Sur l'histoire moderne des théories de la valeur et de la plus-value,* Paris: Anthropos, 1970; Vol. IV, *Les échanges socialistes* (forthcoming); and Vol. V, *La bureaucratie . et la révolution,* Paris: Anthropos, 1972. Together, Friedmann and Naville have edited an important collection of articles on the sociology of work: *Traité de sociologie du travail,* 2 vols., Paris: A. Colin, 1961-62.

permitting an understanding of 'the facts.'

But, however much the reaction of many young sociologists against 'rhetorical sociology' seemed justified in a period when profound changes were disrupting French society, it must be regretted equally that, because of their static method, they have eliminated from the field of sociological research [both] contradiction and the concept of 'possible consciousness'[27] that the quantitative interview will never uncover but which real social history causes to explode into the perfect world of questionnaire studies.

Alain Tourain, in his henceforth classic study, *Sociologie de l'action,* has justly remarked that: "the labor movement expresses the needs of the historical subject in industrial society. Trade union action is part of the general process of surpassing class relationships and consequently contributes to the emergence of a type of society in which, in principle, the creative consciousness and its need to consider every social reality as the product of labor appears."[28]

In certain periods and on the basis of superficial observations, this universal historical dimension of the labor movement has been challenged and it has been reduced to the role of a regulatory mechanism of a society whose essential structures it accepted. According to such theories, far from being the "historical subject of industrial society," to use the expression of Alain Touraine, the labor movement would in fact abandon its own direction to a technocratic stratum disposing of negotiating powers equivalent to those of industrial and financial leaders and presenting relatively similar sociological characteristics. In multiple forms, this theory of the evolution of the trade union movement into an institution ensuring a specific function in industrial society and contributing to its capacity to integrate all tensions and contradictions has largely dominated American industrial sociology and has become widespread in Europe.

Of most of these theories one may say what has been written of the celebrated theses of Selig Perlman (*A Theory of the Labor Movement*)[29] who greatly influenced them, that they appear like "a descriptive rationalization of a trade union model in a particular situation" but that "upon analysis they prove to be useless in

27. See Lucien Goldmann, "Conscience réele et conscience possible," *Transactions of the Fourth World Congress of Sociology,* 1959. The distinction has its origins in Lukács' *History and Class Consciousness.*

28. Alain Touraine, *Sociologie de l'action,* Paris: Seuil, 1966, p. 345.

29. New York: Macmillan, 1928. —SM

explaining the variations in density of trade union action."[30]

Despite their desire to escape the positivism of concrete industrial sociology, the functionalist theoreticians participate explicitly in its essential motivations. If the apologetic intention of the system presently dominant in industrial society is less clear here, functionalist sociology identifies itself as conservative sociology in its treatment of the importance of factors of 'change,' which 'are considered there only as deviations.' If functional analysis 'is sociology,' it is in the sense that Linnaeus is 'natural history.'

Social stratification, for Talcott Parsons and his disciples,[31] is the sum of relationships among individuals, according to norms of 'efficiency,' of competence, which are those of American society of the time. In this sense, even more faithful to the 'liberal' American mythology than Perlman—who at least knew the American labor movement and the social reality that he confronted—Parsons and the functionalists who use his methods establish an absolute correspondence between the situation attained temporarily by American organizational capitalism and the drives of the individual personality, whose social nature is expressed and may only be expressed through adaptation of the individual to existing structures. This equation leads Parsons to reject as the same 'deviation' pre-capitalist ideologies and those which oppose the present order in the name of what society is becoming. The notions of functionality and dysfunctionality, concerning which Robert K. Merton admits that they explain society's processes of adaptation only in relatively open structures permitting social mobility,[32] express like basic technical principles the naive belief of the greatest American sociologists in the perennity of their social system.

It is not a question of systematically revoking the accomplishments of functionalist methods but of contesting the elevation of useful research methods into dogmatic science, into integrative ideological truth (which was the role of Talcott Parsons in particular).

Herbert Marcuse, echoing on this point C. Wright Mills, has perfectly described in *One Dimensional Man* the 'sideslip' by which a methodology intended to be essentially empirical was transformed into an ideology of acceptance of a particular reality: ". . .by virtue of this limitation—this methodological injunction against transitive

---

30. L.M. Tremblay, *La Théorie de S. Perlman*, Québec: Université de Laval, 1965, p. 45. —SM

31. Talcott Parsons, *The Social System*, Glencoe, Ill.: Free Press, 1951. —SM

32. Robert K. Merton, *Social Theory and Social Structure*, Glencoe, Ill.: Free Press, 1957. —SM

concepts... —the descriptive analysis of the facts blocks the apprehension of facts and becomes an element of the ideology that sustains the facts. Proclaiming the existing social reality as its own norm, this sociology fortifies in the individuals the 'faithless faith' in the reality whose victims they are..."[33]

The contempt for history and for totality, the rejection of the concept of social class as the central concept in conflicts in social history, in a word, the positivism manifested by American sociology stems not from the reality of American society, as some who wished to organize the 'peaceful coexistence' of functionalist and historicizing sociology still thought recently, but from the reality that America wished to be; a sociology of wishful thinking which so successfully concealed their own social reality from the American ruling classes that functionalist sociology broke down with the 'American dream' in the tear gas grenade bursts of the Chicago convention and the flames of the black ghettos.

It is true that, curiously, it is in the Soviet Union and the Eastern bloc countries that functionalism is today conquering an emerging sociology, while at Columbia, Berkeley and elsewhere, the best methodologists are discovering what their 'objective science' harbored of ideology and are assimilating, in the light of their brand new political experience, the traps of 'false consciousness.'

In the high international circles of sociology there reigns a curious atmosphere of 'peaceful coexistence' in the style of Yalta which simple concern for diplomatic correctness does not suffice to explain.

Thus it is that today a new generation of Soviet researchers are throwing themselves upon the accomplishments—supposed or real—of empirical American sociology which has, at least so it seems to them, the merit of 'studying the facts.' A derisive vengeance of the history of ideas, to be sure, but behind which one can not help but see the bidding of the new organizers of production, of a bureaucracy in the process of becoming technocratic, not without violent shocks.

It remains true that between the Charybdis of the subjectivism of the Stalinist epigoni and the Scylla of technocratic neo-positivism, the reintroduction of the Marxist dialectic into the sociology of 'facts' is, in view of the realities of organization capitalism, one of the conditions of the elaboration of the perspectives of socialism.

Does a Technological Alienation Exist?

Marx considered the development of the process of labor

---

33. Marcuse, *op. cit.*, p. 119. —SM

fragmentation as one of the essential characteristics of capitalist production. But at the same time that he stigmatized the material and moral consequences of the worker's loss of occupational autonomy in large-scale industry, he considered that, liberated from the rites and mysteries by which the 'know-how' of Medieval journeymen was transmitted, the workers' occupations and the workers' condition gained in clarity. In his mind the image of the proletarian who 'has nothing to lose but his chains' was linked not only to the workers' loss of economic initiative but also specifically to the loss of this occupational autonomy: "Modern Industry rent the veil that concealed from men their own social process of production, and that turned the various spontaneously divided branches of production into so many riddles, not only to outsiders, but even to the initiated. The principle which it pursued, of resolving each process into its constituent movements, without any regard to their possible execution by the hand of man, created the new modern science of technology," wrote Marx in *Capital*. [34]

In fact, with the disappearance of the worker's occupational autonomy, the producer saw himself dispossessed of the sole property left up to him by the capitalist system, the ownership of his professional skill. The disappearance of the old stratum of polyvalent skilled workers was to be slow; in the Latin countries particularly, the resistance of old urban structures, already strongly developed in the Middle Ages, and the persistence of the economic and political pre-eminence of a petty bourgeoisie whose objective interest was to restrain the process of concentration slowed by several decades the generalized application of technological processes already strongly developed in the Anglo-Saxon countries and in the United States. Marx was not wrong in thinking that the archaic stratum of skilled workers, although it had been at the origin of the first forms of labor organization, situated its resistance to capitalism on a level which was scarcely different from that of the petty bourgeois artisans attached to archaeo-capitalist modes of production. It was necessary, according to him, to break the last link which preserved the individual character of production, so that the working class could form itself fully into an autonomous class.

Nevertheless the formation of large semi-qualified laboring masses exercizing activities in which creative work was not only reduced economically to the condition of a commodity but moreover to that

---

34.   Karl Marx, *Capital*, Vol. I, New York: Modern Library, 1906, p. 532. —SM

of object in the technical process itself, had other consequences for the evolution of the labor movement than those which Marx had at first envisaged. To be sure, in a first stage, the brutal homogenization of the working class, the disappearance of occupational initiative and of the individualization of work, contributed largely to the formation of a working-class consciousness tending to modify fundamentally the character of the relations of production. But the very resistance of the proletariat, the development of the political and trade union organization of the working class as well as the exacerbation of competition among capitalists, including technological competition, led the system to a whole series of adjustments tending to escape "the accumulation of misery at one pole" which the author of *Capital* foresaw. Today the most dogmatic theorists of the labor movement are nearly in agreement in admitting there is no longer any absolute pauperization of the working class in the advanced capitalist countries. Wishing at any price to avoid having this class pose overall problems for the organization of social production, capitalism more or less consciously diverted the workers' demands from the sphere of production toward the private sphere, that of consumption. While the generalization of the methods of labor fragmentation separated the producer from his product, a separation was also created between man at work and man away from work [l'homme privé]. Between the system of work organization based on the loss of worker initiative and the tendency of large Western trade union organizations to take no interest in production organization and to content themselves with obtaining wage increases usable only in the sphere of consumption, we must recognize a close dialectical relationship. The worker in the period of mechanization ceased not only, as Marx foresaw, to feel himself to be an individual producer, but comes to the point of ceasing to consider himself a producer at all.

This tendency to abandon demands bearing on the nature and content of production in order to settle for demands realizable in a world of consumption itself determined and oriented by the mode of capitalist production is not alien to the development of reformist influences in the whole of the Western labor movement, whether the predominant influence there belongs to Social Democratic or to Communist organizations. From this point of view, in fact, the practice of social struggle during the second quarter of the twentieth century has scarcely been different in England and France. 'The struggle for the beefsteak,' i.e., the struggle to obtain greater means of consumption, but within the framework of needs created by capitalist industry, and parliamentary and electoralist practices in political action, were equally widespread on the other side of the Channel. To be sure, in the organizations claiming to be Leninist, the reference to total revolution was never dropped. "One day there will be bread and roses for all." But this reference tended more and more to become a formality.

It would be dangerous to consider that the development of dogmatism and opportunism within the Western labor movement was only the product of bureaucratic practices of such and such a group of leaders, the sad heritage of 'Social-Democratic treason,' or 'the negative consequences of the cult of personality.' In fact, the bureaucratization of the labor movement in Western countries was the consequence and not the cause of one structure of the working class, itself determined by the technical mode of organization of capitalist production. It is remarkable that Marxist authors never linked the phenomena of economic concentration and capitalist bureaucratization to the characteristics of capitalism's technical organization of work. Lenin, for example, considered in 1923 that the Soviet Union had everything to gain from the introduction of the Taylor system in its enterprises.[35] He saw the future of industry in the creation of large industrial units organized in the assembly line mode and believed it possible to reconcile this dehumanizing mode of production with the flowering of socialist man. In fact, it seemed to him that as soon as the ownership of the means of production and decision power in productive organization had been returned to the producers, the system of work organization could remain the same as it was in the most advanced capitalist organization. Of course Lenin was at that moment preoccupied with the problem of the creation of large industry in the Soviet Union, the material base of Socialism, and it was legitimate that he sought the modes of production apparently most profitable, those which could most rapidly bring Russian industry out of its archaic routines and its proverbial unproductiveness. But it is not without interest to note that it was almost at the same moment that, in the capitalist countries most advanced in the use of labor mechanization, sociologists and social psychologists were demonstrating the fragility of the conceptions of Taylor and Henry Ford, even from the strict viewpoint of capitalist profitability. The celebrated Hawthorne experiments led by Elton

---

35.   V. I. Lenin, "The Immediate Tasks of the Soviet Government" (1918), in *Collected Works*, Vol. 27, Moscow: Progress Publishers, 1965, p. 259. — SM

Mayo, then the experiments of the group dynamics school were showing that producers deprived of creative initiative tended to produce less than the producer to whom this initiative had been restored. Certainly, and it is curious that few Marxists have been tempted to reflect on this contradiction, the warnings of American industrial sociologists have not fundamentally modified the organization of the technical relations of production in large American industry. For forty years now, all the large firms of that country have permanently maintained sociological and social psychological research teams, in whose works they have absolutely no interest, except to extract a few minor improvements about which a great amount of noise is made but which are not fundamentally different from the methods used in modern agriculture to augment milk production or egg laying.[36]

One may ask in these conditions whether the resistance of capitalist leaders to the restitution of workers' initiative, be it strictly in the domain of the technical organization of production, and be it at the expense of productivity, does not correspond to a confused consciousness that the mechanization and fragmentation of labor are, all things considered, the system most adequate to the non-contestation of the capitalist production system in the firm. In a work, to safeguard the famous power of decision of the employers, capitalism needs a production system in which the producer is reduced to the condition of object, and it will maintain this system even if, from the strict point of view of productivity, it appears today not to be the best.

Is the New Working Class Revolutionary?

Organization capitalism realizes to the maximum degree the fundamental contradiction already analyzed by Marx: that between the constantly increased socialization of the productive forces and the private character of the ownership of the means of production and exchange. In this sense, organization capitalism's recourse to socialist techniques appears less a reinforcement of its internal structrues than the fruit of a compromise which it has been obliged to reach with the requirements of the development of the productive forces. The equilibrium of organization capitalism can thus be assured only to the extent that it succeeds in obtaining the voluntary support of the

---

36. Cf. Loren Baritz, *The Servants of Power. A History of the Social Scientists in American Industry*, Middletown, Mass.: Wesleyan University Press, 1960 and Matthew Radom, *The Social Scientist in Industry; Self-Perception of Role, Motivation and Career*, New Brunswick: Rutgers University Press, 1970.

classes contributing to production. In a word, the objective contradictions of the structure are such that they render the opposition forces contesting the nature of the relations of production infinitely more dangerous than in the past.

It is, of course, on a similar judgment that Herbert Marcuse bases his analysis of 'one-dimensional man.' But concerning capitalism's objective needs, he concludes that 'political containment' is henceforth accomplished and that, according to the brilliant but perhaps too hasty formula which he used during a debate with André Gorz and myself at the University of Mexico in 1966, "the cop is today in the head of the worker consumer."

Citing my study of Caltex in *One Dimensional Man*, he finds, quite contrary to my own conclusions, proof that "the new technological work-world thus enforces a weakening of the negative position of the working class. . ."[37]

In the same way his pessimism makes him accept as an unquestionable proof that "the declining proportion of human labor power in the productive process means a decline in the political power of the opposition. In the view of the increasing weight of the white collar element in this process, political radicalization would have to be accompanied by the emergence of an independent political consciousness and action among white collar groups—a rather unlikely development in advanced industrial society."[38]

Curiously, if one sticks to the insults directed at him by the highest officials of all the Communist parties, Marcuse's pessimism is shared on this point by the leaders of the Communist Party. For if they of course reject violently the Marcusean idea that the working class can no longer be the bearer of the revolutionary ideal, a simple study of the texts would show that this is simply because Marcuse and the Communists are not referring to the same historical period. Starting from the American situation, Marcuse admits, like every man endowed with common sense, the diminishing qualitative and quantitative importance of the traditional proletariat. Therefore, in expressing his radical pessimism, he takes his stand principally on the new strata of workers, white collars among them. The Communist leaders continue and will undoubtedly continue for a long time to take into account only the traditional strata of the working class which, moreover, they tend to count according to the hardly Marxist criteria used by the *INSEE* [National Institute of Statistics and

---

37.   Marcuse, *op.cit.,* p. 31. —SM
38.   Marcuse, *op.cit.,* pp. 37-38. —SM

Economic Studies]—notably without imagining that the same occupational classification has quite different meanings, depending on the level of advancement of the industry. But so far as the 'new strata' of industry and services are concerned, their distrust is at least equal to Marcuse's. Certainly after having denied the existence of these new strata of the working class for an entire period or having rejected them to the rank of the traditional worker 'aristocracy,' the Western European Communist leaders have finally admitted the possibility of letting these strata play a certain role in the labor movement. Nevertheless, the last publications relating to this question in the sphere of so-called 'orthodox Marxism' show that it continues to refuse fully to consider them as a developed and integrated fraction of the working class: "One can argue for an infinity on the problems of the notorious 'new strata:' whatever their intrinsic importance, they cannot furnish a basis for a socialist politics. To avoid adventurism, we will put first what is actually essential: the struggle between the owners of the means of production and the producers, the wage earners who own nothing except their labor power."[39] In this text, the last one he wrote before his death, Maurice Thorez arbitrarily assimilated the new working class to the 'new middle classes' which, he correctly noted, include both elements linked to the process of production and therefore objectively linked to the condition of the working class, and parasitic elements, objectively linked to the condition of the exploiting classes. But one cannot help wondering why the fundamentally antiscientific notion of 'middle class' which Marxism has always condemned was then reintroduced into the debate. In reality, the reticence shown toward the new strata of the working class, technicians, researchers, and skilled workers in automated firms, only reflects the incapacity of traditional labor organizations to adapt their action to the new organizational forms of capitalism and to elaborate an offensive strategy for the passage to socialism in the economically developed countries.

Is the new working class revolutionary? If one means by this a revolutionary consciousness in the traditional sense of the term, expressing itself by *the will to take political power first, by any means and whatever the price, and then only in a later phase to organize society in a new manner, it is incontestable that the new working class is not revolutionary.* It is not, in these conditions, because it

---

39. Maurice Thorez, *"Notion de classe et rôle historique de la classe ouvrière,"* presented to the *Semaine de la pensée marxiste*, March 13, 1963. —SM

offers two preliminary conditions for the transformation of existing structures: the first is that the transformation of economic, political and social structures cannot be made at the price of the destruction of the existing apparatus of production, nor even of its serious weakening—"the machine is too dear to break."

Secondly, because on the one hand it has experienced the negative consequences of a political seizure of power which is not accompanied immediately by a transformation of structures and the social hierarchy, and on the other hand it feels itself now in a position to achieve some elements of these new social relations, it has a tendency to pose as preliminary to the slogan 'we must take power,' the question 'to do what with it?'

But if one understands by revolutionary the concern to fundamentally modify existing social relations, then the objective conditions in which the new working class acts and works make it the vanguard par excellence of the revolutionary socialist movement. In fact, the more the importance of the sectors of research, creation and supervision develops, the more human labor is concentrated in the preparation and organization of production, the more the sense of initiative and responsibility develops, in short, the more the modern worker reconquers *at the collective level* the occupational autonomy which he lost in the phase of mechanization of work, the more tendencies towards demands for control will develop. Modern conditions of production today offer the objective possibilities for the development of generalized self-management of production and of the economy by those who do the work. But these possibilities clash with the capitalist structures of production relations and their profit criteria based on short-term returns to the owners, and also with the companies' techno-bureaucratic structure which appears more and more as a brake on the harmonious development of their productive possibilities. The recent social conflicts which developed in the last few years in the Western world, and the strike of May, 1968, crowning this series of movements, have shown that the advanced sectors of the working class were no longer content to make wage demands, but were led to enter into conflict with the techno-bureaucratic structure of the decision centers of the economy to the extent that the latter no longer appeared justified by the requirements of technical and economic development but appeared on the contrary as a remnant destined to protect the privileged status of existing hierarchies. The evolution of the Western European labor movement reflects the new characteristics of this new consciousness:

nearly everywhere it is the evolution of industrial sectors where the new working class predominates which bends the activity of union organizations, until now characterized by purely reformist action, toward a fundamental questioning of the capitalist system of production; whether it concerns the technicians' or chemical products unions, or these new unions of industrial designers whose development has caused the British Trades Union leadership to swing to the left, or the German chemical and automobile unions, or the Belgian gas and electricity unions, or finally in France the chemical, technicians', oil and metallurgical federations, or reformist organizations like the *C.F.D.T.* was yesterday and the majority of the *F.O.* still is today.

Precisely because it is located at the center of the most complex mechanisms of organization capitalism, the new working class is led to recognize the inherent contradictions of this system more quickly than other sectors. Precisely because its elementary demands have been largely met, the new working class is led to pose itself other problems which cannot find their solution in the sphere of consumption. Its objective situation thus places it in a position to grasp the faults of modern organization capitalism and to become aware of a new way of organizing production uniquely capable of satisfying human needs which cannot be expressed in the present structural framework. Its action tends to be in fundamental opposition not only to capitalism but also to any technocratic formula for the direction of the economy. The hierarchical structure of industry is challenged with each partial demand for control. It is true that, until now, the totality of these demands have not been coordinated, and does not constitute a general line of action susceptible of modifying the relationship of political forces within Western societies. But this situation stems more from the organized labor movement's incapacity to formulate an offensive strategy based upon advancing anti-capitalist structural reforms, than from temptations for the new working class to let itself be 'integrated' into the neo-capitalist system. In fact, this temptation, if it exists, will not withstand the deepening of the contradictions of neo-capitalism itself. The modern working class has an immediate interest in uninterrupted technical development and its results: a substantial reduction of work time, the reconquest of occupational autonomy, job rotation, more varied activity. Capitalism, on the contrary, tends to brake the development of the productive forces to the extent that their development has as its principal result to lower the rate of profit continuously and to the degree that it increasingly involves recourse to socialist types of economic instruments whose effects capitalism is not certain to master.

One of the problems which arises in the elaboration of an offensive strategy founded on the objective possibilities of action by the most advanced fraction of the working class obviously lies in the difficulty of coordinating the struggles of this sector with the sectors of labor linked to more traditional activities. Although the new working class sees its numbers grow from year to year and its place in the productive apparatus confers on it a logistical importance greater than its numerical importance, it still constitutes only a minority of the working class and *a fortiori* of all the lower class strata. Nevertheless these different sectors of society are not isolated by any Great Wall of China. Just as the most advanced capitalist industry has a tendency to influence the most backward forms, the behavior of the new working class influences that of the other sectors. Demands bearing on the control of production organization, on the guarantee of job security, on the refusal of bureaucratic methods of direction of the economy, have become widespread today to the extent that they appeared first in the advanced sectors of industry.

May, 1968 has, moreover, given a first response to this question. In drawing nine or ten million workers along in a general movement, despite reticences and reservations, not to say more, the advanced sectors of industry and the services proved that it was possible, at least in action, to cause the working masses of traditional sectors to go beyond the narrowly defensive and corporatist vision they had of their own interests. To be sure, the braking elements coming from the old workers' consciousness, an alloy of resignation to a capitalist type of industrialization and of a religious type of attachment to 'revolutionary' party which justifies not making a revolution "while projecting the Unhappy Consciousness as absolute" [Hegel], still largely carried the day in May 1968. While being eroded, it is true.

The vanguard forces of the labor movement did not yet have control of their own ideology. Torn between the fervor of the students — whose action but not whose language they understand (the action was contemporary while the language carted out all the old skins abandoned by the labor movement in the course of successive moltings, from Bakunin to Trotsky) — and the corporatist demagogy of the traditional labor movement, they had to invent, day after day, their own forms of action, their own demands, even their own language. [This was an] incontestable weakness, which came fully into play when the repression was relaxed and thereby ceased to be the simplifying magnetic pole which united heterogeneous forces. But *"ce n'est qu'un début."* The historical problem brutally posed in May by student and working class youths, by the sectors most linked to new economic and technical developments, will become increasingly well defined. Students, these future producers, will learn that it is because science is today a factor of production that they must conquer the technocratic university and place it at the service of society—and of themselves.

From a diffuse consciousness of this role of science and the university, the young technicians and workers reacted to the student movements. Living permanently in the process of modern production, they lived, without knowing it, the prodigious anticipation of Marx, tracing, in one of his most striking formulas, the fundamental contradiction between the mode of production engendered by large-scale industry and the system of production it persists in maintaining. "In this transformation [automation, which he describes as well as John Diebold, but a century earlier —SM], what appears as the mainstay of production and wealth is neither the immediate labour performed by the worker, nor the time that he works—but the appropriation by man of his own general productive force, his understanding of nature and the mastery of it; in a word, the development of the social individual.... The theft of others' labour time upon which wealth depends today seems to be a miserable basis compared with this newly developed foundation that has been created by heavy industry itself."

The technicians and workers of advanced industry will entirely cease to feel like strangers toward these 'sons of the bourgeoisie' headed for modern forms of proletarianization who are today students. And the latter will cease to repeat the self-satisfied and grossly paternalistic phrase "we don't want to be your future exploiters." As if the future semi-skilled workers of scientific research, the economists, the econometricians tending computers, and the sociologists recording fragmentary interviews had anything to exploit except their own psychological and material misery! The student-worker alliance will not establish itself as Marcuse thinks—I should say, thought before May, 1968—between the proletariat of Zola's *Germinal* and the students of 1848, but between the diverse

---

40.   Karl Marx, *Grundrisse*, New York: Harper & Row, 1971, p. 142 (edited and translated by David McLellan). —SM

strata of professionals of modern production, producers of sciences and techniques more than of products, in order to found the true industrial society, rid of its capitalist and technocratic archaisms.

February 10, 1969

Post-May 1968:
Strikes for Workers' Control[1]

In going beyond 'legalist' demands and 'organized' forms of action, the May struggles launched new models of spontaneous workers' control actions which are continuing to develop in numerous conflicts and of which the author made an inventory during 1969: movements for control over employment, taking control of work conditions and classifications, of work organization and of hours.

Thus since May, 1968 social conflicts have changed in form and content; the rank and file directly controls the struggles which it begins, counts on the *fait accompli* rather than negotiation, and in this way challenges the employers' authority and imposes a workers' control upon the management.

For French trade union organizations, the movement of May-June 1968 was a severe 'object lesson.' Whatever their analysis was at the moment of the conflict, whether, like the *C.G.T.*, they continually tried to reinsert the movement into the classic forms of 'conflictual participation' (cf. the Grenelle accords), whether they recognized, a bit slowly, the new character of the movement and rallied to it by advancing demands for self-management (the *C.F.D.T.*, notably in metallurgy and petro-chemicals), or whether they quite simply 'forgot' the movement, like *Force Ouvrière*—which manifested its presence only through its 'minorities' (Federations of Chemicals or Technicians, Departmental Union of Loire-Atlantique)—all the union head offices had to record the fact that the mass movement of May-June, 1968, begun among the rank and file, had thrown union legalisms overboard, had put forward demands which were not integratable by the social legislation of the capitalist system—and so not negotiable in terms of 'loyal relations of social partners'—and revealed in their forms of action models of workers' collective

---

1. This article first appeared in *Sociologie du Travail*, No. 3 July-September, 1970, and is reprinted here with permission.

participation in the struggle which largely overflowed the occupational and minority structure of the union organizations.

But the exceptional conditions of the launching of these conflicts, the fact that they developed from an initiative outside the working class (the student commune with its barricades and university occupations), the fact also that very quickly the distinctive character of the workers' struggle—including the embryo of 'workers' power' in the firm—had been covered again by the overall political conjuncture, all these did not permit carrying the analysis through to its end. To understand the essential characteristics of the labor movement in May-June, 1968, it is necessary to follow, as did Alain Touraine,[2] the subterranean currents which have come to light since 1960 in limited conflicts in the advanced sectors of industry, to understand the tie between the self-management demands of the new categories of technicians or of those becoming 'technicized' and the revolt of the young workers arbitrarily disqualified by the system of employer authority, and to sift out of the fusion of these two poles of workers' contestation the coherence which was the strength of the general strike and swept along or reduced to silence the traditionalist currents of the labor movement.

The majority of the union leaders—if I except a part of the confederal [national] leadership of the *C.F.D.T.*, or more precisely the men in this confederation in charge of the 'political sector,' and elements who had remained in the minority in their organizations (such as Barjonet or Labi)[3]—refused to probe the historical significance of this overall change in the forms and motivations of social struggle and applauded, in their innermost selves, the obsessional analysis given by Raymond Aron,[4] which saw in this movement which brought the established power within a hair's breadth of total dislocation, a 'collective psychodrama' in which the French, bored with the society of abundance, for a few days gave

---

2. *Le Mouvement de mai ou le Communisme utopique*, Paris: Seuil, 1968. —SM [English translation: *The May Movement, Revolt and Reform*, New York: Random House, 1971.]

3. Maurice Labi was formerly secretary-general of the Chemical Federation of F.O., representing the left-wing of that union. In 1971 he took his Federation out of F.O. and joined the CFDT. André Barjonet was formerly a high official of the C.G.T. and the best known labor sociologist of the P.C.F. In May 1968 he left his official functions in the C.G.T., quit the P.C.F. and joined the P.S.U. The pamphlet he wrote at that time explaining his actions had a large audience.

4. *La Révolution introuvable, réflexions sur la Révolution de mai*, Paris: Fayard, 1968. (English translation: *The Elusive Revolution; Anatomy of a Student Revolt*, New York: Praeger, 1969.)

themselves a 'revolutionary fête,' as the Romans gave themselves circuses.

In fact, as early as 1969, the principal unions, reverting to their old habits, envisaged the resumption of action in very traditional forms — according to the scheme of 'listing of demands,' 'action days,' 'warning strikes' — ending in these eternal 'October meetings'[5] of which one hoped only, considering the quantitative dimension of the May, 1968 strike (the only dimension they wished to grant it), for results less disappointing than those of previous meetings.

But the October meeting did not take place... Starting in September, 1969, the strike of the operating personnel of the *S.N.C.F.* [nationalized railways] caught short the negotiators of the 'second Grenelle:' by rudely intervening in the government's project for reform of the *S.N.C.F.* — i.e., by obstructing the decisions of the company head, the State itself. The strike of the operating personnel raised workers' demands to such a level that the government could no longer take the risk of a general negotiation.

The strike of the operating personnel, more spectacular because — owing to the structure of the enterprise — it entailed a general paralysis of the rail network which made it impossible to consign it to the inoffensive fourth or sixth page of the daily papers, was nevertheless only the development of a more general movement which, since the end of spring, 1969, had touched, branch by branch, firm by firm, an entire series of nerve centers of industry and the services: steel, automobiles, aerospace, air and sea transports, etc.

Improperly baptized 'wildcat strikes' by the mass press, these movements had their start in the theoretical experience gained by the working class in May-June, 1968. This time, the movements came entirely from the working class itself, without the student movement (on the wane since what it considered as the failure of the May movement) having the slightest part. They gave themselves objectives directly linked to the life of workers in the firms. In May-June 1968, workers in numerous places verbally asserted a desire for self-management, but except for certain well-known examples — *CSF* in Brest, *Rhône-Poulenc* in Vitry, the Nantes region — the demands officially advanced did not go beyond the stage of traditional demands. The will to take the organization of production in hand remained implicit, reflected particularly in the refusal to resume

---

5. When representatives of the unions would meet with representatives of the employers' association and present their demands.

work when the traditional demands had been met.

On the contrary, the movements of 1969, less assertive in their overall challenge to the capitalist system of production, attacked the concrete structure, geographically and sectorially defined, of the production relations of particular enterprises or industrial branches.

This tendency was all the more significant in that it was not peculiar to France. The so-called 'wildcat' strikes of the workers of Hamburg, Schleswig, and Bremerhaven, those of the Flemish miners of Limbourg, the eruption of the Italian "creeping May" and, still more spectacular because it broke out in the model firm of the model country of social integration, the iron-miners strike in Kiruna in Swedish Lappland—all demonstrated a new orientation of social movements in all of Western Europe, revealing a profound crisis of the 'unionism of conflictual participation.'

For lack of any 'participant observation' permitting us to catch the non-traditional aspects of these movements in action, the information we have recorded for this article does not pretend to be a sociological study; it nevertheless seems useful to us, in the context of this special issue devoted to the movements of May-June, 1968, to bring into relief through 'current events' the respects in which it constituted a true change; how, since May-June, 1968, social conflicts have changed in form and content.

The set of conflicts which we have enumerated here seems to us to exhibit one basic trait: the active intervention of the rank and file (unionized and non-unionized) who lead and supervise their struggle themselves, which can lead to management's being *confronted with the fait accompli*. They do not negotiate, they *take*—with any later negotiations being likely to be settled only by management's ratification of the workers' collective decisions.

Here are some very recent examples of demands for which conflicts of this type have been conducted. Some of these actions include only the aspect of 'self-direction of the conflict' by those involved. Others include a second aspect which derives from the first: confronting [management] with the *fait accompli*.

The classification which we have established is empirical. It is almost a rule, in fact, that several very different demands are advanced in the course of the conflicts; we have retained the demand which seemed to us dominant and determining for the form of conflict chosen.

1. Gaining Control over Firing

Since May, 1968, individual or collective firings have been very numerous. On the one hand the employer has sought to rid himself of a certain number of 'ring-leaders.' On the other hand, he has made the working class pay for the attempt to rationalize production (plant closing, manpower reductions, concentrations and mergers entailing the elimination of 'duplicate jobs').

Many movements since 1968 have had as their objective not to contest firings 'legally'—which ends in the best of cases with the payment of indemnities—but to prevent them entirely. Let us cite a few examples at the elementary level of these movements which refuse 'the absolute authority of the head of the enterprise.'

C.O.D.E.R., Marseille, metallurgy, November 1969

This firm employed a particularly 'selective' hiring system: before final hiring, workers and employees were engaged only on the basis of a provisional work contract, renewable each month for six months. Thus, in 1969, one thousand (of two thousand) workers left the firm before the signing of the final hiring contract: a type of temporary work contract well-fitted to those factories of semi-skilled workers (of which *Citroën* is the model) which voluntarily pursue a particularly high turn-over rate.

In May-June, 1968, an action committee backed up by neighborhood organizations took charge of the strike—successfully.

In November, 1969, the work contracts of two workers labelled as ring-leaders were not renewed. [There was a] massive work stoppage in the shops *and also among the white collar workers*, affected by the contract but also fighting for the workers, in terms of the workers' positions. General strike. First demand: rehiring of the two fired workers. Second demand: a one-month limit to the provisional work contract, followed by final hiring. The strike also extended to other demands: wages, year-end bonuses...

The strike lasted eleven days. [It was] decided and led by the rank and file in complete democracy. A complete victory on the two demands.

Etablissements Quillery, La Garenne-Colombes, automobile equipment

Of six hundred workers, three hundred were Algerian. Following the firing of an Algerian worker, his compatriots and the French workers in the *C.F.D.T.* launched an unlimited strike (which lasted

17 days).[6] Despite the refusal of the *C.G.T.* to join the action, management capitulated, annulled the firing and paid fifty per cent of the strike hours.

Etablissements ALMES, Alpes-Maritimes, Nacryl buttons

For years the management of the employer had been catastrophic. He survived only by paying neither his contributions to the Social Security nor his taxes. The *U.R.S.S.A.F.* [*Union de Recouvrement de Sécurité Sociale et Caisse de Sécurité Sociale et Allocations Familiales*], to which he owed nine hundred thousand francs, placed the firm in receivership. A parallel company founded by the employer, *SECOM*, offered to take over the business on the condition that a part of the personnel be fired in November, 1969.

Response: strike and occupation [of the factory] and a demand that all personnel be taken back, even at the cost of a reduction in hours. After a few days, *SECOM* gave in. It took everyone back, even those last hired, on the basis of a forty hour week. This conflict showed the workers the importance of solidarity; after their success and to consolidate the results obtained, they became union members.

The three examples of winning struggles given here are not isolated; in many middle-sized firms of the same type, similar struggles were begun without attaining the same results. They are worth noting in that they took place in peripheral firms not having a determining influence on production. These firms use slightly skilled labor, often with a majority of foreign workers or women. In all cases, unionization followed rather than preceded the conflict.

The struggle against employer arbitrariness here takes a principally defensive character: as in some other forms—of which we shall see examples below (struggle against work rhythms, job insecurity, arrangement of hours)—they do not lead directly to control over management, but they teach workers not to accept the norms of capitalist exploitation, more oppressive here than elsewhere, as a given.

In large factories already possessing an old union tradition, the struggle against firings took on a more serious character. It was not different in kind.

---

6.   Unlimited strike: one in which no stopping date has been pre-set; as opposed to several other types, which last for short pre-determined periods.

SNECMA, Villaroche and Corbeil, Paris region
[airplane engines], 1969

The conflicts of November had their origin in plans for 755 firings. At the Villaroche factory (near Melun) the organization and supervision of the struggle by the workers themselves took the following forms: (a) daily general assemblies which decided the next day's action (continuation of the strike); (b) formation of work groups organized by different services of the factory and charged with bringing programs to the general assembly.

The foot-dragging of the unions prevented the extension of this experiment to the other plants, notably Corbeil. At Voillaroche, it also prevented the establishment of a strike committee elected by all, despite the desire expressed by the six work groups. Also noteworthy were the political support contributed by the *P.S.U.* sections and groups of the branch and the information role played by street demonstrations.

Many other examples could be cited: the October, 1969 conflicts at the *Société métallurgique de Normandie* in Caen, those of the *CECEBA* (aluminum windows and curtains) at Maxéville, Meurthe-et-Moselle...

Traits in part new characterize the recent period. These are, in general: an immediate strike decided upon by the rank and file before any negotiation. Occupation of the premises, an active organization of solidarity in the neighboring enterprises, and a political explanation of the necessity of the conflict.

Manufrance, Saint-Etienne, arms and cycles

Finally, the most spectacular of the conflict movements against a collective firing was that of *Manufrance* (the famous arms and cycle factory of Saint-Etienne). Following a conflict bearing on wages and work conditions for women workers, the workers occupied the factory on November 17th. The management responded by firing 1,180 workers and employees, including all the shop stewards, out of a total of 2,400. On November 26th, at the call of the *C.F.D.T., C.G.T.,* and *F.E.N.,* all the factories of Saint-Etienne struck and the workers occupied the streets of the town all day. The pressure of other local employers and the municipality (a stockholder in the company) forced the *Manufrance* management to accept on December 4th not only the annulment of firings and a contract including a part of the demands but also an important advance of union rights in the company: an increase in the number of hours accorded to stewards, in-plant meetings for union news, collection of dues and sale of union publications during work hours, direction of social welfare activities by the plant committee.

This process of collective reaction has moreover been confirmed in many other firms: as employers have a tendency to react to thrombosis strikes (strikes in a shop which block, with a minority of strikers, the entire production of the factory or group) with a generalized lock-out, hoping thus to dissociate the mass of workers from the strikers, the workers respond with the occupation of the factory. It was like this at *Renault* in Le Mans in November, 1969.

Workers' reactions to firings, individual or collective, are not something new and cannot strictly speaking be classed as "workers' control" actions. What is new, on the other hand, is the form they have taken since the beginning of 1969: the workers impose the retention in the shop of the fired workers; the latter consider the firing as null and void. Then the workers stop work and occupy the premises to force the annulment of the measure. They do not let the delays of the judicial mechanism, which first confirm the workers' departure from the factory—and thereby remove any bite from the action of solidarity—come into play.

But this is nevertheless only the most elementary form of the actions recorded during 1969. The other movements we have counted can be classed into four principal categories which are directly related to the notion of workers' control, as they challenge the employer's *exercise of the right to manage*. It is a matter of gaining control over: (a) classification, qualification, minimum income; (b) work rhythms, output, productivity; (c) work organization, job sheets, work-post ratings; (d) the arrangement of hours.

2. Gaining control over classification, qualification, minimum income

Peugeot at Sochaux [Doubs], drying oven operators [automobiles] There are forty, classified O.S. 2A, the equivalent of O.P.1.[7]

---

7. According to a classification system which became law in 1945, French industrial workers are divided into three principal categories:

   M. *Manoeuvre* (unskilled);

   O.S. *Ouvrier spécialisé sur machines* (semi-skilled);

   O.P. *Ouvrier professionnel* (skilled).

These are in turn internally subdivided into *M1, M2, O.S.1, O.S.2, O.P.1, O.P.2,* and *O.P.3,* and further distinctions (e.g., *O.S.2A*) are often added. For further information on French occupational classification and payment systems, see François

Their work requires six months of on-the-job apprenticeship and some technical courses. Their work continues for three eight-hour shifts each weekday and they must assure all-day service on Saturdays, Sundays and holidays. As in all heat-processing shops, they work in an unhealthy atmosphere.

November, 1968: three of their fellow-workers, no longer [physically] able to hold their post, were declassified and demoted to O.S.1 and O.S.2. The operators then formulated their demands: no declassification in cases of physical incapacity, and the option of leaving the post after ten years of service while keeping the O.S.2A classification. A petition to this effect was signed by all.

Faced with management's refusal, and after having agreed among themselves and with their shop stewards, the operators struck. They continued nevertheless to ensure the security of the ovens and emptied them to avoid complications.

The management, sensing the cohesion of the strikers and fearing that this bottleneck-strike might paralyze the entire plant, then agreed to a discussion. This was carried out by the shop stewards accompanied by representatives of the strikers. The latter followed the evolution of the negotiations from the dining hall. The essential part of the demands was granted, and notably the veto on de-qualification.

Peugeot at Sochaux, Spraypainters

One hundred sixty spraypainters, one hundred of them classified O.S.2A, encouraged by the success of the strike in heat processing, submitted analogous demands. They paint car bodies, an enclosed job, very disagreeable and unhealthy. They demanded: (a) after five years, a guaranteed salary in case of sickness or accident; (b) after ten years, the option of leaving the post while preserving the base pay, the classification and, partially, the minimum income. The spraypainter, if he quits his position, used up by his work, loses these various advantages.

These demands, approved by all [spraypainters], were partially rejected by the management. In particular, they entirely rejected the guaranteed income. After consultation, the spraypainters decided to strike. The next day, they specified their demands: after ten years of work in the painting cabin, retention of the hourly wage rate of 5.51 and of the premium of 0.41. The management refused.

Sellier and André Tiano, *Economie du Travail*, Second edition, Paris: *Presses universitaires de France*, 1970.

Without spraypainters, no more production: 16,000 workers (of 29,000) were soon locked out. At the end of a week, faced with the determination of the spraypainters and the sympathy of public opinion for the strikers, the management sought to restart the painting line with *cadres* and foremen.

The discussions remaining at an *impasse*, the spraypainters decided by secret ballot to provisionally abandon the demand concerning the premium of 0.41 and to hold the line on the questions of rate, qualification and reconversion. They won satisfaction on these last points and voted to return to work.

In this strike it is necessary to underline: (a) the self-direction of the conflict by those concerned: fourteen spraypainters accompanied the nine shop stewards to the discussions. All decisions were taken collectively; (b) the great effort to inform the other workers in the plant and the population; (c) the veto over declassification.

These two conflicts took place in sectors where the strike paralyzed the factory's production. This was an important element in their success. Gaining control in less crucial sectors would have become more difficult.

3. Gaining control over work rhythms, output, productivity

Caterpillar, Grenoble, farm machinery

At the end of October, 1969, a certain number of workers stopped work to defend their work conditions. These are the facts: three workers on one line, which included about twenty operatives, were summoned individually by the shop supervisor. The latter informed them that they would no longer be on three machines but on four. The operation amounted in practice to an increase of a third in the work rhythm.

Back on the line, the three informed their fellow workers and, after discussion, they all decided to stop work thirty minutes early to put together an information sheet to be distributed the next morning at the entry to the plant.

The next day, the line operatives were convoked by the shop supervisor to explain their dissatisfaction. A list of demands, on which all collaborated, gave multiple reasons why their work conditions were bad. They concluded by demanding that a certain number of slack periods be taken into account. In fact, this amounted to challenging the system of 'bonuses.' The management backed down and pledged to re-examine the problems within a month.

So, it was won and work could start again without difficulties. Not entirely. The next day the line operatives noticed that the management was trying to stir up the workers of the other departments against them. The latter reproached the operatives for having implicated them in explaining why they had slack periods. The operatives decided to respond to this maneuver of the management by posting a declaration, signed by all the workers on the line, which affirmed that the other departments were not responsible for their work condition, denounced the management's attempt, and underlined their solidarity with the other workers.

The 'human relations' official of the plant convoked the signers and demanded they withdraw their declaration from the bulletin board: they refused. The management then posted a text in which it denied the accusation brought against it, while claiming that it was not in its interest 'to maintain a situation prejudicial to productivity.'

Let us underline a few special traits of this conflict: (a) the complete democracy which reigned among the rank and file; (b) the refusal to negotiate a compromise over problems of work rhythms; (c) the undercutting of the maneuvers of the management; (d) the political news diffused on this occasion by the south Grenoble *P.S.U.* section.

Renault at Flins, Paris region. Automobiles

In October, 1969, in the upholstery shop, the workers imposed their own rhythms. They went from 288 pieces to 255 [per day]. The action spread in this form or in other forms to other shops.

These actions were always decided upon by the rank and file.

Peugeot at Sochaux. Automobiles

In March, 1969, the workers of the body assembly line launched a strike among the rank and file which mobilized the plant for three days. The reason for this strike was a change in work rhythms imposed by the management.

In a sorting center of the Post Office in Paris, the workers modified the division of labor among the teams, thus confronting the management with the *fait accompli*.

At the *Pirelli* factory in Oulon the workers themselves reduced the work rhythms without prior negotiations.

The same thing [happened] at *Renault* at Cléon, the same thing among the copying-machine personnel of the civil service, the same thing in September at the Thomson plant in Angers [electronics]. Each time the decisions were made by the rank and file.

It is rather difficult to separate the problems of work rhythms, or output, or productivity from problems linked to the organization of work, to its control and remuneration. We have nevertheless brought together in the following paragraphs some actions conducted with control in mind where the predominant aspect seemed to us to be wages.

4. Gaining control over job sheets, work-post ratings, wages

S.C.A.L.-Groupe Pechiney (formerly FROCES), Isère, aluminum.

Six hundred workers paid by the hour work aluminum. The May [1968] conflicts there were particularly sharp. The firm was one of the last to resume work.

The victories of May were threatened by the new management: hours and vacations, changes of post without wage compensation, reorganization of each job to increase work rhythms, alignment of wages with those of other plants of the trust. On January 10th, unlimited strike; on January 23rd, occupation of the plant to reply to maneuvers aiming to use a minority of workers paid by the month against the strike.

From the beginning of January, the workers paid by the hour in maintenance and in certain production shops had spontaneously decided not to turn in the 'production sheets' which, given to the foremen, permitted supervision of output. On January 12th, a slow-down strike began and on January 16th, there was a strike by the maintenance workers.

The decision for an unlimited strike on January 20th was made by a secret vote of 533 to 16; the strikers ran their own strike.

It is necessary to note: the taking of control over the 'production sheets;' the practice of democracy among the rank and file; the confrontation with management which led to the occupation of the premises.

C.O.D.E.R., Marseille, Metallurgy

June, 1969: conflict broke out spontaneously in one yard. Two demands were advanced: (a) bonuses: to stop the output race, the workers asked, in addition to the variable bonus, fifteen hours of fixed bonus; (b) the production sheets: these were collective and given to the head of the work team. Result: the bonuses obtained on one day for a job were diminished the next day for the same job. The workers demanded that the sheets be individual and that they be given to each worker.

After an eleven-day strike, the workers obtained collective supervision of the work sheets. We should note that this strike provoked very negative reactions in certain neighboring plants [whose unions were] controlled by the *P.C.F.*

Renault, at Le Mans, Normandy. Automobiles

The GG shop mounts tires for the models R4, R6, and R16. In February, 1969, conflict broke out there over the [system of] rating each work-post. The extreme diversity of criteria aimed at the division of the workers.

This spontaneous strike threatened the other *Renault* plants with a technical shut-down. Against this strike, the management mobilized the *cadres*, went to court, went to see the strikers at their homes. Tie score: the negotiations began without any sanction. But the conflict resumed under different conditions in December.

Renault, at Cléon. Automobiles

September, 1969: work conditions and manipulations of the wage hierarchy were at the origin of the conflicts.

Three types of action: (a) as soon as the time study man arrived, production stopped; (b) if the shop was not fully staffed, production was proportionately reduced; (c) in case of modernization of equipment, hours were reduced by advancing quitting time.

At the same time, commissions to control the wage hierarchy were established and the workers collectively decided to post their pay sheets.

During the negotiations that followed, delegates of the striking workers joined the union representatives.

Saint Frères, Amiens. Sugar refinery

An arbitrary raise for 'good workers' immediately suggested to all that the company could pay more.

At the end of March, 1969, action began at once among the rank and file: the night of March 31st, the Flixecourt plant went on strike. The next day, work stoppage extended to the other *Saint Frères* plants of the region.

At the end of a fifteen day strike, union supervision of the 'production averages book' and of the pay book was obtained.

Nessi Frères, Pont-à-Mousson group. Construction

The promotions which were to be given in the fall were not granted. A shop steward posted his pay note. Many workers did the same. It was noticed that at a given work post, the gap could be up to 200 francs a month. The lesson will not be lost.

UNELEC, Orléans. Metallurgy

A disagreement over lunch room price increases led the workers to demand and obtain the opening of the account books. The poor management of the lunch room came out into broad daylight.

Manurhin, Arsenal-Vichy. Machine tools

After having compared wages among the shops, one sector noted that it was underpaid regarding bonuses. A grievance was submitted, which resulted in the release of 500,000 francs in favor of this sector.

The workers, after being informed, demanded the posting of each worker's wages to avoid the arbitrary distribution of this sum. The management refused, invoking the right to secrecy, but the union obtained for its stewards the right to examine the individual pay sheets. In each of the four shops a supervisory commission on the preparation of these sheets was created; the workers pledged to show their sheets to each other. This supervision began July 1, 1969. It seems to be working satisfactorily.

Freitag, Marseille. Chemicals

On the occasion of the March 11th strike: (a) a wage commission was imposed on the employer; (b) on March 11th [there was] work with the management on revision of the bonus coefficients [for each post] with an obligation to furnish the list to all of the personnel; (c) this list showed that 80% of the coefficients should be changed.

When work resumed, the management went back on what it had accorded: explanation to the workers, remobilization, strike threat. At the beginning of July, the management gave in.

Alsthom, Tarbes. Heavy metallurgy

In November, 1969, conflict began for wage equality with the plant at Belfort. After a twenty-four hour warning strike, a new form of conflict was adopted: the reduction of productivity. The use of this weapon, which requires a perfect accord among the rank and file, is rather uncommon for a wage question.

Let us also mention here the very numerous strikes at *SOLLAC* [steel] which were, in fact, a challenging of the entire system of renumeration.

5. Gaining control over hours of work

Electricité de France, Rennes

March, 1969: after a general assembly, the *EDF* employees of Rennes decided to impose a reduction of hours. Each day they left twelve minutes early.

From Rennes, the action spread to Saint-Brieuc, Brest, and other plants in the west of France. Note in these actions: (a) the decisions made in general assemblies; (b) the break with the traditional actions of pre-May, 1968; (c) the direct confrontation with the management which was preparing to cut wages at the time of the next pay check.

ELF-Union, oil

The workers assigned to fixed posts proposed putting into action for a three month trial a rotation system which they had developed together. The management refused.

November 17, 1969: strike at Grandpuits [near Paris]. November 18th, strike at Gargenville. November 20th, strike at Feyzin [near Lyon]. These demonstrated the workers' desire to control their work conditions and to not leave this burden to the technocrats. At the end of November, the fixed-post workers of *ELF-Union* won satisfaction and obtained rotations which were the product of collective discussion.

In February, 1970, faced with the failure of discussions, the railway workers of the Lyon-Chambéry electrified line put into practice the five day week and their own work schedules by themselves.

To these movements of diverse types, directly concerned with control objectives, it is of course necessary to add some of those which attracted the greatest attention.

Stewardesses and Stewards of *Air France* late January, 1970

The flight personnel unions had already conducted several strikes including, this time, two twenty-four hour strikes on all lines, in order to obtain the unions' right to sit on the juries charged with granting stewardesses and stewards their security and life-saving certificate. The granting of this certificate, formerly effected by the government, became the responsibility of the companies alone on November 21, 1969.

"Behind this tumult," protested the companies, "the unions are trying to get *control of hiring*. The companies cannot give in to this grave threat," the director of Air France explained to the press.

Steel

Steel strikes, notably those conducted in September and November at *SOLLAC* at Thionville and at *USINOR* at Dunkerque had as their goal a revision of the wage hierarchy and, above all, the more general use of payment by the month. Both presented identical characteristics: instead of launching a 'traditional' limited strike, the movements started in the nerve centers: among the automated rolling mill operatives and the computer services at *USINOR* and the rolling mill workers at *SOLLAC*. [Actions proceeded] from bottleneck strikes to slow-down strikes, with explosion phases when the employers, forced to the wall by the 'technical' shutdown which the stoppage of certain essential installations provoked, threatened to fire everyone. In fact, these movements called into question the national round table agreements for steel, an agreement signed by the unions in a 'trough of the wave' period, when the threats to the very existence of the Lorraine steel basin spurred them to seek any type of guarantees and led them to take seriously the 'let us save ourselves together' slogan that the steel employers were offering them.

The strikes of the Commissariat of Atomic Energy in December successively hit Saclay and the production centers of Marcoule and Cadarache. Launched in spectacular fashion by the hunger strikes of Saclay, they called into question the 'reorganization' plan adopted by the Commissariat under governmental pressure, a plan ending in the elimination of 1,600 jobs.

The strikes of the operating personnel of the *S.N.C.F.*, a part of the switchyards of Achères and those of the Paris-Lyon-Marseilles line (at Dijon, Avignon, and Lyon), which notably reached the engineers of the semi-automatic electrified lines, were of an identical type. It was a question here of opposing the *S.N.C.F.* reconversion plan, which aimed to reduce drastically the number of railroad jobs by closing secondary lines.

The operating personnel, without pronouncing themselves on the more or less well-founded reasons for the proposed line closures, observed that the elimination of jobs projected by this measure in no way translated into a diminution of hours worked by the operating personnel on 'profitable' lines. But they had been demanding for a long time two persons (instead of one) at each post on the electrified lines, the reduction of the number of hours per shift and kilometers assigned to each of them, and finally an improvement of the sleeping posts for the operating personnel. The demands made for each category were thus inserted into the reorganization plan.

Paradoxically, the operating personnel had intervened in this way not over the general objectives defended by unions which aimed to arrange and reduce the overall extent of firings, but over their own demands; and this time it was not a question of bonuses but clearly of an offensive struggle for a real diminution of the duration of work.

This rapid glance at labor conflicts occurring since the month of May, 1968 allows us to delineate, while awaiting a deeper analysis, a certain number of observations:

(a) Wage demands strictly speaking (struggle for increase of the base wage) are rarely the principal object of the conflicts. Naturally, they translate themselves only rarely into strike movements. Everything happens as if wage negotiations, because they are accepted by the system, are somehow abandoned to 'union technicity,' at least where the latter is recognized by the employers. Whence the feeble impact of general slogans such as 'the return to the sliding wage and price scale:' it is a question here of a demand the workers know they cannot act on directly in any case; it is beyond their control.

(b) But if general wage demands are abandoned to technical discussions between the 'social partners,' the way in which each individual wage is determined is not. Faced with the increased—and very often artificial—complexity of types of remuneration, the workers seek to control the fashion in which these are set up. This demand is oriented in two sometimes contradictory directions:

One tends toward the simplification of forms of remuneration, which guarantees elimination of employers' arbitrariness. The only demand completely accepted by the entire working class during this period was for payment by the month.

But on the other hand, innumerable forms of 'extra wages,' institutionalized for years, such as pay for risk, unhealthy work conditions, tiring work, etc., continue to exist. It is here that demands are led to change in kind and to bear upon the conditions of work themselves.

(c) Discussion of work conditions has been, of course, integrated into collective contracts for a long time. But the fact remains that at this level it is always transformed into a discussion of the amount of wages. Traditional unionism has given up fighting for effective transformation of work conditions and has transformed their most scandalous aspects—accident risks, unhealthy conditions, nervous tension—into so many particular wage advantages. Strikes which break out on these points and tend to impose changes in work conditions unilaterally—slowing work rhythms, refusing a certain type of work, etc.—thus inevitably take place outside union organizations. The workers do not depend on unions for the resolution of this type of problem.

(d) This spread of 'wildcat strikes' concerning objectives not covered by usual union practice in no way signifies a 'hostility' of workers toward their organizations: quite simply, they have the impression that it is a question of something not in the unions' domain.

It is in this manner that one can explain the role sometimes played at the start of these actions by political groups (despite their small numbers) carrying out a role traditionally belonging to union activity. I do not mean to speak here of the factory cells of the *P.C.F.*, whose action is limited in general to propaganda activity and which are more a back-up element for the *C.G.T.* plant locals than the contrary, but of the various 'ultra-leftist' groups (Maoists of the *Gauche prolétarienne*, Trotskyists of *Lutte ouvrière* and of the *Alliance des Jeunes pour le Socialisme*) or the sections and factory groups of the *P.S.U.*, active today—and this is the case only since May, 1968—in all the large enterprises. The role played by these political groups, a role often magnified by the attacks mounted against them by the employers and the *C.G.T.*, must be seen in perspective. It is the expression of the crisis of traditional unionism whose institutionalized forms of action (the strike with advance warning decided by consultation with all workers) appear as inadequate as the type of ('consumption-oriented') demands it advances.

This does not signify workers' disaffection from the unions themselves. The best proof of this is that—and this is true for France as well as for the so-called 'wildcat' strikes of Germany, Italy, or Sweden—almost everywhere it is union militants who have been the activists and spokesmen in the strikes. Although not assured of the support of the branch and national organizations, and sometimes fought by them, the strikes went through 'union channels' at the grass roots; they tend in fact to strengthen the plant or firm-level locals in relation to the vertical and horizontal organization of the national confederations. Moreover, all struggles undertaken with control as an aim have been negotiated through union channels, with the union organization finding itself 'controlled' during negotiations by delegates emerging directly from the strikers' general assemblies.

(e) If we further analyze the diverse aspects of the struggle for control, we observe that, depending on the enterprises, it includes in fact two different approaches:

(1) In modern sectors of production with a high organic composition of capital, the content of these conflicts can lead to a desire to take managerial control itself. Implicitly, the autumn strikes in aeronautics (*SNECMA*), the *S.N.C.F.* (the operating personnel), atomic energy (Saclay, Cadarache, Marcoule and Le Hague) called the general orientation of the enterprise and its management policies into question. It was a matter here in all cases of sectors directly or indirectly related to the State sector, and all strikes attacked measures which favored the progressive 'privatization' of this sector.

The governmental counter-offensive starting with the *accords de progrès* which were begun precisely in the State sector can appear as having in part the aim of countering this tendency while orienting it toward 'consumer' aspects through re-emphasis on the well-worn theme of 'profit-sharing.'

But linking the determination of wages to the [quality of] management of the firm risks spontaneously orienting the unions themselves toward demands for control of management: the determination of production costs, and thus of control of supply and equipment markets, that of fixed investment as well as of distribution markets, indeed even the determination of the ends of production, come in as factors in wage determination.

This type of contractual relation dissipates the mystifying notion of a free labor market. The objective integration of workers into the firm, thus institutionalized, facilitates the passage from 'trade unionist' consciousness to the consciousness of the managing class—the will to acquire control of the enterprise by and for the workers—and thus to a new political awareness, as this demand develops at the level of large national sectors and against the policy put into effect by the State.

(2) The struggle for workers' control in the more traditional sectors of production and services takes on a more defensive character. The struggle against infernal work rhythms, and for job security,

improvement of work schedules, and control of wage-setting norms, does not lead directly to control of management, but teaches the workers not to accept as a given the norms of the employers' exploitation, which are most oppressive precisely in these sectors.

In the proper sense of the term, it is still a matter of 'economic struggles' which do not question the ends of production: how could it be otherwise, as they take place most of the time either in particular sectors of a firm which have no economic autonomy, or in subcontracting firms?

They are thus none other than struggles of resistance against capitalist exploitation. But even the terms of this resistance are put in *non-integratable* demands. The struggle against productivity, that is to say here, against physical super-exploitation, disequilibrates the competitive system in which the modern sector of production prospers. In refusing to let their demands for dignity in life be transformed into wage demands integratable at the cost of a slight inflation, in refusing to seek a few cents more for risking their lives and health, the workers of these firms are challenging the system of unequal development of the French economy, the 'internal' colonial pact which ensures both the proliferation of small and middle-sized firms and the super-profits of the big firms.

These struggles demonstrate at the same time — and for the first time in a longwhile — the revolt of the traditional working class against what Paul Lafargue denounced, 'this strange folly which has seized the European working class: the moribund passion for work pushed to the exhaustion of the vital forces of the individual.'[8]

This is the most direct product of the trauma that May, 1968, left in the working class consciousness: if demands oriented toward control experienced a *qualitative* development in the modern sectors of industry in May, 1968, one could find indications of it in social conflicts since 1956: these are the elements that I analyzed in 1963 in *La nouvelle classe ouvrière*. On the other hand, the questioning of the ends of labor, the transcending of the simple wage demand, is an entirely new fact in the unskilled working class.

The two movements in fact rejoin and support each other. And both call into question the 'unionism of conflictual participation.'

---

8. *Le droit à le paresse*, Paris: Maspéro, 1970, p. 121. (First published in 1880.) —SM [There are several English translations, the first by C.H. Kerr & Co., 1917, and recently reprinted. *Radical America* has also published this essay in pamphlet form.]

PART II:
The New Working Class

"Preface" to *Le Pouvoir Ouvrier* [1]

The essays brought together in this volume—of which several have not been previously published in France—were written between 1964 and 1971. The choice of these essays was determined by the convergent character of the problems posed. Nonetheless, written with a concern for immediate intervention in the action of the workers' movement, these essays are all profoundly marked by the period in which they were written. It is often the case that in such circumstances the author "rectifies" the old essays in order to bring them to the "taste of the present," and to demonstrate that the "line" of the author has remained unchanged, a-temporal and immutable in the midst of the inclemencies of the social struggle. Just like the Russian painters have taken the habit of redoing every ten years their commemorative paintings of October by erasing the heroes who have fallen into the "garbage heap of history," so many political authors give in to the temptation of hiding their old writings when these no longer correspond to the present evolution of their thought.

The mummification which the most impetuous and, in practice, the most unpredictable revolutionary leader has undergone has, alas, not been confined to his body: one has only to look at the ravages exercised today by a "neo-Leninism" which accumulates hectically citations from *What Is to Be Done?* and those of *State and Revolution,* as if Vladimir Illitch were that imbecile whom the movement of the masses between February and October 1917 had taught nothing. Theory makes no sense unless it returns ceaselessly into social praxis: this is an old injunction, but one which precisely in Marxist thought—be it "institutionalized" or intending to be institutionalized—is treated like the republican slogans on our town halls.

---

1. This Preface, written May 1, 1971, for the publication of *Le pouvoir ouvrier* (Paris: Anthropos, 1971), is published here with the permission of Serge Mallet. The present volume includes the essays printed in *Le pouvoir ouvrier* with the exception of a programmatic essay written for the National Congress of the PSU in 1971. We have also printed here several essays not included in that volume.

I am not the least bothered to say that while remaining basically in agreement with the essentials of the theses expressed before May 1968—especially since the problematic which is laid out there could not have been seriously formulated otherwise at the time—I consider them to be surpassed in certain aspects. Between them and the articles which follow them came an event whose lessons we have not yet fully assimilated: the Movement of May, 1968. With regard to many of the discussions contained in this volume,[2] and especially to the 1963 polemic with Herbert Marcuse, the Movement of May and what followed it has categorically decided: it informed the pessimism of those who despaired of the revolutionary capacity of the working class in the developed countries. It clarified the famous sea-serpent debate about "integration" by clearly establishing the distinction— unknown to philosophers—between *objective* integration into the mechanisms of production (the enterprise taken in the sense of an integrated productive complex)—an integration which facilitates the demand for control at the general social level—and *subjective* integration which leads the workers to assimilate their needs to those of capitalist management. Experience has proven that the more the production processes are "socialized," the less the workers had a tendency to confuse the ends of capitalist production and the socio-economic role of the production process.

May 1968 also showed that it is from the elements of the working class tied to the most advanced mechanisms of capitalist production that the new revolutionary ideology is organized: the struggle for control against the patronal autocracy, against the "reified" hierarchy and the bureaucratic organization of work are today assumed, sometimes in voilent forms, by the "backward" sections of industry; but they are the result of the "diffusion of the model" which I analyzed in 1963 which leads the workers of the archaic sectors to adopt the behavior and perspectives of the workers in the determinant sectors of the present, even when their objective conditions in production don't permit them to obtain the same consequences.

But at the same time we have here to integrate into the analysis of the social dynamic that positive role of the negativity which Alain Touraine correctly stressed in his book on the Movement of May: "Although the procedure of the elements of the working class who are the most integrated into modern production must pass through a

---

2.   "This volume," —i.e., *Le pouvoir ouvrier*.

'reformist-revolutionary' phase where the reserves of monopoly capitalism permit it to have a certain 'elasticity' towards these elements, the advancing of demands for control by the 'backward' sectors of the capitalist mode of production—whether it be workers in manufacturing firms or the middle peasantry—has inevitably the character of a revolutionary rupture—and that rupture radicalizes in turn the elements of the advanced sectors. The entire evolution of the social movement since May 1968 in France and in Italy especially confirms that dialectical interaction between the workers of the 'advanced' and the 'backward' sectors." Whereas from January 1969 through May 1970, the return of the social movement after the pause of the immediate after-May was the act of the advanced sectors (electronics, petroleum, chemistry, metals, aerospace, atomic energy, etc.), the relay was taken up after the Fall of 1970 by the workers of the sectors in difficulty (Fougères, Ferodo, Batignolles, mines de l'Est, etc.).

But the fundamental change for a revolutionary strategy which has come since May 1968 is not in that enlarging of the front of the anti-capitalist struggle to the strata that until now have been the least combative of the workers. It is much more in the profound rupture of the inter-class alliance which was postulated by the "reformist-revolutionary" strategy. The text "Socialism and Technocracy" which, if it was written in direct reference to the Yugoslav situation, exposed at the same time in clear terms what was at the time the strategy of the PSU at the time of the "Colloque de Grenoble," and what was at the same time the strategy of the left of the Italian Communist Party (which since then has formed the group "Il Manifesto") and that of the PSIUP. The strategy of the "structural anti-capitalist reforms," according to the term of André Gorz, included the possibility of detaching—for a transitory period which would be fairly long—a large part of the high state technocracy, of the "technostructure" as Galbraith would say, from the capitalist system in order to associate it with the workers' movement in a conflictual alliance which, after the overthrow, would lead to a situation of double-power.[3] This essay was without ambiguities on the risks which that association carried, and showed a certain clairvoyance as to what was its principal weakness: the refusal of the technocracy to share the power of decision, which implied an

---

3. In a long discussion of the Movement of May, Mallet remarked that the strategy which he had proposed to the PSU would have led precisely to these results. Mendès-France would, in effect, have been the French Kerensky.

accentuation of the class struggle — though in a subterranean sense —
after the seizure of power. We lack totally a Marxist scientific
analysis of the phenomenon of the "cultural revolution" in China —
our Chinese comrades having, as opposed to western Marxists, a
tendency to have a practice very much in advance of their and at the
same time a manifest incapacity to theorize that practice. But if we
recall the themes developed and put into practice by Mao Tse-tung
in his Yenan Writings, collected under the title *The New
Democracy*, and if we note that one of the basic reasons for the
success of the Chinese Communist Party in the military and
economic domains was the massive rallying to the Chinese revolution of the scientific and technical intelligentsia trained in the
West — then one can ask whether China has not decided in its own
manner, in 1967-68, the conflict which today countries like
Yugoslavia and Algeria face. At a certain point in the development
of the productive forces in a non-capitalist system, the new forces
created in the people by this same development enter into conflict
with the state technocracy and its ideological and political allies.

As concerns the countries of Western Europe, the radicalization of
the demands for control advanced since 1968 by the working class —
prematurely, some will say, but social history does not bend itself to
the rules of calculation of the planners — has traced a dramatic
demarcation line between the "progressive" sectors of the
technocracy and the revolutionary current. The rallying of the
conservative majority of the "men of the clubs"[4] to the conservative
government in France and in Italy — whether they find themselves
like Giolitti in the Finance Ministry of a Center-Left itself less and
less to the left, or in the cabinet of M. Chaban-Delmas — does not
imply in the least that they have renounced that modernization of the
industrial structures which was the bible of modern Saint-Simonian-
ism, but that they have decided to form it in the sticky mold of the
old conservative structures. From Turgot to Edgar Faure, the history
of France is cluttered with the corpses of those reformers who reform
nothing. It seems that General de Gaulle, to whom no one would
deny a certain "sense of history," cried out in May 1968: "What can
you do? In this country a revolution is needed in order to make a
reform!" But in this case it is not in the least a case — as the General

---

4.   There exists in France a tendency for politicians who are out of power in their
own parties to form "Clubs" for reflection and discussion — no doubt in imitation of
the pre-1789 period. As the context of Mallet's remark indicates, the members of the
Clubs tend to have a technocratic orientation towards politics.

believed—of who knows what French particularity: the failure of Kennedy and that of Wilson, the failure of technocratic reformism is the reflection of that profound contradiction: in order that there be a social change, the masses must take into their hands the will to change. That change may well be at the beginning behind the objective needs of the masses. But as the movement develops and radicalizes, as the resistance of the old structures hardens, the masses become aware of their own objectives. And the reforms have then to choose their side.

May 1968 was one of those moments where the positions of the ones and the others are clarified: the progressive technocracy which flattered the will for control of the working class and the minor technicians as long as they did not put into question the "profitable" management of the enterprise became afraid when the new working class began to question the management in general, that is the entire system of goals, of control and hierarchy. May 1968 and its results have effectively "rejected" the majority of the elements of the technostructure into the conservative camp. And, in the immediate present, the rupture of the "Alliance of Grenoble" may well make the struggle against the system more difficult. But that too is the result of an extraordinary advance in the consciousness of the class.

The technocracy has lost confidence in its capacities to orient a technically skilled working class towards "a new society" which it would control as did the liberal petite-bourgeoisie in the Third Republic. Its difficult alliance with the most reactionary forces of rentier capitalism isolates it at the same time from its virtual social bases. It leaves the field free—over against the reactionary camp, and isolating outside the social dynamic that great rusty machine which is the communist party—for a restructuration of the revolutionary workers' movement not in terms of the old schemas but starting from the realities of the class struggle here and today. It will be permitted to the militant which I am to note that the evolution of these writings corresponds grosso-modo—some times going ahead of it—to the movement of my party, the PSU: from the PSU of Grenoble to that of the Workers-Peasants' Assemblies there is not a continuity but an incontestible, qualitative change.

But like all political and ideological phenomena, this change is nothing but a reflection of those changes which upset in its depths the social basis of this country. One must recognize in the present that which we inherit from the past, for good as well as for bad. But one must especially recognize what is born and develops. After having been in advance of the social movement, the PSU runs the risk of falling behind it. It must change in order to remain faithful to itself.

Socialism and Technocracy [1]

Western neo-capitalism represents a powerful attempt at adaptation by the capitalist system of production and exchange in order to resolve its principal contradiction, which derives—and let us remember that this is the foundation of the Marxist critique of this system—from the "increasingly social character of the productive forces" and the private character of the "appropriation of the means of production and exchange." Nevertheless, two contradictory tendencies—I mean to say objectively conflictual—appear here. The first, which has predominated during the last fifty years, especially in the United States, is an attempt at "private planning of production and exchange" by the formation of integrated production units of a monopolistic type. Nevertheless this attempt, as Lenin recalled in *Imperialism, the Highest Stage of Capitalism*, clashes with the very nature of capitalism. Far from evading the classic crises of the capitalist system, the struggles among the giants of production aggravate them. The great crisis of 1927-1933 appears from this point of view as the consequence of this gigantism of industrial trusts. The second, which Engels had analyzed so lucidly as the ultimate consequence of capitalist concentration, is the development of state capitalism, of which Roosevelt's "New Deal" on the political level and the economic theories of J.M. Keynes on the theoretical level appear as the first generalized expressions in the developed capitalist world.

Western neo-capitalism, as it dominates in Western Europe and as it tends to assert itself in the U.S.A. through diverse phases of advance and retreat, is a combination of these two models of organization.

According to whether monopoly capitalism has reached a more or less advanced stage of organization, more advanced in the U.S.A. than in Western Europe, for example, the relations of the capitalist

---

1. This article first appeared in *Sozialism* (Belgrade) in 1967 and is reprinted here with the permission of the author.

organization of the state to private capitalism will be different. So it is that in the U.S.A. state capitalism exerts its influence principally by means of government purchases, especially military ones. The failure of the grandiose plans of American state capitalism as elaborated under J.F. Kennedy and carried further by Lyndon Johnson under the banner of the "Great Society" demonstrates the inadequacy of such procedures. Through the influence of fiscal policy and government purchases alone, the American capitalist state showed itself incapable, to orient the American trusts toward the industrial development of the Deep South (and thus to resolve the race problem), to resolve without serious tension the problems posed by the development of automation, to reconvert the brutal imperialism practiced by the U.S. trusts in Latin America into a structural imperialism permitting the development of dominated but efficient national industries, to organize the rational growth of American cities, to control the sectorial growth of the economy, etc.

In fact, the elements of "private planning" in the U.S.A. appear to be both sufficiently powerful to defeat the state's attempts at control and inadequate to parry the risks of self-destruction inherent in the subordination of collective to private interests.

For diverse reasons in which the two World Wars and their economic and demographic consequences, space limitations, and the political role of the labor movement play the principal roles, in Western Europe the monopolies were never able to reach this size and the role belonging to state capitalism was thereby reinforced to the same degree.

Not only has the latter tried, with variable success according to the country, to master the orientation of large firms through fiscal policy, but in order to reinforce its control, it was led to create its own economic sector. The weight of the state economic sector in industry, credit organisms, services, and agriculture is continually becoming stronger. This was particularly true in France and Italy, where the state sector bore the principal weight of the economic expansion of the years 1950-1963. It is beginning to be so in West Germany, as the takeover of Krupp by para-state groups has just shown.

It is primarily in the latent conflict between the state capitalist sector and the monopolistic sector that the principal sources of contradiction of Western neo-capitalism will be found in the near future. In effect, monopoly capitalism which still essentially controls political representation, tends to push the state sector toward "service" sectors hardly profitable in themselves, and to secure for itself, according to the celebrated formula, the "privatization of the profits" by leaving to the state sector "the socialization of the losses." But the state capitalist sector develops its own productive dynamic at the same time that it creates a particular strata of wage-earners—cadres and upper-level management included—who exert pressure on it so that it will assure its own profitability despite capitalist interests.

A second series of contradictions comes from the general socialization of all activities—agricultural, commercial, artisanal, intellectual. The reconversion of these social strata attached to archaic forms of economic organization is one of the principal questions that neo-capitalism has to resolve. These social strata, struggling first to maintain an outmoded status, are subsequently led to demand a social status other than that of direct or indirect wage-earners under capitalism.[2]

Finally, the contradictions between Western European capitalisms and American capitalism constitutes a third element of structural weakness in the capitalist system of Western European countries. It partially overlaps, moreover, certain elements of the first two series.

If we take the case of France or Italy, we can say from now on that the struggle for control of an entire class of big firms is already no longer between the state capitalist sector and the private *national* capitalist sector, but between the state sector and the private American *international* capitalist sector, which tends to have hegemony over the private national capitalist sector.

The offensive strategy of the labor movement must therefore be, in the first place, to use itself as a lever in these contradictions of a so-called "neo-capitalist system" which, far from being a completed system, appears much more as a transition phase full of explosive contradictions. The historical evolution of Western Europe depends to a large extent on the ability of the labor movement to make use of these contradictions for a qualitative modification of the relations of force in its favor. This strategy might thus, during a first stage, schematically define itself through an overall struggle to modify the relations of force in the economic domain, to enlarge continually the sector directly or indirectly controlled by the state, to subordinate

---

2. Mallet analyzed in great detail the situation of the French peasantry from this point of view in *Les Paysans contre le passé* (Paris: Editions du Seuil, 1962). Cf. also, the essay, "La société politique française en 1963," in *Le Gaullisme et la gauche* (Paris: Ed. hons du Seuil, 1965).

private national capitalism to the state, and to prevent the penetration of American capitalism.

The novel character of the situation in the Western European countries is that this phase, which the orthodox Marxists considered as *deriving directly from the political conquest of power by the labor movement,* appears at the present as *necessarily preceding* that conquest. This situation suggests a process of objective alliance between the labor movement, bearer of socialist solutions, and the relatively autonomous forces generated by state capitalism. The most important of these forces is the technocracy itself relying on the confused aspirations of the intermediate social strata which, although having acquired in fact a status identical to that of workers, have not yet realized all the consequences.

But this strategy clearly harbors an immense risk, that of seeing the state-technocratic groups, placed in a position of strength in this confrontation with national and foreign private capitalism subordinate the labor movement to their own ends—ends which, let us not forget, intend to change the *form* of capitalist exploitation, *not its fundamental content.*

To make this analysis concrete, it would be necessary here to study the countries of Western Europe one after the other: each of them in fact shows an identical tendency of this type, but in the form of very different policies whose results may be very different.

In Great Britain, this tendency appeared in the Labour Party's coming to power on the basis of "structural modernization" of old Victorian England. But the tendencies toward state capitalism included in "Wilsonism" found themselves weakened by the unconditional submission of the labor movement (trade unionist above all) to the technocratic ideology and its political expression. No longer having to "protect itself on the left," Wilsonism had a tendency to seek such compromises on its right (as much with the financiers of the City as with the U.S.A.) that it sacrificed a good part of its own objectives—objectives that unofficially "socialist" governments have achieved better elsewhere because they had to answer to the opposition of the labor movement.

In Italy, this strategy officially justified the constitution of the Center-Left govenment. The results were better for a time, because of the opposition force represented by the Italian Communist party and the *C.G.I.L.* [*Confederazione generale italiana del Lavoro,* equivalent of the French *C.G.T.*] as well as the left wing of Italian socialism. Nevertheless, the fact that the majority of forces representing the labor movement found themselves excluded from the governmental coalition created a negative situation by weakening the resistance of the Center-Left to the pressures of reactionary Italian and American forces. The dialectic of political competition led the Italian Socialist Party [P.S.I.] to align itself on the most backward wing of Christian Democracy and not on the advanced wing close to the state technocracy (led by Fanfani).

Finally, in France, (I will not go into the German question, the Kiesinger-Brandt experience being too recent to draw any conclusions) the conflict between the tendencies toward state capitalism, unambiguously expressed by General de Gaulle and Michel Debré with its incontestable consequences for foreign policy, and the aspirations of French private capitalism which is fairly open to a policy of subordinate collaboration with American capitalism, took place essentially *within* the governmental majority, the forces of the Left being excluded from this debate.

Thus, in none of these three of the four big powers of Western Europe did this *conflictual* alliance between the socialist movement and the state technocracy (which marks the requirements of the transitional phase at these countries' level of development) materialize politically.

In Great Britain and Italy, this situation risked compromising even the devlopment of state capitalism and, at the same blow, putting an end to the economic autonomy of these countries, which would become second zone economies dominated by American capitalism. In France, it isolated the trends toward state capitalism and toward the economic independence of the wage-earning masses who were the necessary support for it and, by the same token, rendered them *politically* fragile.

Without overestimating the role of theory, it is undoubtedly necessary to attribute these situations partly to the socialist movement's lack of reflection on the problems of the *ways to pass to socialism in the developed countries*, that is, to guesswork and dogmatism, the twin maladies of the labor movement.

Undoubtedly, in Italy and France, reflection on these problems has been underway for a decade but it would be premature to conclude that it has reached the upper levels of the political leadership and even less the masses. It is also true to say that the problems posed are highly complex as soon as one wishes to explore them on the level of political practice. But this is another reason to approach them with frankness and courage.

But to conclude—tentatively—on the fundamental point, I would nevertheless formulate a few propositions, while asking readers to interpret them with care.

1) The prospects for a passage to socialism in a relatively near time in the countries of Western Europe are objectively included in the contradictions of neo-capitalism. From this point of view, the labor movement ought firmly to deplore the pessimistic tendencies which tend to confuse the working class' aspirations to a higher standard of living and to an acceleration of the technical and scientific process with any "subjective integration into the capitalist system." The Communards of 1871 and the Kronstadt sailors aspired fully to have access to the consumer goods offered to their bourgeoisies. There are some stale odors of an anti-technical "Rousseauism" presently floating in leftist intellectual milieux which are particularly dangerous, even when they hide behind "Third World romanticism."

2) It would be illusory to believe that the passage to socialism, despite the already advanced level of productive forces, will be accomplished overnight, following a successful insurrection or an electoral victory. This passage will in fact probably last *an entire historical period*, during which it will sometimes happen *that the level of progress toward socialism will be more advanced on the level of political power than on that of economic and social structures, and sometimes the reverse.* It was the two opposed faces of the same dogmatic illusion which led Stalinist dogmatism to consider only the political factor and Social-Democratic opportunism to consider only the social structures. And it is a third error to believe that the two factors develop at the same rhythm.

3) During a long historical period, there will be *conflictual co-existence* of state capitalist and socialist forms, perhaps even a continuation of a relatively important (although subordinate) private capitalist sector. Socialist theory must at the same time keep from:

　　a) denying the inevitability of state capitalist (or technocratic) forms;

　　b) likening them to socialist forms (on the pretext that private capitalism has been eliminated).

4) In the advanced capitalist countries of Europe, *the alliance of the labor movement and the technocratic tendencies, and of the social forces which sustain them, is an absolute necessity in order to reduce the influence of national and foreign [American] private monopolistic capitalism.*

5) Nevertheless, *the success of this alliance requires the political, organizational, and social autonomy of the labor movement in relation to state capitalism,* and of the social and political forces which embody these tendencies. This is valid both for the period of "opposition" and for the period of "passage to power."

6) The struggle of the labor movement takes place simultaneously in all sectors of social life. Without waiting for "the taking of power" in its pure form, or even the coming to power of coalition governments, the labor movement must thus enter into a determined struggle *to enlarge to the maximum all the forms of democratization of political, economic, and social decision-making.* It must strive to create, under conditions of partial domination by state capitalism, the instruments of socialist decision-making on which it will rely for:

a) developing the germs of socialist society in a second phase;

b) assuring itself bases for opposition to the "progressive" technocracy in the immediate future.

7) The clarity of objectives, the permanent elucidation of levels of action, and the accurate and public delimitation of acceptable compromises determine the labor movement's capacity for autonomous action, permitting it to avoid both an inevitable lack of patience and stagnation in compromises.

8) The permanant coordination of the labor movement must encompass all the forms of its action (political, trade union, economic, cultural organizations, etc.); and the *general political direction of the movement* (different from the action of the political organization strictly defined) *can only be the result of this coordination.*

I am of course not unaware of the difficulties involved in a transcending of the old reform-revolution dilemma, a dilemma in the name of which, in Western Europe, the "reformists" have made fewer reforms than neo-capitalism and the "revolutionaries" have turned away from revolutionary prospects each time they apeared. I would add that the confrontation of different points of view among the diverse (political and trade union) fractions of the labor movement of the various countries of Western Europe and of these with the other fractions of the labor movement, especially those of Eastern and Southeastern Europe, is each day more urgent.

Bureaucracy and Technocracy
in the Socialist Countries[1]

Preface to the Reader

This article developed out of two speeches presented by the author last year, one in August at the Korcula Summer School in Dalmatia, where since 1963 Marxist philosophers and sociologists from the East and the West have held annual meetings, and the other in September at the Colloquium in Hercegovina (Montenegro) organized by the Institute for Social Sciences in Belgrade and the Gramsci Institute in Rome, at which sociologists from all the Eastern countries (including the USSR) discussed "Social Stratification in Socialist Countries."

The last part of the article, "The Technocratic-Bureaucratic Antagonism and the Imperial Contest," was written later, in July of this year, after the advent of the "Czechoslovakian Spring." The latest events in Czechoslovakia do not make necessary any revision of the article. If it did not predict them, it nevertheless analyzed the context in which they occurred. That context is one of the dual conflict within the socialist countries: a conflict for power between the bureaucratic class and the new technological elites of "Soviet" society, and between the "imperial consciousness" of the Soviet Union and the desire for a self-managed socialism on the part of the new intellectual, technical, and industrial working classes of the European People's Democracies. The recourse to armed intervention, taking into account the risk to the cohesion of the "world socialist camp" and to peace itself, signified that the dual conflict analyzed in these pages had reached a point of contradiction where "'the ammunition of critical exchange is ready to give way to a critical exchange of ammunition."

As socialists, we may be saddened that the resolution of internal contradictions in the socialist camp is accomplished by resort to brutal military force. But, as Marxists, we shouldn't be too surprised. If it is true that force is the midwife of social revolution, the passage of Eastern countries from the primitive stage of state capitalism to

---

1. This article first appeared in *L'Homme et la société*, Oct.-Dec. 1968. The present translation, adapted from Anna Frankel's version in *Socialist Revolution*, is reprinted from the *Spokesman* by permission.

that of realized socialism can scarcely be imagined without a long, painful process of prolonged struggles and sharp conflicts. In the end, the most important thing is not this or that episode in the historical struggle, but that the masses of the "socialist" countries rediscover political struggle and that the desire for socialism, contrary to what happened in Hungary in 1956, no longer be discouraged, but rather affirmed with a new vigour.

The author of this article has been convinced for many years that there is no society in existence that is truly socialist. The "socialism" of the Eastern countries, even in its liberal version, is to socialism what the monsters of the paleolithic era are to present animal species: clumsy, abortive prototypes.

It is essential, now that Western youth are once again engaged in the struggle for socialism, that the face of socialism in the East be placed in its proper historical perspective.

From this point of view, the "Springtime of Prague" corresponds to the "Commune of May" in France.

In Warsaw as in Berkeley, in Belgrade as in Turin, in Prague as in Paris, the red flag represents the aspirations of humanity to exercise in full its creative freedom. —S.M.

Self-Management and Socialism

The concept of self-management cannot be studied abstractly in terms of an ideal and timeless society. The degree to which economic and social self-management is practiced is one of the most significant indices of the level in the development of the new social relations among human beings that socialism seeks to achieve. Yet fifty years' experience in states that claim to be socialist shows the extent to which the concept of a socialist society can be altered and modified to match the level of productive forces attained in a country where a political revolution has occurred. A political revolution can modify the character of the ownership of the means of production, but it is not sufficient for modifying the nature of social relations. In order that management, not only of the means of production and exchange, but also of the society as a whole, cease to be the domain of a minority felt as oppressive by the majority, the political revolution must be accompanied by an equally profound social revolution, one in which the relations of "the governed" give way to relations of egalitarian co-operation. The development of self-management as a substitute for administrative management does not result in a particular form of socialism, but is an absolute imperative for a socialist society.

Of course, there can be specific national or historical forms of self-management. But there can be no socialism without self-management — in the larger sense of social self-management and not in the narrow sense of the management of autonomous units of production.

Fifty years after the October Revolution, twenty years after the passage to socialism in Eastern Europe, fifteen years after the success of the Chinese revolution, the development of worker and social self-management remains embryonic in all socialist countries. Even in the Federated People's Republic of Yugoslavia, the only country that made self-management its fundamental social principle, its realization seems to be undergoing retardation rather than advance.

The Marxist masters had thought the transition from political to social revolution would be very short, because for them the "withering away of the state" was to begin the very day that the working class seized political power. But today, the concepts of bureaucracy and technocracy, concepts developed by Western sociologists outside the context of Marxist analysis, are accepted as operational concepts by Marxist sociologists of the socialist countries in order to analyze their own society.

Most of our colleagues in Eastern Europe analyze even the process of economic reform now taking place in all Eastern European countries as the product of a conflict between the state bureaucratic class that presided over the development of heavy industry during a period of authoritarian planning and a new class of economic directors who are fighting for the economic and social flexibility appropriate to industrial diversification and who want to create a large class of consumers capable of influencing the quality and orientation of socialist production.

Technocratic-Bureaucratic Conflict in the Socialist Countries

The sociologists of The Institute of Social Sciences in Budapest have proposed the newest and most challenging conception of this conflict in the socialist countries. They see the development of socialism taking place by means of an alliance of advanced socialists and the technocracy against the archaic bureaucracy, which has slowed down the historial development of the socialist countries and has kept them in a outmoded phase of development in which the bureaucracy's political monopoly will be secure. The passage of economic-political power from the bureaucratic stratum to the technocratic stratum would represent an essential element in the passage from one phase to another in the development of socialism.

But how can the appearance of a bureaucratic or technocratic stratum be integrated into the concept of a socialist society? Bureaucratic and technocratic strata have no place in a fully socialist society—even if they constitute necessary phases in its development. What, then, are the social and organizational forces at the heart of those countries with a socialist structure that will assure passage to more democratic forms of social management? Such a passage is an indispensable condition for the abolition of exploitation and the liberation of collective and individual creativity.

The answer to these various questions can only be sketched here, especially since the necessary materials for such an analysis are still not at our disposal. The explosive development of the social sciences in the socialist countries indicates that we will be able to see the deeper nature of these societies more clearly a few years from now, and perhaps to elucidate in a more realistic fashion the complex relations of their economic infrastructure, social structures and political superstructures. But we can begin to make some observations now in the light of the loosening of bureaucratic constraints that has taken place in Eastern Europe since the days of Stalin.

The Formation of the Bureaucracy in Socialist Countries

Socialist political regimes in Eastern Europe all came about under socio-historical conditions different from those foreseen by Marx. In some countries, the Marxist-Leninist wing of the workers' movement found itself in the leadership of democratic movements that did not initially have socialist objectives. In Russia and China, the political revolution occurred in the frame-work of an agrarian revolution for land and peace. In Yugoslavia, it was the expression of a movement for unification and national liberation. In the other Eastern European countries, it was exported into the country as a consequence of the Red Army's military victories and the refusal of traditional political forces to collaborate with it. Whatever the case, the political revolutions were never principally the product of a revolutionary class, which in these countries was still too small to constitute a decisive political force. (Only Czechoslovakia was a relatively developed industrial nation, but the 1947 revolution, effected for reasons of the USSR's international strategy and initially against the will of the Czech Communists, deviated from the historical process that was in course since 1945.)

The Formation of Bureaucratic States
from the 17th to 19th Centuries

In all socialist countries, the seizure of political power by the workers' movement (under Communist direction or by the Communists alone, according to the case) occurred within the framework of a particular historical situation which Western Europe had experienced between the seventeenth and nineteenth centuries. The framework was one of a proto-capitalist phase of development. It was characterized by the advanced formation of bureaucratic centralized states, which made possible the establishment of the first capital reserves, the primitive accumulation of capital forced on the back of the peasantry and a fraction of the old pre-capitalist middle classes, and the creation of a capitalist market extended to the whole population.

Victorian England, Napoleonic France and the Germany of Bismarck constitute examples of this phase, whereas the Czarist and Austro-Hungarian empires had just entered it in the beginning of the twentieth century. Beginning with the formation of finance capital as a fusion of banking and industrial capital, the forms of the bureaucratic state entered into conflict with the development of the productive forces and inhibited the formation of the financial market and the initiative of the free market. The Russian revolution appeared as a brutal rupture in the process that had had a much slower evolution in Western Europe.

Liberal Capitalism and the Bureaucratic State

The Bolsheviks were confronted with the need to raise the level of development of the whole of the backward Czarist empire to that attained by the industrialized regions of Russia where the revolutionary movement had crystallized. The Bolsheviks, contrary to the profoundest thoughts of Marx and Engels, did not move to destroy the bureaucratic Czarist state. On the contrary, they used its structures to make possible a gigantic leap in industrial production. But that leap was limited precisely to those sectors of the base (steel production, energy production) that in the nineteenth century West were under the control of the bureaucratic state rather than private capital.

The Formation of Stalinist Bureaucracy

Stalinist Bureaucracy, as a ruling caste, is the historical product of the leap beyond and over the phase of liberal capitalism. In addition, its formation appears as an amalgamation of the old "urban revolutionary" class, transplanted after several years of partisan struggles into the backward conditions of the Russian countryside, and the old Czarist provincial bureaucracy, which had rallied to the new regime all the while retaining the essence of its old habits. In the resulting bureaucratic detour taken by the new regime, one cannot be certain that these latter "leftovers from the past" weighed more heavily than the neophytes. (The publication of the Archives of the Party Committee of the town and region of Smolensk casts a harsh light on the struggles that the central power had to wage against former revolutionaries turned Oriental satraps.)

In 1922, Lenin, in his testament, unequivocally expressed his fears about the rise of this new bureaucratic class. He feared that it would become a new ground for something he detested very much—Russian national chauvinism: "We call ours an apparatus that in fact is still basically foreign to us and represents a hash of bourgeois and Czarist holdovers, which were absolutely impossible for us to transofrm in five years because we lacked the help of other countries, and because we were preoccupied militarily and were also fighting famine."

"In these conditions, it is completely natural that the 'freedom to leave the union,' which seemed to us a sufficient statement of policy, should appear in fact as a bureaucratic formula incapable of defending the people of other races in the USSR against the invasion of the authentic Russian, the nationalistic Russian, the chauvinist, the idiot, and the oppressor, which is what the typical Russian bureaucrat basically is. Nor can it be doubted that the Soviet and sovietized workers, who are a small minority, will also drown themselves, like flies in a bowl of milk, in this ocean of Russian national rabble. . . .

"Have we taken careful enough measures really to defend the Soviet peoples of other races against the typical Russian slavedriver? I think that we have not taken these measures, and that it was really incumbent upon us to have done so and to do so." (December 30, letter to the Central Committee.)

The total nationalization of economic activity that this class directed through the state apparatus gave it, in the absence of any opposition from the workers, an economic base of power quite superior to that of the old Czarist bureaucracy. The basis of this power was a still archaic undifferentiated heavy industry, which by its nature was susceptible to non-economic control. (From the same point of view, one must understand the apparent failure of the collective farm [*kolkoz*] system. Its essential object was less to give a socialist structure to the peasantry than to impose upon it a framework of production which, as in the old mode of Asiatic production, would allow a rigorous tax assessment distined to assure both the development of heavy industry and the maintenance of the bureaucratic stratum.)

In the European states detached from the Czarist or old Austro-Hungarian empires, as in the Balkan countries recently liberated from the Ottoman empire, a national bourgeoisie arose too late to control primary economic development; foreign imperialist capital had already conquered the most important positions. Political power, in Hungary as in Poland, in Rumania as in Yugoslavia, took the form of an unstable equilibrium between the old bureaucracy and still strong feudal elements.

The Bureaucratic States in Central and Eastern Europe

Nowhere, not even in Czechoslovakia, did the national bourgeoisie find itself strong enough to create liberal democratic political structures or a semi-independent capitalist economy. The political revolution took place between 1945 and 1950 under the direction of Communist cells, which had little real influence in the country and could do little to modify the position of the bureaucracy. The very weakness of the working class and of its militant core, which had gone through twenty-five years of uninterrupted fascist repression, favored the creation of a bureaucratic stratum, a stratum formed in part from elements of the old bureaucracy which had allied with the regime and in part from new notables of peasant origin. In most of the People's Democracies, with the exception of Czechoslovakia and Yugoslavia, the revolutionary elements that arose from within the intelligentsia and the working class constituted from the beginning only a small group of militants. The purges of the 1947-1953 era were to reduce them still further. As a result, the process of penetration into the Party of a bureaucratic stratum of "*parvenus* of the revolution" was even more extensive and rapid than in the Soviet Union.

Thus, the roots of the bureaucratization of the socialist state in both Stalinist Russia and in the People's Democracies between 1947 and 1955 go back to the bureaucratic structures of regimes that predated the October Revolution and the establishment of the People's Democratic states. But it would be misleading to draw a straight line from the bureaucracy of the old regime to the new bureaucracy. The Czarist bureaucracy (and the various national bureaucratic classes that came into power in the Balkans and Central Europe after the break-up of the Austro-Hungarian, Czarist and Ottoman empires) had to share its power with still powerful feudal classes, and thus had to seek the aid of foreign capital in order to organize industrial development. The assumption of power by the Communist parties ended the power both of the feudal classes and of foreign capital.

The new bureaucracy, heir to the traditions and often the personnel of the old one, was nevertheless able to achieve, although with difficulty, a primitive accumulation of capital. Whereas the Western bureaucracies had achieved this for their bourgeoisies toward the middle of the nineteenth century the Eastern countries, economically backward in comparison to their Western competitors, had little success in doing so. We must thus recognize the positive character of the bureaucratic phase through which all the socialist countries passed. This explains the popularity that the bureaucracy enjoyed, despite its police methods and its despotism. The resistance of the Soviet people to Nazi aggression was the surest measure of this.

The Historical Function of the Bureaucracy

The October Rvolution notwithstanding its socialist aspirations, and the political revolutions that occurred in Eastern and Central Europe after 1945, allowed the bureaucratic stratum, as a social expression of primitive state capitalism, to play an historic role in the passage of agrarian societies to the primary phase of industrial society. It was a passage that these countries, because of their "historical lag," could not achieve in the framework of traditional capitalist structures.

This interpretation of the historical development of the socialist countries supports Lenin against Kautsky, when he asserted that because of the imperialist character of the states first entering the capitalist era, the automatic passage from feudalism to capitalism had become impossible for most backward countries. But this interpretation also supports Kautsky against Lenin, when the Austro-Marxist argued that because of the insufficient development of its productive forces, the direct passage to socialism was impossible in Czarist Russia.

What conclusions can we now draw from this interpretation? 1) The first phase of socialism — what Marx and Engels as well as Lenin called the "dictatorship of the proletariat"—implies the withering away of the state beginning as soon as power is seized. Insofar as the bureaucratic phase in socialist countries implies the continuation of the exploitation of man by man (which need not be tied to the particular process of capital accumulation, only one of the diverse forms it has assumed) this bureaucratic phase should not be confused with the "first phase of socialism."

Socialism or Society in Transition

Although certain conditions indispensible to the realization of socialism, especially the nationalization of the principal means of production and exchange, have been realized, others equally important, such as the democratisation of economic management and of the state apparatus, were not set in motion during this period. We are thus led to speak of a society in transition toward socialism and not of a socialist society. This historical revision of vocabulary would have extraordinarily positive consequences for the revitalisation of the concept of socialism in Western European countries. 2) Just as discussions now in progress on the question of "the Asiatic mode of production" make it appear that humanity had two different models for the dissolution of primitive community, namely the ancient (or slave) mode of production and the Asiatic mode of production, so we can accept the hypothesis that the capitalist mode of production was the West's own way of passing from agrarian civilization to industrial society. The fact that it arrived first in Western Europe and the United States is precisely the reason why other societies were prevented from taking that path. At the same time, the arrival of capitalism in Western Europe engendered the diffusion of Western life style, models and products that everywhere sapped the base of the ancient agrarian societies, just as the imperialist development of the Greek and Roman slave societies doubtless counteracted tendencies in this direction within Eastern Mediterranean societies. 3) The revolutions of the Eastern countries and Central Europe—the first and most powerfully affected by this diffusion—found the framework for non-capitalist and non-imperialist development in the pre-existing structures of the bureaucratic state. The socialist revolutions in some ways liberated the productive tendencies of the state bureaucracy, tendencies which couldn't develop in the West because of the growth of finance capital and the political weight of the middle class, but which existed embryonically in the beginning of the capitalist era and permitted its development. 4) Whatever feelings of sadness it causes us, history—since October, 1917—was neither with the anarchist peasants or Makhno, nor with the sailors and workers of the libertarian commune of Kronstadt; instead it was firmly with the Bolshevik centralisers who, from Trotsky when he was in power, to Stalin, created the conditions for the liberation of the productive forces by giving power to bureaucracy. The Russian people, as Gorky's hero Thomas Gordeiev expressed so well, did not reproach the Czarist bureaucracy for its very existence as a bureaucracy, but rather for its impotence in assuming effectively its historical task.

The Appropriation of Surplus Value by the State: The Foundation of Bureaucratic Power

There exist thousands of definitions of "bureaucracy"—from that of Stalin, of whom Trotsky said that "when he spoke of it (and he spoke of it often), he had in mind only the bad habits of bureau employees," to that of Bruno Rizzi, who gives it the characteristics of an autonomous class. In fact, however, there is only one definition, crude as it is, that encompasses all bureaucratic situations: bureaucracy is, above all, the reign of the tax collector, the treasury, to whom a social group, large or small, delegates the power to appropriate, through civilian or military constraints, the surplus value created by the work of the state's subjects. The policeman, the judge, and the soldier are in the last analysis only the secular arm of the treasury. When the level of the productive forces and the level of demographic growth are more or less in equilibrium and the maintenance of the ruling classes, including the bureaucracy itself, can be handled by an appropriation which the populace finds supportable, then the weight of the bureaucracy in the society is weak and its autonomous power insignificant. When, on the contrary, the level of production is insufficient to assure both the maintenance of the structures of production and the standard of living of the ruling classes, the weight of the bureaucracy becomes oppressive. Feeling the consequences of popular discontent, the bureaucracy seeks to obtain a maximum of political autonomy, and to set itself up as a ruling class.

The key fact in the evolution of Western countries is that the capitalist system of production created a process of appropriating surplus value that in theory dispensed with the role of the bureaucracy as an intermediary. The young Marx based his vision of capitalism's destruction upon this meaning of the capitalist mode of production: the overthrow of capitalism would at the same time relegate the state to "the museum of history." The substitution of the private ("voluntary") appropriation of surplus value for state appropriation had already begun to undermine the principal function of the state. The working class, by altering the legal status of the owners of the means of production, and by transforming their private property into productive property, would transform itself into the collective user of the surplus value produced by itself through the process of industrial accumulation; and, it would thereby bring an end to surplus value itself, as the product of the exploitation of man by man.

But we know today that the historical fulfillment of this process has been postponed to a future time, because of the new qualitative and quantitative needs created by the liberation of the productive forces of heavy industry. We also know how state capitalism set itself up as the regulator of the whole economy in substituting itself for liberal capitalism. But that is another subject.

In any case, if we accept these premises for analyzing the internal evolution of socialist countries, we also observe that the conditions foreseen by the Marxist authors did not yet exist, and because of the existence of a more developed foreign capitalism, could never have exsited. The primitive accumulation of capital required the reinforcement (not the withering away) of the state bureaucracy as an agent for the appropriation of surplus value—that is, it required external control exercised by the bureaucracy over economic mechanisms, and in particular over the private production of the peasantry. The political weight of the bureaucratic class was made that much stronger. For the first time in the history of European societies (if one leaves aside the Creto-Mycenaen era in which it seems that the Asiatic mode of production dominated), the bureaucracy found itself in the position of directly managing the economy.[2]

Eliminating External Control
over the Mode of Industrial Production

The realisation of the bureaucracy's objective condemned it to eventual death. As Eastern European societies were transformed from agrarian into industrial societies, the number of direct producers of surplus value (industrial and agricultural wage earners,

---

2. Nevertheless—contrary to the theses of Milovan Djilas in *The New Class*—the essential part of the bureaucracy's power is extra-economic. Its control is first of all political control. Stalinist or Rakosist "voluntarism" is a caricature of this. —SM

and workers in productive services) increased accordingly. The appropriation of surplus value through external control became an obstacle to the internal growth of productive forces, and began to appear more and more as an anachronism.

It is from this point of view that one must understand the revival of "the market," the autonomous management of enterprises, and the decentralization of the planning apparatus. The autonomous management of enterprises on the scale of capitalist enterprises of the same kind makes it possible for the directors of these enterprises to escape fiscal control by means of self-investment and to establish direct, unmediated relations among themselves. It is a means of giving economic initiative to the directors of the enterprises and of taking it away from the centralized state bureaucracy. In a word, it isn't a question of eliminating the appropriation of surplus value, but of eliminating the external control over the mode of industrial production.

The technocratic stratum appeared at the head of this offensive. It constituted itself as the upper class of economic directors, who passed from a position as specialised employees of the state bureaucracy to becoming principally responsible for economic activity. This stratum developed as industry in the socialist countries grew and became diversified.

Among the financial techniques that began to come into use were accelerated amortization, self-financing, free disposition of saleable stock reinserted into the balance sheets of assets and liabilities and free from taxation, and interenterprise loans. From this point of view, "economic reform" in the USSR, Czechoslovakia, and Hungary seems to have gone in the direction followed by European liberal capitalism in the nineteenth century, where political control over the producer classes gave way to economic control, and where the state itself was gradually reduced to the role of policeman. The partisans of Mao Tse-tung, viewing these developments, speak of the "restoration of capitalism" in the USSR. But, in so doing, they reflect an archaic conception of a bureaucracy placed in conditions identical to those of the Stalinist bureaucracy of the first five-year plans. One may just as well maintain that "the free society of producers" that the First International inscribed on its flags is hardly conceivable without the exercise of intelligent initiative by individual enterprises.

Technocracy as Tied to the Uninterrupted
Development of the Productive Forces

We cannot ignore the particular character of the technocratic stratum in socialist countries, where there is no private ownership of the means of production, and where such a stratum cannot expect to find support in perpetuating itself indefinitely. Nor can we ignore the fact that the liberation of the internal accumulative mechanisms of large-scale production tends increasingly to bring the majority of workers together in a concern for self-management. The maintenance and development of the privileges of the technocratic stratum are founded upon the uninterrupted development of the productive forces. Stagnation or regression brings an end to its power and influence. The technocracy does not prosper simply by virtue of its position. In this sense, its power is totally different from that of the state bureaucracy. The struggle between them that ensues is between a technocracy that bases its power on internal economic mechanisms—on the growth of the productive forces—and a bureaucracy installed in fossilized structures—using police control as a response to its incapacity to master the new economic processes. The echoes of this struggle have been heard in all post-Stalinist literature over the last ten years—from *Not by Bread Alone* to *Engineer Bakhirev.*

In restoring to the economy its guiding role in the development of new social and cultural relations, the technocracy reinforces the specific weight of the direct producers of social wealth. The technocracy has neither the means to buy its labor force—because it is not the owner of the means of production—nor any power to control work by force, since it does not control the police or judiciary. The struggle waged by Soviet technocrats, allied with liberal intellectuals, against such leftovers from the Stalin era as the "corrective labor camps" is symbolic. Stalin's concentration camps, like those of the Nazis, appear to them a caricature of relations of production that bureaucracy spontaneously led to: the negation of the natural effects of the economic dynamic, physical control substituted for "economic stimulants," the radical suppression of the requirements of the consumer, the voluntarism of the bureaucracy that became a law for the economy, and an economy geared towards prestige efforts upon the success of which the bureaucratic stratum could flatter itself.

The Qualitative Development of the Productive Forces

In this struggle, the technocracy today carries within it the future possibility of socialism, in which "the administration of things will replace the administration of men," without itself being socialist. I would like to recall again an important factor in this struggle: the technocracy, as a homogenous social group and as the sum of the particular interests of each technocrat (including cultural, scientific, and professional interests), finds its strength in the qualitative development of the productive forces. Preoccupation with such development is fundamentally foreign to the bureaucracy. The technocracy is first and foremost interested in the development of the most modern forms of technology (such as automation), in the continuous rise in the level of qualifications of the working class, and in the generalised development of scientific research. In this way, it tends to accelerate the process of the generalised formation of a class of worker-technicians. One might say that the process that brought about the formation of the Soviet technocratic class is the same that led to the constitution of a "new working class," technically qualified and deeply integrated into the process of production.

The Development of the Technocracy Creates a "New Working Class"

One of Lenin's most dramatic errors (in company with Trotsky and Stalin) was not seeing the consequences that the introduction of the assembly line would have upon the political and social consciousness of Soviet workers. The resulting technological alienation would only strengthen the hold of the bureaucracy upon a working class which would remain a minority. On the other hand, the third industrial revolution that the Soviet technocrats are working feverishly to bring about fovors an awakening of consciousness on the part of the working masses and a desire to control the management of the economy. Within Socialist countries, during the present period, the restoration of the rights of the consumer—that is, of the producer outside of the sphere of production—will have similar effects on the development of social self-management.

The formation of the technocracy in the Soviet Union and in the People's Democracies takes place within legal relations of production identical to those in which the bureaucratic stratum flowered: relations of production of the "state capitalist" variety. The exploitation of man by man has not been abolished: the state appropriates from labor a profit going far beyond the "general expenses of society." Social equality is very far from being established; there still exists the relation of dominator to dominated and of rulers to ruled; and the accumulation of capital remains the motor of the economy's development. The fact that the Twenty-Second Congress characterised the Soviet State as "the State of the Entire People" (an expression of Lassalle's that Marx considered an expression of "state capitalism")[3] proves furthermore that the Soviet theoreticians are more conscious of this fact than is generally believed.

The Two Phases of State Capitalism

However, state capitalism in the bureaucratic phase differs profoundly from state capitalism in the technocratic phase. In state capitalism of the first phase, the 1924-1955 period in the USSR and, roughly, from 1947 to 1955 in the People's Democracies, the bureaucracy had no other economic function than to apportion among the vital sectors of heavy industry and the civilian and military bureaucracy the appropriations taken from the mass of the population, and principally from the mass of private producers in the country and small towns. The bureaucracy was occupied with the organization of scarcity.

The economic management of state capitalism in the present phase must be described in completely different terms: private producers have almost completely disappeared, and the increasing majority of salaried, urban workers has created large masses of modern consumers, requiring a qualitative diversification of products distributed. Furthermore, the relative scarcity of the postwar years encouraged considerable private savings for which people today are seeking an outlet not in capital investment (which is removed from individual capitalist initiative) but in consumer goods. The development of the automobile industry in the USSR and the People's Democracies proves that this demand has been stronger than the will of the politicians and the planners.

One might regret, however, that the model of consumption found in Eastern countries resembles so much the model developed in capitalist countries—one which subordinates the realization of social needs to the realization of individual ones. This is one of the most serious consequences of the bureaucracy's impotence in organizing

---

3. In the *Critique of the Gotha Program.*

an "abundant" society: poverty, inconvenience, and the defective functioning of collective equipment all render inevitable the search for comfort at an individual level, just as the maintenance of official salaries at a rate inferior to economic growth is responsible for widespread moonlighting and camouflaged forms of adding to one's income.

This tendency imposes on the economies of Eastern countries a double task: to satisfy the individual demand that has already appeared and to forestall the growth of this tendency through a qualitative improvement in collective equipment.

Technocratic state capitalism must respond to the inevitable need for industrial diversification, to the need for the multiplication of service jobs and for better qualified personnel to fill them. It must respond to the need for a generalized development of pure and applied scientific research that no longer concentrates on certain sectors considered essential by the bureaucracy.

It cannot avoid establishing competition among enterprises in order to watch over the profitability of investments—a rich society whose needs are well-developed can less afford waste than a poor society. It must guard against the over-development (however inevitable) of certain sectors, and must seek the maximum utilization of reserves. In a word, state capitalism in the second phase can no longer count on any extra-economic control. This is the profound significance of the "goulash socialism" that the peasant Khrushchev promised, but whose precise costs—far different in nature than a robust Muzhik soup—were left to the industrialist Kosygin to assess. The autonomy of the enterprises, the criterion of profitability, the actual costs of production, and the growing demand of a technically and culturally maturing working class cause the rigid framework of bureaucratic planning to burst, multiply the centers of decision-making, and engender in Soviet and Eastern European society polarities that contest these divisions.

The industrial, scientific or technical technocracy, conscious of these processes, finds its present strength and succeeds in winning over the old bureaucracy only because it appears as the representative of the desires and needs of "the whole society."

The danger lies in just this fact. For the bureaucracy at first played a positive role in relation to the needs of an agrarian society moving towards industrialization, only to become an obstacle to its development later on. In going back to 1936-1937 to find the beginning of "the negative period of the cult of personality," Soviet theoreticians and rulers admit explicitly that since that period the phase of bureaucratic state capitalism had ceased to be necessary. (The new Soviet constitution of 1936 was, moreover, the theoretical recognition of this fact.) Unfortunately, the bureaucracy had been developing all through this period without any opposition. Neither the workers' opposition, broken in 1938 when the unions were chastened,[4] nor the purged Bolshevik Old Guard, nor the terrorized intellectuals were in a position to express at that time the objective aspirations of Soviet society. One cannot consider as positive this unnecessary prolongation of the bureaucratic phase, even taking into account the danger of world war; for the Soviet Union was very poorly prepared for the World War by the Stalinist bureaucracy— politically, diplomatically, and militarily.

The Dangers of the Uncontrolled Exercise of Technocratic Power

The dangers of the uncontrolled exercise of technocratic power aren't the same as those that flow from an all-powerful bureaucracy. But those dangers are no less real, nor are they less of a constraint upon the development of the socialist process. The bureaucracy is voluntarist, while the technocracy is empiricist. The technocracy has the tendency to follow the "spontaneous" currents in the economy, currents that international commerce orient more in certain directions than others. And the concern with short-term profit leads it to renounce with ease objectives judged beyond reach.

Recognizing the Working Class, but Subordinating It

The technocracy's orientation toward establishing new social relations is ambiguous: on one hand, it knows that in a modern industrial system requiring qualified personnel, one can no longer do without the support of the working class. The introduction of new technology requires the integration of workers by contract. Neo-capitalist Western society has come to recognize the importance of that integration. It is all the more important in a society where "socialism" remains the governing ideology and goal, and in which the private ownership of the means of production does not set up a legal barrier between the worker and the enterprise. The technocracy is thus led to seek the "participation" of the workers in

---

4. Mallet's date is unclear. The Workers' Opposition group was broken by the time of Lenin's death. The 10th Party Congress (1921) defeated Trotsky's attempt to militarize labor, but the unions were brought to heel and the use of "experts" was sanctioned.

the functioning of the enterprise. We should not forget that the bureaucracy, the reflection of a state which proclaims itself a workers' state, freely considered itself as the reflection of the workers themselves and was so much the more determined to refuse them the right to speak, in the name of the bureaucracy's "representative" status. The technocracy does not share this charismatic power. It sees itself as different from the working class which it is thus constrained to *recognize* as a partner in the realization of economic objectives.

On the other hand, the technocracy has the tendency to transform this recognition into subordination: it will accept a better distribution of salaries, multiply individual incentives, abandon to workers the management of the collective social part of the salary—the social services of the enterprise—but in the name of its special competence, it will refuse the workers access to economic management itself. It wants sole decision-making power over investments, market retail prices, and production orientation. In order to secure this power, the technocracy of the socialist countries, just like its Western counterparts, will have the tendency to redirect the workers' demand for managerial power toward the satisfaction of their consumer needs—needs that it holds the power to orient.

In the most evolved Western societies, these relations already exist in a popular mode: they come under the name of "collective bargaining." But Western technocracy (European or American) is protected by capitalist relations of production and appears officially as the management of the capitalist class. That fact causes the paradoxical development within the working class of a conflicting set of feelings about these relations that encourages it to go beyond the simple higher wage demand. The technocracy in socialist countries can take refuge behind "the collective ownership of the means of production" and appear as the manager of the property of "all the people." This gives it an "objective" character that Western technocracy has difficulty in imposing.

Resistance to Technocratic Reform

Socialist countries have not escaped from the law of unequal regional development any more than capitalist countries. As long as there was a situation of general scarcity and as long as the centralized bureaucracy used extra-economic controls as a means of collecting taxes, this gap between more and less developed regions remained small or was passively accepted. The style of life of the Muslim regions of the Soviet East or that of the primitive mountain communities of the Caucasus were so different from that of the urban centers that no comparison could be made.

The creation by the bureaucracy of a unique market of consumers, the homogenization of social classes, the administrative uniformity inherent in the whole bureaucratic apparatus, and the transplantation of entire populations to production sites chosen by the authorities have fundamentally changed this situation. Because the ruling bureaucratic stratum draws its power from the total appropriation of surplus value, it imposes a relative homogenization of living conditions and style of life. In the meantime, the artificial character of general distribution has only masked the unequal development without correcting it.

Moreover, the quantitative character of production has allowed the old industrial regions to age and fossilize without the leaders of these regions noticing this fact. The supremacy of political power over the economy has thus allowed zones of technical backwardness to develop whose level of revenue is only maintained through subsidies. Besides, bureaucratic decisions have created costly enterprises without consideration of retail prices. There are the notorious "political factories," destined to transform the consciousness of the peasant masses, to pull them away from the agrarian mode of life and thus attach them to "socialism."

Social Difficulties of Economic Reconversion

The reconversion away from this past is an absolute necessity in order to permit the passage of the economy of countries with socialist structures to a qualitatively superior level. But the reconversion creates important social contradictions.

"Administrative socialism" assured to the working classes a dull security: salaries were miserable, but jobs were assured. Consumer goods were rare, expensive, and of mediocre quality, but work was most of the time not very tiring. The material handled by the workers was antiquated, but they worked routinely with it as they had learned to do ten or twenty years before. The absence of any renovation of equipment or techniques excused workers and technicians from the effort of permanent readaptation which the modification of techniques entails. Paradoxically, the socialist bureaucracy, after having exalted constructive effort in its ascendant phase, after having distributed medals to the "Stakhanovists" and "Oudarniks," had come to the point of letting laziness and an "I don't give a damn" attitude corrode all the gears of production. The economic reform upsets all these habits; its brutal application is causing veritable social crises. In certain cases, it throws out of the productive circuit elements that cannot adapt to the changes; in others, it also throws out those who have not had the time to adapt. Because it sometimes affects not only entire enterprises but whole regions and economic sectors, it provokes serious ruptures in the equilibrium among regions. The experience of developed capitalist countries has demonstrated that the rigorous application of the laws of economic competition can in time destroy the very seeds of reconversion in a region undergoing structural crisis.

The Bureaucracy Rediscovers Its Political Base

When the "political factories" that were opened during the last ten years in Yugoslavian Bosnia and in Slovakia begin to close by the dozens, the managers and the young of these areas will experience the fate of older workers. The whole region will risk falling back into the state of underdevelopment from which it had only—through state subsidies—superficially emerged. There is a real possibility that barely extinguished national passions will reawaken, inflamed by this state of affairs.

"Poujadist" reactions on the part of the old working class, with its inadequate education, its inability to readapt, "nationalist" reactions of marginal regions that falsely believed they were on the road to industrialization—these are some of the elements that give the old bureaucratic stratum a mass base that it has not enjoyed for many years. One has seen Hungarian workers longing for the times of Rakosi, Serbian workers rallying to the Rankovitch banner, and Novotny and his followers have found among a part of the Czech working class a base that has permitted them to hold out for long months against the "technocrat offensive."

A more intensive analysis permits us also to perceive contradictions that are dependent upon those mentioned above but even more significant: the first was revealed when the economic reform brought to light an informal network of communication and exchange that had grown up within the inequality tolerated under the apparent uniformity of bureaucratic production. This network brought with it numerous opportunities for illegal and semi-legal economic activity. One example is the Kolkhoz peasants near large urban markets who, because of the complex distribution mechanism for agricultural products, found ways of realizing, thanks to the free market, more than sixty to seventy percent of their total revenue on their private plots—to the detriment of the Kolkhoz. Another is the extraordinary proliferation of small dealers on the black market; still others are the systematic thefts in the factories, and the clandestine manufacture of scarce consumer goods. All these "little interests" weigh against the reform.

The "Pseudo-Equality" of the New Social Differentiations

The second and even graver contradiction, because it upsets the basis for collective consciousness, is the apparent extension of social inequalities engendered by economic reform. The privileges of the bureaucratic stratum were hidden beneath its status as a servant of the State, which protects it from public attention. In the beginning, these privileges were limited to a narrow layer of the population, living above and outside the daily life of the masses. Below this layer, small-time profiteers of the bureaucracy were obliged to conceal their gains. They continually risked discovery from an unexpected change in management that might bring to light their illegal practices, with the usual ugly consequences. Most of the population thus lived in a relatively egalitarian climate, an equality based upon equal poverty to be sure, but poverty is better tolerated when it is general.

Economic reform, in restoring to work the norms of effective social labor, does away with this dull egalitarianism. It diminishes the revenue of certain less productive industrial sectors and raises that of others. The disparity of revenue, along with the new opportunities given higher incomes to buy consumer goods heretofore considered luxuries, becomes a visible phenomenon in daily life. It is more difficult not to have a car when one's neighbor has one; it is more difficult than when cars were reserved for managers of the regime who only used them when escorted by motorcycle police... The Pobeda of one's neighbor is less tolerable than the Mercedes of the Party secretary or of the Trust director.

Condemned to irrelevance by economic evolution, the old bureaucratic stratum is thus finding within the inheritance of its own social system a new means to survival:

—It ties its own fate to that of elements of the population who found the means to live well by selling their illegal or semi-legal services, an exchange which the bureaucracy had tolerated as an escape valve but which the reform tends to eliminate.

—It can appeal to the socialist consciousness latent in the population against the deepening process of social differentiation.

—It can find a mass base in underdeveloped or artificially developed regions, as well as in regions that are declining because of antiquated techniques.

—It can give singular expression to the fears of the most backward sectors—the oldest but most numerous—of the working class, threatened by job and status insecurity.

It would thus be naive to believe that "objective necessities" will be sufficient in themselves to liquidate rapidly the bureaucratic system. On the contrary, the system finds a new political vigour precisely in the struggle waged against it and in the social consequences of the attempt to eliminate its own inheritance. Its new strength is analogous to that manifested elsewhere and in other conditions by reactionary groups on the defensive: one need only think of the depth of resistance of the old labor force of the archaic capitalist enterprises in France when they rallied to Poujade, or the difficulties encountered by American neo-capitalism in imposing political structures adapted to the level of the productive forces of the largest capitalist country.

But at the same time, "economic reform" is no longer the occasion of academic jousts or of devious conflicts within the State apparatus, but is becoming an open political conflict. The "economic reformers" of the USSR did not originally seek an open conflict with the reigning bureaucracy. They participated to a certain extent in the bureaucratic process; they belonged to the same "new elite" that emerged from the revolutionary process, and their evolution is a result of the differentiation of functions within the bureaucracy. This leads them to desire structural change rather than to 'seize power." In this respect, the socialist technocrats strongly resemble their capitalist counterparts who disdain, by their very nature, any thought of assuming political responsibility for the changes that they wish to make, and who spend their lives searching for charismatic leaders, from de Gaulle to Kennedy, who will impose upon the politicians and the conservative capitalist elements the changes which they deem necessary.

Another reason for fearing an open conflict with the bureaucracy is the technocracy's fear of social and economic disruption. Caring little for public discussion of the consequences of the reforms, jealous of its directorial functions, it would prefer, if possible, to "convince" the ruling apparatus of its good intentions, and to maintain the hierarchical structures in which it exercises its power, structures which sharp political battle might topple.

The Soviet Union still seems to be in the stage of conflict in which the antagonism between the old ruling group and the new one has not come out into the open. The weak state of "public opinion," the conformity of the press, the influence of the army, which arbitrates in the name of national defense, all mitigate against open conflict. But, perhaps the most important factor is the extraordinary solidarity that the sense of responsibility for world empire gives to the ruling groups. Imperial consciousness has always succeeded in smoothing over the sharpest social contradictions, as long as the Empire remains intact.

Imperial Consciousness as a Factor in the Reduction of Internal Conflicts

But things are not, nor can they be the same in the People's Democracies of Eastern Europe. Several factors play a role in accelerating conflict there, so that it is in Eastern Europe, and not in the Soviet Union, that the evolution of societies with a socialist structure will take the most explosive forms.

1. The People's Democracies are today largely open to Western tourism and commerce, and thus are confronted (more than the USSR) with the need for *qualitative* changes in the organization of production. The passage from a massified, quantitative economy that assures everyone their elementary needs, but limits the satisfaction of these needs to the amelioration of the standard of living, to a diversified, qualitative economy that permits choices, has become a demand of the masses in Prague, Budapest, Belgrade, and Bucharest.

2. The Russian Bureaucracy, or as Lenin would say, the "Great Russian" bureaucracy, is a national bureaucracy. The bureaucracy of other Eastern countries appears more often than not as the executive of the wishes of the Russian bureaucracy. The tendencies toward "decentralization" and toward the autonomy of industrial management has a peculiar character there—this internal autonomy will lead in time to an external national autonomy.

The return to "economic rationality," the reestablishment of market mechanisms, the diversification of production, all appear as different ways of correcting the situation of political dependence through indirect economic means, and at the same time gaining some autonomy for economic decision-making.

In this regard, the struggle of the technocracy tends in the People's Democracies to become a national struggle: the reform not only calls into question local bureaucratic power, but it also undermines the relations of political and economic domination established between the USSR and the small European countries belonging to the "socialist camp." The plans for economic reform in both Rumania and Czechoslovakia are directly at odds with the structure of Comecon, which authorizes relations among socialist states only at the level of central ministries.

The above explains more clearly the ambiguous relations between the Soviet technocracy and the Eastern European technocrats. In certain ways the Soviet technocrats wish—or at least wished in the beginning—to see the People's Democracies *experiment* with models of economic reform. Both the objective technological and economic conditions (cultural and technical level on the average more advanced, industrial traditions more widespread, markets both more homogeneous and less extended, more advanced national integration nearness to Western Europe) and the political conditions (weakness of the national bureaucratic class) allowed the European People's Democracies to move through the *stages* upon which the Soviet reformers could then build. The interest shown by Soviet economists in the Yugoslav economic reform, the encouragement of Kosygin himself for the Czech reformers, notably for Ota Sik, are incontestable proof of this.

But the consequences of economic reform in the People's Democracies for relations in the socialist camp were not slow in appearing. The first conflict with the Ceausescu government in Rumania concerned the level of autonomy of Rumanian industrial production and the nature of its trade with the West. The economic reform introduced in Hungary led it to multiply its inter-enterprise relations, not only with socialist countries such as Yugoslavia and Czechoslovadia, but with Austria, and the German Democratic Republic. The Czech reformers never hid the fact that managerial autonomy also signified for them liberation for their international activities. The dismantling of the bureaucratic system of national planning brought with it the dismantling not only of the heavy and unreal Comecon apparatus, but also that of the bilateral systems preferentially tying each of the People's Democracies to the Soviet Union. And the attempts made by the reformers to give Comecon another status and to create within it a sort of little Common Market of Danubian countries were not received any better by Soviet planners than were the overtures to the West made by Bucharest, Prague and Budapest.

In comparing Comecon with the Common Market, we in Western Europe forget too easily that Comecon more closely resembles an association of the diverse Common Market countries taken together with the United States of America.

To this disproportion among "equal partners" in Comecon is added the backwardness of the Soviet economy which, with the exception of certain privileged sectors (notably in military production) finds itself incapable of putting into play the mechanisms of "structural" domination by which the USA controls certain capitalist economies (Great Britain, Canada, Italy, and to a certain degree, Germany, France and Japan). These would include the ownership of patents, selective investments, organic integration of peak industries into large trusts, etc. The Soviet empire, from the point of view of its methods of economic domination, rests very often on the level of classical colonialism, especially with regard to the appropriation of raw materials.

Soviet technocrats, no matter how good their intentions with regard to reforms in the People's Democracies, can't go beyond a certain threshold of "liberalism"—that which would allow the economy of Central Europe to break out of the Soviet economic orbit. This will remain the case as long as the Soviet Union does not have the means to replace political and military forms of domination with economic ones. This stage will not be possible until the Soviet Union itself achieves its own economic reform, if it can do so. In the meantime, the People's Democracies are expected to "mark time."

One should not even exclude the possibility that the USSR might attain a level of economic and political liberalization which it would deny its satellites. After all, neither "liberal" Great Britain of the nineteenth century, nor Republican France exported their own interior models to their colonies or their zones of influence.

But this contradiction between the rhythm of passage from the bureaucratic to the technocratic phase in the USSR and the rhythm she is willing to accept in the People's Democracies is full of consequences:

1. First, in the Soviet Union itself: the limits that "the imperial consciousness" imposes upon technocratic reformers in the USSR in their fight with the old bureaucracy reinforces the contradiction. It cuts them off from the non-technocratic intelligentsia, and from the students who welcome the audacity of the Eastern European Communists as worthy examples to imitate, being less receptive than their elders to Russian nationalism.

These limits oblige the technocrats to accept the weight of external controls: traditional military force, unusable in a world war, but playing a necessary "gendarme" role in the Empire along with the "ideological edicts" of the bureaucracy. An example of the latter is the unfolding of the "anti-Zionist" wave in Poland, and the anti-Semitic propaganda used almost continuously against the Czech and Rumanian reformers, that doesn't stop at the borders of the USSR. (The father of the Russian economic reform, Liberman, is "more Jewish" than Ota Sik.)

The "imperial situation of the Soviet Union as a consequence acts as a brake upon the passage from the bureaucratic to the technocratic phase, just as, *mutatis mutandis*, the arrival of neo-capitalism in France and Great Britain was slowed down by ten of fifteen years by the imperial character of French and English capitalism. Kosygin clearly does not have the audacity of de Gaulle, who understood that the reformation of old French capitalism depended upon "auctioning off the empire."

2. The limits upon economic reform brought about by the USSR's imperial position affect the character of the struggle in the People's Democracies between the technocracy and the bureaucracy. They give this struggle an open character and force the technocracy to seek popular support—to build a mass base that, in turn, transforms the nature of the passage from bureaucratic to technocratic control.

But this transformation can certainly take different (and less pronounced) forms. In Rumania, for instance, the modern technocracy that has captured the leadership of the Party and the State has not fundamentally modified social and political relations. The "liberalization" of the economic life is scarcely perceptible except to the new generation of administrators, high-level technicians, and scientific executives who control the "islands of modernity" in a country that for the most part is still backward. These islands are found in the lost recently developed sectors of Rumanian industry—for instance, petro-chemicals. National feeling, reinforced by old animosities toward Slavic and Russian peoples, is enough for the moment to assure the reformist regime the popular support it needs to resist Rumania's powerful neighbor.

But the example of Yugoslavia demonstrates that in the long run national feeling is not enough. The Yugoslavian leaders, who in 1945 proclaimed themselves "the best Stalinists in the Balkans" have subsequently formally instituted worker and social self-management, which, even if limited in practice has allowed for fairly extensive free discussion and criticism. They have, for instance, tolerated the existence in such journals as *Praxis* of veritable poles of intellectual contention. This process will probably occur in Rumania too.

But the transformation is naturally even more rapid in countries that are more industrialized, such as Hungary and above all, Czechoslovakia. Here, the struggle for "the economic reform" cannot avoid becoming a social and political struggle of great amplitude. The *de facto* liquidation of a large part of the Stalinist bureaucracy in Hungary, its incredible loss of prestige in Czechoslovakia, leads it inevitably to seek the direct support of the Russians, and their direct or indirect intervention in blocking reform. This can be seen very clearly in the actions of the people around Novotny. The bureaucracy also tends to assure itself a direct political base in that part of the population, especially among workers, who might fear the consequences of the reform. But by the same token, the "reformers" are obliged to seek not simply popular consensus, but the true support of the masses, support that can extend to active political struggles.

It is here that the technocracy, by nature cautious about political action, finds itself obliged to seek support among new strata of the population — among workers and technicians in advanced industries, high school and college youth, and among intellectuals. Henceforth, the processes underway in Czechoslovakia will go beyond the conflict between the bureaucracy and technocracy. The extensive questioning of authoritarian socialism that is proceeding there has spilled over the confines set by economic reform, and has begun to raise the problem of social self-management. One can see, for example, the convergence between the analyses made by Ota Sik's people and those made in France by Charles Bettleheim.[5] For these two Marxist economists, socialist society has not yet reached the stage of development of which Marx dreamed where it is possible to generalize the process of social autonomy but the socialist management of large autonomous and coordinated units already holds within it the possibility of such a future.

In proclaiming that *"social self-management must be achieved at the level of the real socialization of the process of production,"* Ota Sik indicated what roads could lead to a society not entirely socialist — i.e., completely self-managed — but that would allow for

---

5. Several of Charles Bettleheim's works including a lengthy exchange with Paul Sweezy, have been published in the journal *Monthly Review*, and in book form by Monthly Review Press (New York).

large sectors of concrete self-management in areas where activity specifically conditions the future of the country—precisely those areas where the working class has both the desire and the ability to exercise self-management.

From this point of view, the process of self-management envisaged by Czech reformers goes beyond the legally larger framework of Yugoslav self-management. Yugoslavia, which has decreed the self-management of all industrial enterprises, whether service or commercial enterprises, has at the same time limited the possibility for workers' councils to coordinate their activities at the level of branches or trusts. This enlargement, envisaged between 1959 and 1962, was bitterly fought by the Yugoslav bureaucracy, which saw in it the threat of "dual power."

It is true that this power given to the workers' councils would essentially have affirmed the authority of the largest and most modern enterprises, and would have in some manner given these sectors hegemony over less advanced sectors of production. But this situation would at the same time have reactivated the life of unions in the economically weaker sectors.

The possibility of seeing temporary antagonisms between sectors of the working class expressed in terms of real social conflicts—as has already happened between various federal republics—would perhaps require a verbal retreat from the conception of a socialism free from social contradictions. But it would surely be a real advance toward a democratic and self-determined socialism, in which the masses participate actively in political life, instead of abandoning their fate to the obscure manoeuvres of "ruling elites."

The beginnings of political activity along the most advanced sectors of the Czechoslovakian working class—those that prefer the risks of real self-management to the illusory security of bureaucratic planning, is far healthier in nature and furnishes much more cause for hope than the mysteries that surround decision-making in the Kremlin. Theoretical research on the roads to socialism must now emerge from the academic arena and "descend into the street."

Because they were forced to seek public support to resist pressure from the Russians, the Czech technocracy consciously or unconsciously opened the way to a practical—active—experience of socialist democracy. Economic reform is tending to become social reform. The actors are no longer the directors and high administrative functionaries, but rather the most dynamic forces of Czech society. The passage from the bureaucratic to the technocratic phase, because it is happening as open political conflict, is unleashing a new process that undermines the possibility of a prolonged hegemony for the technocracy, and opens the opportunity of social self-management.

Such is the tremendous historial importance of the changes now occuring in Eastern European countries. They seem to prefigure those that will happen sooner or later in the Soviet union. Of course, the final realization of these possibilities also depends upon the possibilities of socialist revolution in Western Europe, but that is another subject.

PART III:
Workers' Control

Yes, Power Could Have Been Taken[1]

Reread in the light of the results of the first and second ballots of the elections,[2] the analysis of Jean Dru, published in *Le Nouvel Observateur* of June 26th,[3] loses much of its credibility. It was, in effect, implicitly based on the prospect of a strengthening of the electoral position of the *Parti communiste français* [*P.C.F.* or P.C.] and an almost unchanged renewal of the dissolved Chamber.

The second stage of the struggle between Gaullism and the Left did not end in a "tie," as Jean Dru foresaw, but actually in a retreat by the Left with respect to 1967—a retreat which expressed a political defeat: the abortion of the May movement. The collapse of the Left's electorate in the major industrial regions, where the struggle was most intense, bears witness to the extent of the disappointment at the enormous gap between the strength of the movement and the results obtained. So it would be absurd to infer from this result a proof of the "political immaturity" of the working class. The workers who abstained in disgust, the wives of workers who voted Gaullist upon observing the uselessness of their sacrifices, are not guilty of any "political incoherence;" the guilty ones are those who thought they could win the elections by selling out the strike. Less great than in 1958,[4] the defection of this half or three-quarters of a million voters has the same significance: *a lack of confidence in the possibilities of the Left's coming to power.*

It is only fair that the necessary critique of the Left's organizations deal first of all with the attitude of the Communist Party and of the leadership of the *C.G.T.* But Jean Dru's analysis of this is far from

---

1. Article published in *Le Nouvel Observateur,* July 24, 1968.
2. In the French multi-party system, all parties may present candidates at the first ballot, but only the two leading vote-getters are eligible for the second ballot.
3. A second article by Jean Dru, slightly correcting the view of the first one, was published in the July 10th number of *Le Nouvel Observateur.* —SM
4. In 1958 the Constitution of the Gaullist Fifth Republic was ratified by a 79% majority. It was this that led Mallet to quit the P.C.F. See Mallet's analyses of the home, "Pour un programme d'opposition" and "Perspectives nouvelles," now in *Le Gaullisme et la Gauche.*

being a critique. It appears on the contrary as a justification of the tactics and strategy of the *P.C.F.* whose sole error was not to have given an "intelligent" version of their position.

This analysis is based on three postulates:

First: the students' struggle and the workers' struggle were two distinct phenomena. While the student struggle was directed by a "tiny, more or less occult collective," that of the workers remained from one end to the other oriented and controlled by the Communist Party. This is to forget that the occupation of the factories was the chronological and political continuation of the barricades of the Latin Quarter, and not the opposite.

Second postulate: the working class never formulated demands other than those which the *C.G.T.* expressed on its behalf. These demands were satisfied in large part and the working class was able to return to the factories with "their heads high." It was only through the conscious effort of the party cells that the workers came, toward May 30th, to the slogan "people's government," and so to a political conception of the struggle. This is to forget the anticapitalist character that the strikes took from the beginning, the working class's rejection of the Séguy-Pompidou accords, [the Grenelle accords of May 27] and the dismantling of the strike front by the opening of sector by sector negotiations.

Third postulate: faced with the prospect of a confrontation with capitalist power on May 30th, the Political Bureau [of the *P.C.F.*] determined that "the conditions for the isolation of monopoly power were not fulfilled." Why weren't they? Essentially because of the *F.G.D.S.*'s [*Fédération de la Gauche démocrate Socialiste*] foot-dragging in responding to the [*P.C.F.*] proposal for a *P.C.F.-F.G.D.S.* meeting: "Except to court disaster," writes Jean Dru, "one undertakes a crucial test of power only with reliable allies and after choosing the most propitious terrain." But the allies were not reliable and De Gaulle occupied the principal terrain: legality was on his side. Having thus enclosed historical possibility in this vicious circle—capitulation or insurrection—Jean Dru comes to his conclusion: one can only take power legally, i.e., electorally. For this, [there are] no other means than to reinforce the pragmatic cohesion of the forces of the Left.

Hit First at the Left

Jean Dru became, a few years ago, the spokesman for an "Amendolist" line in the French Communist Party. Like the Italian Communist leader Giorgio Amendola, he sought the paths of a durable alliance between a Communist Party rid of its "revolutionist jargon" and a modernized Social Deomcratic group. This alliance, combining all of the "non-monopolistic" strata of the nation into a large electoral majority, was to lead to a durable "bi-polar" socialism. The *P.C.F.* remained, in this vision, the acting left wing of a coalition in which the *F.G.D.S.*—or its replacement—remained the right wing.

One sees that this analysis easily fits the official platform of the party. In reviving it today, on the occasion of the May events, Dru adds only one corrective: he doubts the *F.G.D.S.*'s ability to be the second shutter of his false window. None would dispute this point: the May events showed clearly how little this grouping, conceived essentially on an electoral base, weighed in a situation which was not electoral. And the hesitations of its leadership finally stem less from their rightist bent than from a realistic appreciation of their weakness opposite a Communist Party backed up by the *C.G.T.*

If socialism must be founded on a two party alliance, it is necessary that it be the alliance of two forces equal in fact, i.e., in the balance of real forces, including in the factories and in the street.

Now it was precisely this which was being built in the month of May. So it is to render a very poor service, finally, to the cause Jean Dru supports, to defend the *P.C.F.*'s attitude during the crisis, an attitude which was based on the desire to prevent the appearance (on its right or its left, no matter) of another real force. While contenting himself with deploring the acrimonious tone of the *C.G.T.* toward the *C.F.D.T.*, Jean Dru pretends to be unaware that these attacks were entirely in conformity with an unchanging political line which, from the denunciation of the ultra-leftists and "adventurers" to the denunciation of Pierre Mendés-France ("the politicians who wish to deprive the people of their victory"),[5] led the P.C. to give priority to the fight against the other forces of the Left and finally to prefer, at each turning point in the movement, a dialogue with a Gaullist power which accepted the role of the Communist Party as the official opposition.

Simply to read the newspapers of the period and *L'Humanité* in particular[6] gives clear proof that the *P.C.F.* took the political

---

5. The reference here is to the *P.C.F.*'s warning statement issued after Pierre Mendès-France's appearance at Charléty Stadium on May 27th.

6. For a detailed account of what *L'Humanité*, the P.F.C. newspaper, was saying during the May events, see Marc Goldstein, "Le P.C.F. du 3 mai au 16 juin 1968," *Les Temps Modernes*, November, 1968.

initiative only on two occasions, when it saw itself forced to do so in order to avoid being outflanked: first on May 16th, by enlarging and coordinating the strike movement—*after* the occupation of *Sud-Aviation*, *Renault*, *Rhodiacéta*, and other big firms; and secondly on May 29th, by calling a mass demonstration with the slogan "people's government"—after the demonstration at Charléty Stadium and the launching of the candidature of Pierre Mendés-France for the presidency of a transitional government.

As In Warsaw

One can understand that the events which agitated the students from March 22nd, when a hundred "*enragés*" occupied the administration offices at the University on Nanterre, until May 3rd, date of the occupation of the Sorbonne by police forces, had dumbfounded the Communist Party. For a long time, it had no longer had close ties with the student milieu. On two occasions, in 1956 and 1964, it had to dissolve its student organizations. Its mistrust toward the "sons of the *bourgeois*" is long-standing: on October 27th, 1962, it had denounced the "provocations" of *UNEF*, [*Union Nationale des Etudiants Francais*] which called for the first demonstration against the Algerian war, and *L'Humanité* at the time had already brandished the specter of a "military *coup d'état*."

Moreover, it is necessary to admit that, with the exception of a few leaders of the *P.S.U.* [*Parti Socialiste Unifié*] (not all), the rest of the Left remained fairly closed to the student movement. The *C.F.D.T.* [*Confédération Francaise Démocratique du Travail*] accepted, without reacting, a *communiqué* from its teachers' union, the *S.G.E.N.* [*Syndicat Général de l'Education Nationale*], condemning the "*enragés* of Nanterre" in terms fairly close to those of *L'Humanité* and *Le Figaro*.[7]

More serious is the fact that the P.C. did not understand the mechanisms by which a minority movement becomes a mass movement. If on the morning after the police were stationed in force in the Latin Quarter it had sensed that the mass of students had joined the "dozen enragés" and that the teaching staff, Nobel laureates in the lead, were shifting to the students' side, its reticence of the first days would have been forgiven. But it required hundreds of wounded for it to decide to demand the evacuation of the police forces [from the Latin Quarter]. If there was, as Dru claims, a 'conspiracy' by a secret general staff "to force the P.C. to act," one

---

7.   *Le Figaro*: The leading intellectual conservative newspaper in Paris.

must admit that the conspiracy succeeded: on May 11th, the morning after the taking of the *rue Gay-Lussac* barricades, the *C.G.T.* had to call a general strike and Séguy had to march alongside Cohn-Bendit. *But the night of the barricades, with its 376 wounded, would not have happened had Séguy, forty-eight hours earlier, brought the backing of the C.G.T. to the movement. If there was any "adventure" during this week, the responsible party was the P.C., which knew very well that the weight of its intervention would have sufficed to make Monsieur Fouchet [Minister of the Interior] and his truncheon wielders cautious.*

It is not serious to claim, as Jean Dru does, that the *P.C.* was afraid of police provocations: in other times, it did not hesitate, on much more futile pretexts (General Ridgeway's visit to Paris in 1951) to hurl against the police much weightier forces who, unlike the students, did not have the moral privilege of fighting to reoccupy their university, their Latin Quarter. Coldly, the *P.C.* thought that police repression would definitively break a movement which it did not control. It kept its troops at arms rest, just as the Red Army on the banks of the Vistula let the Warsaw insurrection be crushed because it was directed by non-Communists.

A Belated Rallying

Unfortunately for it, the *P.C.* had overestimated Gaullist power and it was forced to follow a movement which it had not ceased to denounce. But it did not do so without afterthoughts and the big march of May 13th from the *Place de la République* to *Denfert-Rochereau* could have been like the "funeral service for Charonne:"[8] a token protest with no tomorrow. Two facts that day disquieted the Communist general staff:

1) the pacifist slogans ("Our forty hours," "democratic government," "unity of the left") prepared by the *C.G.T.* sublocals and the party cells were received with an extreme coldness; the young workers of the Communist suburbs carried the signs all right, but they were shouting "power is in the streets."

2) The leaders of the official Left, Federated Socialists and Communists, marched amidst general indifference. Only Mendès-France, marching with the *P.S.U.*, was recognized and applauded.

---

8. After a U.N.E.F.-led demonstration against the colonial war in Algeria in 1962, the police charged a group of demonstrators and by-standers at the subway-station "Chasonne." Deaths and injuries due to this brutality gave rise to a moral outcry.

From this May 13th undoubtedly dates the idea, anchored in the heads of the Communist leaders, that it was all actually a maneuver destined to bring the leadership of the Left a man they feared because of his irreproachable past [Mendès-France].

Nothing in the orders transmitted by the *C.G.T.* the morning after May 13th indicated that the *P.C.* was preparing to recapture, among the workers, the initiative it had lost, partly through its fault, to the student movement. [It seemed that] everything could still "return to order" at the price of some "student antics" which would last until the vacation and of a parliamentary *corrida* without results. So De Gaulle left tranquilly [on his scheduled trip] for Rumania.

But on Wednesday May 15th, the workers of *Sud-Aviations's* Bouguenais plant, near Nantes, occupied their firm and locked in the manager. The movement was launched by young workers of an anarcho-syndicalist tendency and immediately followed by the *C.F.D.T.* The *C.G.T.* only joined in after the event and Georges Séguy deplored the "arrest" of the manager. The example was contagious: two hours after Europe Number One's flash announcing the news, *Renault* plants at Cléon and Flins were occupied in the same fashion. The next day, the *Renault* plant at Billancourt, *Rhodiacéta*, and all the metallurgical plants in Nantes followed the example. The movement reached the *P.T.T.* [formerly the Ministry of *Postes, Télégraphes et Téléphones*, now *Postes et Télécommunications*] and certain sectors of the railroads.

It was then, *and only then*, that Georges Séguy, wanting to control the movement, launched the large disciplined forces of the public sector into the fray: railroad men, miners, postmen; he kept the *Electricité de France* in reserve: "I cut [power] where I want, when I want." At the same time, the *C.G.T.* deposited everywhere the lists of demands for the raising of the *S.M.I.G.* [minimum wage], the return to the forty hour week, the abrogation of the decrees altering Social Security benefits. But the workers, on the contrary, at the beginning of the movement everywhere *emphasized demands for power*: the abrogation of internal discipline, union supervision of hiring and firing, revision of output norms, etc.

"A Dark Machination"

In fact, the cutting edge of the movement was composed of young workers [profoundly dissatisfied with what they had found in the factories][9] . . . . They were the ones who set up barricades and

---

9. See "May-June, 1968: First Strike for Control," in this volume, pp. 56ff, where

attacked the *C.R.S.* [*Compagnies Républicaines de Sécurité*] in January and February, well ahead of the students. It was among them that the influence of certain neo-Trotskyite organizations had penetrated most profoundly, organizations such as *Voix Ouvrière* which popularized notions of worker self-management like those Trotsky had developed in his *The New Course.*[10]

The action of the students, who had obtained control of their universities in a few days of street combats, was the signal for their revolt: proof was given that one could obtain more power through action than by negotiation.

But the movement of the young workers would not have succeeded if it had not been immediately taken up and echoed by another "new" stratum—adult this time—of the working class: that of the modern skilled workers and technicians of the most advanced sectors of French industry: electronics, aeronautics, automobiles, chemicals, and oil.

It was there that another union organization of whose existence Jean Dru seems almost unaware threw in its full weight: the *C.F.D.T.* The latter, at the beginning, had scarcely understood better than the *C.G.T.* what was happening in the student movement. But it had immediately reacted to the workers' upsurge and seized the deep significance of the form taken by the movement: the occupation of factories and the questioning of employers' authority. Contrary to the *C.G.T.*, it advanced, from the beginning, demands for union power in the firm. Its branch unions had, here and there, elaborated some formulas for self-management, and numerous upper level managers had given their support to these projects.

The coming together of the "reformist" *C.F.D.T.*—which the *P.C.* located on its right—and the "ultra-leftist" elements of the working class (Trotskyite and anarcho-syndicalist) visibly surprised and embarrassed the *P.C.* even more than the unexpected development of the student movement. It saw there only a dark anti-communist machination, a demagogic will to outflank it.

What happened in the working class in May revealed how false this judgment was. Starting from the paternalist Christian conception of "participation," Catholic unionism had progressively come to an

---

the same analysis is offered in more detail. We have edited out several repetitive paragraphs here.

10.   Leon Trotsky, *The New Course,* Ann Arbor: University of Michigan Press, 1965 (first published in 1921). —SM

anti-authoritarian conception of unionism and socialism. What Raymond Aron calls "the return of the French workers' movement to its youthful stammerings" [11] is only the result of an objective evolution of the working class condition and of the fact that, in advanced industries, employers' power today manifests itself more through "functional authority" than through the ownership of capital. The fact, moreover, that the most advanced elements of the movement in the matter of self-management demands were found in the nationalized or semi-nationalized sector (*Sud-Aviation, Nord-Aviation, Renault, Saviem, Raffinerie Antar, C.S.F.*) indicates that the workers' contestation, at least in the big firms, was at least as much an *anti-technocratic* revolution as an anti-capitalist one.

The Second Power

Today, the Communist Party can very well play the game of "legalism." But the strikers, by decreeing strikes without advance notice,[12] almost always by hand vote, by occupying the factories, by sometimes locking the managers in their offices, by starting the IBM machines used for the payroll to help the strike committee, by using the administrative services and switchboards to their advantage, by assuring, in certain cases, rations of gas or fuel to services considered essential, by deciding, as at Nantes, to operate the cattle feed factories and the dairies, by organizing market price controls, had gone beyond "bourgeois legality" and ensured from that moment on, in the order established by the workers, the exercise of a certain number of powers which were symbolized by the red flags floating on the roofs and chimneys.

To be sure, this self-management orientation of the strike was neither general nor, above all, clearly specified. In fact, only a few enterprises where the technicians were in the majority (like the *C.S.F.* in Brest or the research offices of *Sud-Aviation* at Cannes and Toulouse) openly formulated the slogan of self-management of the firm. The *C.F.D.T.* contented itself, on the national level as on the industrial branch level, with forceful support of the notions of "union power in the enterprise" or of "workers' control over production."

But just to the extent that the strikers realized perfectly that the prolonged continuation of the strike seriously inconvenienced the

---

11. See Raymond Aron, *The Elusive Revolution; Anatomy of a Student Revolt*, New York: Praeger, 1969. —SM

12. According to a law passed in 1963, there must be a five day advance notice before strikes in the public sector. The law was not observed in 1968, and the unions have considered the law void since then.

population, *the re-starting of services essential to society, under the control of workers and their union organizations, was taking place.* And the concerted development of this process led immediately to situations of "dual power." At Nantes, Caen, Saint-Etienne, the county administrative director [the prefect], isolated in an office in which the telephone no longer rang and guarded by the two or three hundred *C.R.S.* available in the *département* was in fact nor more than the ridiculous symbol of an order which found itself replaced by another. The establishment of this second power had the double virtue of bringing to the side of the working class the majority of technicians and *productive cadres* and of conserving the sympathy of the majority of the population for the movement. Undoubtedly the merchants of Nantes, forced to toe the line by the price controllers with red arm bands, viewed this intrusion into "their business" with a rather jaundiced eye, but the housewives of all circumstances were pleased by it.

It was by an over rigorous respect for the strike considered uniquely as "work stoppage" that the workers' movement alienated sympathy toward it. Were the "adventurers" in this case *C.F.D.T.* dairy workers of the West, who ensured milk collection on the demand of the strike committee, or the *C.G.T.* railway workers of Finistère, who let thousands of tons of potatoes needed in the workers' lunchrooms pile up, and who in this way brought on themselves the hatred of the peasants of Finistère?

I am not saying that the wage demands — to which, from beginning to end, the *C.G.T.* wished to limit the movement — did not interest the working class. But no wage earner had the slighest illusion (even before De Gaulle spoke cynically on television of the "apparent advantages" which his Prime Minister had conceded) on the value of wage increases unaccompanied by powers of economic control, or on an improvement of work conditions unaccompanied by a limitation of employers' power. This is why, at least in the big firms, the workers did not return "with heads high" and scarcely had the sentiment of having won the "great victories" saluted by *L'Humanité*.

Pseudo-victory or Insurrection

To be sure, thousands of workers in small firms, swept along and going on strike for the first time, limited themselves to wage demands (which seemed to them already exorbitant) and could not be induced further. But since when must the labor movement set its pace according to the most backward fraction of the working class? *If the P.C. considered that a "pause" was necessary and that the movement could not immediately open onto a decisive transformation of the relations of production, it was its role to arrange a stopping place on this path.* But it fought tooth and nail (and Jean Dru, who spoke of the "seductive trap of self-management within capitalist society," approved) against all that closely or distantly resembled a conquest of economic power.

Any notion of workers' councils, or workers' self-management, even of organized contestation, triggered frightful allergies among the Communist leaders. And as it developed this workers' strike, launched after and influenced by a student movement seeking control of its universities, strongly threatened, to call into question the famous [system of] "industrial organization" that the *P.C.* fully intended to use, the moment come, for its own purposes.

But this obsessive fear of any true democratization appeared so strongly that it caused a rebirth everywhere of the old mistrust of the *P.C.* De Gaulle made no mistake in emphasizing the "totalitarianism" of the *P.C.* and not its anticapitalism. In a few weeks, the brutality with which the *C.G.T.* had treated the working class reduced to nothing the patient deceiving work of Waldeck Rochet.[13]

No, the alternative was not between demands leading to pseudo-victories (the rise in prices even before the strike's end permitted a sure affirmation that the advantages won would be largely absorbed between then and the autumn) *or insurrection.* The organization, of workers' control without disorder, without street fighting, without conflict with police forces incapable of operating the factories, in *the big firms and in the public services* (like those being set up in the credit organizations, savings banks, postal checking system, deposit banks, national banks), along with control of the borders by the striking customs workers, was more dangerous to the government than insurrection.

Aiming at Mendès-France

The *P.C.* refused this strategy from the first, because it remains fundamentally hostile to any workers' democracy. In fact, if one thing is now clear, it is that there is a profound incompatibility between the authoritarian "socialism" of the *P.C.* and that which we wish to establish. The misfortune is that it is precisely the former

---

13. Waldeck Rochet; head of the *P.C.F.* from the death of Thorez in 1964 until his retirement in 1972.

aspect of socialism which puts off a mass of people—the peasants for example—and that the French, whose memory is not so short, see Stalinist bureaucratism behind the *P.C.*'s homilies about "order."

But this reason is insufficient. For if the Communist Party refused the revolutionary path of insurrection, as well as the reformist-revollutionary path of worker, peasant, and student power, it also refused, on three occasions, the reformist path which would have led to the replacement of the Gaullist government by a transitional government, still capitalist, but marking a break with established power, and thereby weakening the system.

The motion for censure, introduced in the Assembly during the week of the barricades, gained an unexpected importance with the general strike. The announcement of the resignations of Messieurs Capitant and Pisani, [14] the avowed uneasiness of certain other Gaullist deputies, the very clear reservations of the Giscardiens, everything announced a closely joined debate. Placing the government in a minority position, in these conditions, would have enormously weakened its authority. But, on May 22nd, a few hours before the vote on the censure motion, Georges Séguy, interviewed on Europe Number One, affirmed a willingness to negotiate with the government. "With THIS government, such as it is?" "With THIS government." If a few Gaullist deputies had had the intention to vote for censure to unseat Pompidou and make way for another governmental combination, the remarks of M. Séguy would have been enough to recall them to fidelity.

The Grenelle negotiations constituted in fact and above all *a recognition of Pompidou* by the union organizations representing the millions of striking workers. Because of this, they prevented a different political solution which, whatever it was, would have appeared as the sign of a crisis of the Gaullist majoity. That it actually concerned a recognition of Pompidou is even better proven by the abandonment of the struggle for the abrogation of the ordinances altering Social Security benefits, given at the beginning as the principal objective of the strike.

From this starting point, negotiations were organized sector by sector, firm by firm: [the *P.C.*] no longer wished to make a connection between the general strike and the struggle for political power. To be sure, several days later, the *P.C.* and the *C.G.T.*, faced with the massive refusal of the workers and the panic which seemed

---

14. Rene Capitant and Edgard Pisani were left-Gaullist ex-Ministers who resigned as deputies rather than vote for the motion of censure against their party.

to take possession of the government, took a new turn, but this was *twenty-four hours after Mendès-France went to Charléty Stadium.*

The mere establishment of a chronology permits a demonstration of the *P.C.*'s obsessive fear of seeing political changes take place without it and shows that its reactions will always be defensive in the face of the political initiatives of others:

On May 25th, a communiqué of the Political Bureau [of the *P.C.F.*] called in a brief final phrase, for the "multiplication everywhere of Action Committees for a people's government of democratic union." But people's action committees, set up on the initiative of the *P.S.U.*, had already been forming for two days in Paris;

On May 27th, the Political Bureau launched its famous warning: "A large scale maneuver is developing behind the workers' backs. A certain number of politicians and union personalities are supporting demonstrations which have as one of their objectives to protest against the negotiations among the unions, the employers, and the government."

The target was obviously Pierre Mendès-France, he whose name was pronounced simultaneously by Centrists, Leftists, certain Gaullists, and who had been acclaimed at Charléty. This warning announced that, against Mendès, the *P.C.* would continue the strike, creating insurmountable obstacles to the establishment of a transitional government.

The Ultimate Weapon

On May 28th, the *C.G.T.* signed accords for restarting work at the E.D.F.: it was the surest pledge it gave of its willingness to negotiate with *this* government. In these conditions, de Gaulle could not take seriously the May 29th *C.G.T.* demonstration *directed more clearly against a possible Mendès-France government than against the one in place.*

Leaving to see his generals in Germany, de Gaulle knew that the Communist Party would not support another government than his own. To assure himself of it, he had only to read *L'Humanité* and to observe that the *C.G.T.* was abandoning the general strike's ultimate weapon: the total cutting of electricity. In the end, the rejection of single candidates of the Left on the first ballot[15] (which could have changed quite a few things) was only the extension of this policy. These are incontestable facts, public and known by all. One cannot escape them by embroidering on the theme of an "armed

---

15. The communist and socialist parts of the left have agreed on occasion to present a single candidate of the left on the first ballot.

insurrection," which was spoken of by only a few small groups, not even including the Trotskyites or the March 22nd movement.

Having a choice between the upsetting of the Gaullist regime and an alliance in which its power would have been contested—both in the government and in the street—the *P.C.* deliberately chose the continuation of the regime. It is probable that it had not understood, any more than Jean Dru, all the consequences of this choice and that it has underestimated the size of the backlash that the disappointment of some and the fear of others was going to provoke. But it took this risk, which seemed to it less great than that of not being *the absolute force* in a different government.

Paris, July 12, 1968

Workers' Control, Party and Union*

I. Contrats de Progrès or Workers' Control

A. The Crisis of French Capitalism

Since May-June 1968, the French capitalist system has been going through a profound crisis. The monetary crisis of 1969, the political crisis opened by the departure of General de Gaulle, and the social crisis begun by the wildcat strikes of September, 1969 and continued in December by the agitation of the farmers, have been the most alarming indices. It is legitimate to ask whether, along with Italy, France is not the "weakest link" of today's world capitalist system.

The crisis is at once the manifestation of a more general crisis of the world capitalist system which is seeking its "third wind" in organization capitalism, and the consequence of certain character-istics specific to the French capitalist system, particularly its difficulties in passing the new threshold of development necessary for the survival of the system. However, it would take too long, within the framework of this article, which has a different goal, to give a deeper analysis of the characteristics of this crisis; we must limit ourselves to certain practical assertions which no one in the French capitalist circles really disputes. This crisis reflects directly on the solidarity of the political regime: the government which emerged from the "restoration" of 1968 is, in fact, a *weak* government.

B. The Contradictions of Growth

1) On the economic level, it is weak. This does not mean that we are about to have an economic crisis of the classical type (a crisis of overproduction), nor that the forces of production have stagnated: not since 1963 have the order books of business been so full. The crisis of French capitalism is, in certain respects, a "crisis of growth;" theoretically, the "reserves" of French capitalism for economic growth and for extending both internal and external markets remain large. But French capitalism is not able to reconcile the development

---

*This article first appeared in *Critique Socialiste*, no's. 182, March-April, 1970 and May-June, 1970.

of the productive forces and the maintenance of the capitalists' rate of profit. It is precisely in the relation of the productive forces (very roughly expressed by the GNP) to the monetary conditions that this contradiction, characteristic of the entriety of the world capitalist system, manifests itself most acutely. For the past six years, until the recent devaluation [of 1969], it had been possible to maintain the currency only at the price either of "stabilization plans"—that is, a deliberate slowing of growth, as in 1966 and today—or of the artificial entry of foreign capital looking for fiscal protection or speculative profits—entries whose contingent character was shown by the massive exodus of these funds in June, 1968.

In spite of the incontestable breath of fresh air that the revaluation of the German mark represented for the Pompidou regime, the government has been going through a difficult period, marked by: 1) the desire on the part of those social strata actively supporting Gaullism to rid themselves of the costs of *la grandeur* (that is, of the politics of "national independence"), and to enjoy quickly and as best they can the fruits of the expansion realized during the 1950s, even at the cost, as the saying goes, of living off their capital; 2) by the ultimate lack of solidity of the results achieved by Gaullist politics (situation of the franc, stagnation of scientific research, failure of the policy of opening markets in the Eastern bloc and in the Third World); 3) by the latent political fear provoked in the ranks of the upper bourgeoisie by the May, 1968 movement, which has led it to seek easily negotiable investments or to place its profits in a safe place.[1]

In these conditions the Pompidou government, constrained to satisfy its constituents' thirst for profits, and incapable of accomplishing this by an increase in the mass of profits—which could only result from qualitative structural change of the French economy—can only save its political authority by guaranteeing the fleeing capital an increase in the *net rate of profit*.

This is easier said than done: the evolution of contemporary capital continues to be determined by that invariable law that the founder of scientific socialism elaborated in *Capital*: "As variable capital progressively diminishes relative to constant capital, the organic composition of the whole of capital continually increases, and the immediate consequence of this tendency is that the rate of surplus-value manifests itself as a general rate of profit which is

---

1. The crisis of the housing market is the index of that uncertainty as to the future of the system. —SM

continually decreasing as long as the degree of exploitation of labor remains the same, or even increases..." Thus the progressive tendency towards a *decrease in the general rate of profit* is simply *a manner, specific to the capitalist mode of production, of expressing* the progress of the social productivity of labor.[2]

And the result of this law, which pitilessly crushes the weakest of the capitalists, the only way for a capitalist group to realize a *relative increase* of the profit rate, in spite of the necessity of enlarging the constant capital invested in its industrial plant, is to obtain what the economists call the return on innovation — that is, the advantage acquired over their competitors by developing new techniques or new products which benefit from a monopoly situation for a certain period.

The general characteristic of French capitalism is that even if it would like to pocket the benefits on the return on innovation, it does not want to, or cannot, as do its American competitors, risk long-term investments (especially in research) which would assure it these benefits.

The economic policy which [Pompidou's Minister,] M. Chalandon has been pushing with verve — and which the President of the Republic had announced before anyone else, while he was still Prime Minister[3] — aims at securing for private capitalism the profits of the return on innovation made possible by the heavy investments of the state: the state finances the urban infrastructure, but private capital pockets the profits from real estate; the state pays 80% of the cost of turnpikes, but leaves the profits from the tolls and those from highway maintenance to private capital; the state finances 56% of the cost of the *Mercure* short-range carrier constructed by *Dassault*, while *Dassault*, with only 14% of the investment, will obtain the monopoly on domestic commercial aviation, after already having

---

2. *Capital,* Livre 3, tome VI, Section 3, p. 227, Paris: Editions sociales. — SM

3. Replying in the magazine *Entreprise,* no. 458 (June 20, 1964), to nineteen chief executives of the largest French firms, Georges Pompidou defined his "economic doctrine," which noted of course "the immense contribution of the government resulting from all the basic investments in furnishing energy, means of transportation, means of communication..." but argued that "it is desirable, in normal periods, that the state reduce its role to the minimum." "Nothing could be more harmful to all the social classes than declaring war on the profits of business...The state must cease to be that avid consumer of capital that it has been these past years." The ex-*directeur-général* of *Messieurs Frères* [the Rothschild group] thus defined "that half-liberal, half-socialist system which the French system is in the last analysis." But "the role of the state remains crucial...it must be prepared to control social reactions, to avoid tensions." It would be impossible to explain more cynically the theory of the socialization of losses and the privatization of profits. — SM

had the monopoly on military aviation and utilizing, *at a loss*, the nationalized aviation firms as sub-contractors; the state ruins the equilibrium of the plan for conversion of the arsenal at Ruelle (which manufactures a ground-air missile sold to all the countries of NATO) in order to give the patents and results of the research done by the brilliantly reconverted old royal factory to the private firm *Matra*; etc.

Naturally, the workers will be first to satisfy the gluttonous needs of our budget-devouring capitalists by the physical increase of the productivity of labor (which increased from plus 4.9% in 1949 to plus 5.2% in 1967).

However, the possibilities for recovering an additional portion of surplus-value from the productive laborers remains very limited: *on the one hand*, by the previously mentioned tendencies of the evolution of the organic composition of capital—for example, in the petroleum and chemical industries, the share of variable capital (wages and social costs) represents only 6% of the circulating capital of the firm. It is for this reason that we see a tendency for capitalist firms to pass directly on to the state a part of the costs of fixed capital (particularly that of Research and Development), and to make use of the industrially usable spinoffs. *On the other hand*, because there is a relatively incompressible level of appropriation of surplus value. Marx already showed that if the general tendency of wages in capitalism is only to pay the worker the portion of his labor necessary to provide for his subsistence and his reproduction, the notion of subsistence was determined by "a standard of living which is traditional in each country. This subsistence does not only consist in the maintenance of physical existence, but in the satisfaction of certain needs born from the social condition in which people live and have been brought up."[4] We can agree that as the productivity of labor increases, the "historical" part of the value of labor grows in comparison with the specifically physiological part. Finally, the limitation of the real income of the working class—and of the wage-earners in general—will manifest itself through a generalized crisis of buying-power whose consequences will be heavy because they will express themselves in the impossibility of amortizing the investments in fixed capital.

These contradictions are not specific to French capitalism. What is particular to it are the difficulties that it encounters because of its delay in resolving them provisionally through the techniques of

---

4.   Marx, *Salaires, prix et profits*. Trad. Ch. Longuet-Giard, Paris, 1912, p. 93. —SM

"organization capitalism." Since 1950, Western Europe, following the United States, has undergone significant structural convulsions. In diverse forms, a new kind of capitalist society in which the private appropriation of capital ceases to be the unique or essential form of control over the development of the productive forces, and in which the economic intervention of the state becomes the essential instrument of regulation in economic activity is in the process of appearing everywhere.

This tendency already arose in 1935 in the United States as a consequence of the great economic crisis which showed the impotence of the capitalist system to coordinate the growth of the productive forces, to assure the enlargement of the internal and external markets parallel to that growth, and to permit the qualitative transformation of the technical and economic forces which had arrived at a saturation point. In liberal capitalism, even when it arrives at an advanced stage of monopolistic development, the laws of the organic composition of capital, the necessity of appropriating the maximum rate of surplus-value, enter into contradiction, as we have seen, with the necessities of a ceaselessly growing reproduction of capital, and engender stagnationist tendencies, especially as concerns scientific and technical development.[5] The crisis of 1927-1930 and its international consequences brought, with the New Deal, the first appearance of the state as "collective capitalist," whose task was to take the place of private financial capital as the instigator of long-term investments. Nazism, through the theory of Dr. Schacht, the war economy in the U.S. from 1941-1945, and the necessities of reconstructing Western Europe after the war, all developed even more this state capitalism.

2) Mass consumption corresponds to the necessities of enlarged reproduction. The limitation of the world market and the difficulty of enlarging the sphere of distribution of manufactured products contributed to this development. The constitution of an autarchic sector, first in the Soviet Union and then in Eastern Europe, concerned with its own self-development and entering in its turn into competition with the capitalist market, has incontestably aggravated the internal contradictions of European and American capitalism. But the economic theorists of the Stalinist period who correctly—in 1948[6]—put forth this theory did not know how to analyze the

---

5. Cf. Paul Baran and Paul Sweezy, *Monopoly Capital*, New York: Monthly Review Press, 1966, Chapter IV. —SM

6. Theses taken up by Stalin himself in his last work, *Economic Problems of Socialism in the U.S.S.R.* —SM

consequences it would have: unable to enlarge the area of its markets, capitalism sought an increase in the depth of its internal markets. This situation has developed to a point such that—although there exist enormous reservoirs for the extension of the world market in the countries of the Third World, on the condition that they are given long-term loans—American and European capitalist countries have nearly ignored these possibilities of extension and have maintained, up to the present, relations with the underdeveloped countries which are essentially founded on exploitation or on the holding in reserve of raw materials necessary to their own internal consumption.

Marxist economists have often interpreted the considerable importance of military expenditures in the large European capitalist countries as a means of regulating production, of freezing, so to speak, the excess of capitalist production in the form of non-consumable goods. In fact, the evolution of all the advanced countries proves that rather than engendering a stagnation of consumption, the war economy stimulates it in a significant manner through its spending for equipment, its funding for research, etc. which are directly taken from the public treasury.

In countries like the United States or West Germany, the bases of accumulation of scientific and technical capital are sufficiently large so that the costs to the state—which are just as heavy as in France—do not become insupportable to the population (even though the participation of the "liberal bankers of Wall Street" in the Vietnam Moratorium was not an act of pure Puritan philanthropy, and indicates that these costs are beginning to become too heavy. The cut-back in funds for NASA space programs is another important index of this). But French capitalism's backwardness, its inability to resist the competition of those nations which began their growth before it, means that the situation for the French capitalist state is far more difficult.

It is on this basis that at the risk of sawing off the branch on which, politically, it is seated, the French state has been led to reestablish the weakened confidence of big capital through a new internal division of capitalist profits. This is the source of the systematic proletarianization of the small intermediaries (small and middle-sized shop-keepers) and independent producers (farmers and artisans). This is also the source of the increase of the tax burden on the non-capitalist social strata (the "salaried middle classes," *cadres*, civil servants, etc.)— a policy which stirs up against the government the only strata which could assure the capitalist state a mass base. It is also the source of the contradictions within the governmental majority, reflecting the internal conflicts between bourgeois strata.

3) Organization capitalism in question. With this perilous situation is combined a climate of cultural crisis of bourgeois values: authority, hierarchy, family, discipline, thrift. The crisis of values of the liberal bourgeoisie could have been surmounted if another "productivist" ideology of the technocratic type could have been substituted for it. That ideology, which cannot exist without the support of a consensus (the "Great Society") was just what was undermined at its base by the frenzy of appropriation and personal pleasure of the regime's supporters. The technocratic ideology has failed as a "new model of rationality" for lack of credibility: the technocrats themselves are caught, one after another, in the frenzy of short term gain from bank capital, and enter the private sector as fast as possible.

The same failure, the same impasse, is evident in "social policy"—that is, the policy of integrating the working classes into the system. The impossibility of giving tangible satisfactions to the unions in a new Grenelle Accord has ruined the whole carefully designed policy elaborated by Pompidou at the time of the first agreements with the *CGT* in May, 1968.

C. The Different Strategies of Integration

The new style of the social policy offensive of the government—this time marked by the imprint of the social councilors of the Prime Minister [Chaban-Delmas] and not of the President of the Republic—appears in effect as the negation of the policy begun at Grenelle. The Agreement between Pompidou and Séguy tended towards a policy of regular meetings between the "contracting parties of the social order:" the capitalist government and the official opposition, the *CGT*.

The *CGT* promised to hold the workers' movement within the limits of its rights and to concern itself, as in the case of American unionism, only with negotiable wage demands. The strike of the operating personnel of the *SNCF* in September, 1969, calling into question the plan to dismantle the *SNCF*, immediately stopped the negotiators of a second Grenelle short: it raised the level of the workers' demands in such a manner that the government could no longer take the risk of a general negotiation which would have promptly stirred up the desire for strikes. But at the same time, the main source of political equilibrium for Pompidou's regime was ruined, founded as it was on the "conflictual participation" of the

Communist Party as the "loyal opposition" of the system. The *"petite phrase"* of Georges Séguy was the only recognition that Pompidou had not kept the committments he had made at Grenelle and reconfirmed at the time of the presidential election: the system of "conflictual participation," as it has functioned with relative success in the U.S. until the present, presupposes a loyal respect of engagements undertaken on the part of each participant. Pompidou did not keep his promises—though he could object that, outflanked by the strikes of September which did not wait for the planned October meeting, Séguy did not keep his either. It is very difficult to institute such a system when the chief executive of the capitalist state proves to be just as incapable of controlling "his class" as the leader of the "workers' society" is of "disciplining" his troops.

The idea of a *"contrat de progrès,"* such as it is being applied at the *EDF,* is of an absolutely different sort. Certainly, it has the same objective as that sought by Pompidou at Grenelle: to assure the integration of the workers' demands into the system. *"Hic et nunc,"* however, in December, 1969 and at the *EDF,* the idea conceals some rather important fireworks. What is at issue is nothing less than tying the wages and working conditions of the largest firm in France to two elements: that of the growth of the GNP, and that of the growth of the firm itself. We can leave aside the first of these, which is common to all wage discussions; it is the second that is crucial here. For the unions it implies either an effective taking over of the management of the firm, or it's an empty slogan! Beginning with the signing of the *"contrat de progrès,"* every financial intitative of the *EDF* will have to be minutely examined, for it is in terms of the firm's management that wages will be determined. If unable to influence the decisions which commit the firm's assets, the unions will find themselves disarmed in negotiations. Thus, respecting the *contrat de progrès* implies the power to control the decisions that will define its content.

Given the large number of unionized workers at the *EDF-GDF,* this means that from now on, if they don't want to be eliminated from wage discussions, the unions will have to be ready not to "co-direct" but to organize strikes to affect the orientations of the firms management.

This is a doubly explosive situation. First, because the extension of such a procedure into the private sector would carry with it the seeds of a new outbreak of "strikes for control"—intolerable for big capital. Second, because the important role played by the *EDF-GDF* in the equilibrium of the French production system means that union pressure could aggravate the terms of the contradiction between the nationalized and private sectors. The workers at the *EDF* must not let the "socialization of the deficit" be imposed on them.

Thus it appears that the only intelligent attempt at contractual integration of the workers' demands into the system contains factors which are radically disequilibrating for the system—on the condition, of course, that the union wants and knows how to use them. But the habitual rapacity of French capitalists in their relations with their nationalized suppliers leaves few worries on that score: used to treating the state as a "milch cow," the large private users of the *EDF* will know how to apply the necessary pressures on the government in order to ruin the chances of the *"contrat de progrès"* and to create, by their very action, the conditions of a violent social explosion in the firm which is at the very heart of French economic life.

The economic and social councilors of Chaban-Delmas are far from ignorant of the dangers which such a policy harbors on the social level. But they have deliberately made a wager based on the advanced sectors of the economy which are capable, they think, of integrating the demands, if not of the *entire* working class, at least of that part which counts, that part whose weight is determining in the development of a general strike of the masses.

The observer of social struggles can thus situate with reasonable precision the contours of the two governmental strategies, each answering to the differentiated needs of different fractions of the bourgeoisie, each implying a different social partner. The strategy of the Grenelle type, to which the President of the Republic is attached, rests on a "political" vision of the French economy; tying together the wage demands of the advanced sectors and those of the backward sectors, it limits the general increase of wages to bearable dimensions, quickly recuperable at the level of total consumption. At the same time, it prolongs the existence of the backward sectors whose political weight counterbalances their economic weakness. This strategy is by nature *electoral*: it aims at politically controlling the rate of growth of the diverse sectors of the economy, at distributing the surplus-value principally appropriated from the profitable sectors of the economy to a business *petite-bourgeoisie* tied to the dominant political party, and at utilizing the state's economic apparatus as the indirect agent of that distribution. In following a policy of conquering the middle classes, which it began in 1963, in substituting itself for the Radical Party in its regional bastions [inherited from the Third Republic], and again using its practice of specific subsidies at specific times and places—"Pompidouism" is attempting above all else to recreate a tertiary "middle class" as the social support of its regime. To do this it will write off to "profits and losses" the grand international projects of Gaullism: the *force de frappe* and independence with respect to the U.S.

The evolution of Pompidou's politics in the Third World is a sign of this retrenchment. It has given up the planetary goals which led *Renault* [state-owned] to irritate American capitalism in Mexico and Québec, and has withdrawn to the Mediterranean, picking up the ball from and concealing an American intervention there which it does not want.

To this moderately Malthusian policy corresponds the equally broad and electoral stragegy of the *CGT*. Because the *CGT*, like the Communist Party, has decided against a strategy leading to a rupture and in favor of one of electoral development, it will attempt to consolidate that electoral hold on the social plant. It will thus also be led to seek a politics of agreements at the summit, of broad collective contracts, which have the double advantage: a) of assuring it the maximum representativeness of the working class. The *CGT* is losing influence in the leading sectors of production but has, since Grenelle, considerably enlarged its influence in the non-productive sectors (traditional white collar and even school teachers); b) of giving all strata of workers small, but electorally profitable, wage increases. This is the reason that today it demands a sliding wage scale. That does not at all mean, however, that the *CGT* has decided to put forward homogenizing or egalitarian demands. Far from that: the system of collective agreements has the advantage of maintaining the wage hierarchy while tying all the elements of the working class to each other: the progression of wages is made uniform for all—that is, uniformly unequal. And this permits the *CGT* to present itself as the defender of both the unskilled laborers and the engineers.

The strategy of the *contrat de progrès* also aims at a strategy of integration by indexing the increase of wages to the productivity of the firms. But for the attempt at overall integration which is that of the tandem Pompidou-Séguy, it substitutes a policy of selective integration. The policy of agreements at the summit—these poor man's Yaltas—bring together the internal contradictions of the French bourgeoisie and the "contradictions within the people." The social policy of Chaban-Delmas' counselors, on the contrary, goes in the direction of technocratic simplification. It works at the level of the new strata, and is uninterested in the rest. It is said that General De Gaulle, faced with the May eruption, shrugged his shoulders, grumping: "What can you do! In this country, in order to carry out a reform, a revolution is necessary!" Having decided to use the lessons of the aborted revolution of 1968 in order to modernize French capitalism, the *Mendèsiste* team which thinks for Chaban-Delmas wants to kill two birds with one stone: by integrating the new working class of the advanced sectors of the economy into a "tight tissue of contractual agreements" it hopes to neutralize the potential striking power of the revolutionary movement.

The accentuation of the differentiations of income within the working class, which is the inevitable consequence of the *accords de progrès*, effectively contributes to isolating the vanguard of technicians—the vanguard which logistically, whether the backward populists of *La cause du peuple* like it or not, alone has the possibility of transforming a protest movement into a broad revolutionary movement—from the mass of workers and employees of the traditional sectors. The *accords de progrès* will not only limit that integration to simple wage advantages: the agreement at *Berliet* which, because of the ramifications of the firm (owned by *Citroën* and thus associated with Fiat), is the model destined to play the role in private industry which the *EDF* contract played for the public sector, also establishes that "union power" which the *CFDT* demanded in May, 1968.

But it also has its limits. At the advice of the counselors of Chaban-Delmas, the excessive clauses of the contract which limited the right to strike have been given up: the recent experiences in Hamburg and Schleswig-Holstein, and in Kiruna, eloquently demonstrate that all judicial barriers fail when the conditions for a mass strike present themselves. But, at the same time, the unions have agreed that the management of the firm, the organization of work, hiring and firing, are the domain of management alone.[7]

Thus the policy of Chaban-Delmas rejoins that of Pompidou: nothing must challenge the authority of the head of the firm.

However, having established this essential point (which is the basis of the intrinsic solidarity of the entire capitalist system),[8] we still must note that the consequences of the policy of contracts at the level of

---

7. This article was written when the contracts at the *SNCF* [French national railways] and the private automobile firms were signed, confirming this tendency. —SM

8. This is one of the essential points of the doctrine of the "Manifesto" of the Neo-Radical party of Jean-Jacques Servan Schreiber. Audaciously "revolutionary" against the *rentiers*, it does not allow for any structural reforms in the hierarchy of the firms. The *rentiers*, if they want to protect their inheritances, have only to entrust their handling to the managers, or become managers themselves. (Cf. the example of Henry Ford III.)

the firm are fundamentally different from those of any Grenelle, past or future. By raising the income of the advanced sectors of industry, by integrating these pay raises into a creeping inflation, the policy of the *contrats de progrès* tends, as a result, to accelerate the concentration of industry, and to "take the fat off" (as the pet word of the *rue de Martignac* [where the French Plan is elaborated] has it) the unproductive services: the increase in the production costs of small and middle-sized firms which follows the increased buying power of the leading sectors — which, we too often forget, are located *principally* in Marx called Sector I: *the production of the means of production* — will accelerate the process of collapse which has been going on for fifteen years. The inevitable increase of the "possible social level of income" will lead the workers to leave those sectors which are scarcely or not at all productive — and who cares if they revolt beforehand, for that revolt is ineffective, as we know since the strike of the miners in 1963, when the bosses reply was: "Let them eat their coal!" The "new society" leaves outside its net the old France of the *rentier* and the *boutique*, of technically backward manufacturing and the local brick-maker: the old France which paraded down the *Champs-Elysées* one afternoon in June, 1968, and which sent that mass of Pompidouist old fogies to the National Assembly. In fact, the "Swedish model" appears as a totally utopian objective in France. Of course, it is possible to realize a policy of integration in a few advanced sectors, and in that way to dull for a time the combativity of the technologically advanced fractions of the working class. However, it is very late. The hopes awakened in precisely those strata during May, 1968 will not be put to sleep by the sugar pills of "productivity-sharing:" the workers want to know who will direct that sharing. The policy of *contrats de progrès*, established in a specific conjuncture in conditions humiliating to the working class,[9] can easily be "countered" by it: in "interesting" the

9. Let me say clearly and publicly here what I had the opportunity of saying during a meeting of the *PSU* and *CFDT*, to the leaders of that union concerning the responsibility that they took in swallowing the agreement at the *EDF-GDF*, which their branch union signed. As a wage agreement within a firm, the *EDF-GDF* agreement is not scandalous: there have no doubt been far worse. But the signing of that agreement took place in a situation which gives it its true meaning. (1) A strong strike movement had been developing since July. Though fragmented and limited to certain branches, it was centered on demands for control, and was typified by the seizing of victories without negotiations — the sign of an already acute revolutionary crisis. By putting the demands of the working class once more on the legal, institutional plane, the *EDF-GDF* agreement had in France the negative effect that the "bomb of Milan" had in Italy. [Attributed first to an anarchist, Valpreda, later shown to be the work of neo-fascist groups aided by the police, the bomb of Milan exploded in a bank, killing some 60 persons.] (2) The psychological shock which the agreement provoked in the

workers in productivity, one runs the risk of seeing them demand the right to control the norms of that productivity.

But at the same time, this "Swedish model," which we see precisely in Sweden only raises the consciousness of the working class even higher, can only exist for a part of the nation. And in that small country, so strongly centralized, the pockets of underdevelopment constitute just so many explosive factors, capable of spreading to the others. We have just seen this in the sharp upsurge of the farmers' movement.

Thus all the necessary conditions are united so that a profound crisis of confidence concerning Power and Authority emerges, a crisis which touches *all* social strata, including the small capitalists.

In these conditions, the socialist struggle rediscovers, in different forms, the two essential components of its objectives of social transformation: a) to assure a social order more just and more satisfactory for man, the elimination of poverty and exploitation, but also the deepening of freedom and individual creativity—fundamental demands expressed notably in May, 1968; b) but also to insure the realization of a more rational economic model capable of assuring the growth of the productive forces.

D. Recognize the System is in Disequilibrium

In terms of the analysis above, we must pay attention to formulae, often used by ourselves and our allies, of the time: "put the system into disequilibrium." The voluntarist character of this slogan hides the reality: we do not put the regime into disequilibrium (we could not); *it is already there*. The failure of "participationist" attempts like the Edgar Faure Law [on educational reform after May 68] is

---

working class is largely due to the fact that it took place following *a defeat*: the grotesque fiasco of the electrical workers' strike in December, 1969. I concede readily that the responsibility for that failure is due first of all to the *CGT*. Launching an "authoritarian" strike in a sector so central because of its effects on the whole of social life, and doing so just before a scheduled negotiation the terms of which were still unknown among the rank and file, Comrade Séguy conducted himself like a frenetic adventurer attempting by an ultra-leftist move to regain the credit he had lost in opposing, without success, all the strike movements set off since the summer, movements which were animated either by the *CFDT*, or by sectors of the *CGT* influenced by the *PSU* and the ultra-leftists, and which each time ended in success. But the strike at the *EDF-GDF*, with which the *CFDT*, giving in to pressure from the *CGT*, was associated—erroneously—was felt by the workers there, and by the entire working class, as a sharp defeat. In such condition even the best armistice agreement appears as a *capitulation*. (3) But, that capitulation on the field of action was not justified by the total social context. That episode should lead to a serious discussion concerning the limits of branch autonomy in the unions. And lead the union leaders to study the strategy of social war. I propose that the study of Clausewitz be included in the program of the future workers' educational programs such as that of the *CFDT* (the *Ecoles normales ouvrières*). —SM

significant: we were powerless to stop the participation of the teachers and a large part of the students—but nevertheless the law failed.

The strategic and tactical consequences of the analysis that we have made of the regime, of the diagnosis that we have given concerning its state of health, are considerable. It is in terms of an analysis of this sort—although masked by the simplifying rigidity that marks all Theses at a Congress—that the *PSU* has for a long period engaged the largest part of its working class forces in struggles for "workers' control," the strategic axis of workers' struggles.

But we can only make this orientation concrete if we start from the recognition of the contradictions of the French capitalist system—and not from a voluntarist option.

A strategy of workers' control based on the attempt to put the regime into disequilibrium would be a defensive strategy. In our own language, we are paying here our tribute to the "seafaring images" dear to the Trotskyists—to the typically mechanist concepts of "ebb and flow," of "waves and troughs of the wave"—as well as to a superficial analysis of the May Movement considered as a classical type of revolutionary crisis which failed, and not as the first manifestation of a new type of revolutionary situation.[10] The strategy of the struggle for the generalization of workers' control aims both at the *conquest of a position* of strength in the firms and at the *dissolution* of the contralized system of authority, hitting it at its nodal point: the control of the productive forces.

If the French capitalist system were in as good health as its sycophants claim, the struggle for workers' control would be a "reformist" one, and would be illusory because the experience of fifteen years of "participation" in the plant committees and Planning Commissions, etc., has shown that French capitalism refuses absolutely and definitively to "share" the slighest crumb of real power.[11] Or it would be a pure "agit-prop" technique and would have the same fate that this slogan, which was endlessly put forth for forty years by the Trotskyist groups, had in its time: that is, it would remain without an echo.

But because French capitalism *is* in a situation of disequilibrium,

---

10. This is the point of view of Alain Touraine in *Le mouvement de mai ou le communisme utopique* (Editions du Seuil, 1968). It seems to us far richer than the analysis which sees "the tenth failed revolution." SM [Touraine's book is available in English as *The May Movement*, New York: Random House, 1971].

11. Cf., on this subject, in the "*Témoins*" collection of Gallimard, the book of M. Combe, *L'Alibi*, the story of twenty years of the life of a plant committee in a steel company, probably Schneider. —SM

the struggle for workers' control becomes an offensive struggle: it is the concrete challenging through mass action of the authority of capitalist power and the state, a challenge which can continue for a relatively long period. For if it is true that revolutionary "crises" — that is, the moment when the polarization of the opposing forces reaches a point of confrontation where one must give way to the other — are, in effect, very short (as we say during the last week of May), revolutionary situations are, on the contrary, generally of a fairly long duration. It is probable that the new forms of industrial technology and the determining weight of economic constraints will further prolong this process to the extent that they make the recourse to armed action more difficult and more dangerous for all sides.

But our strategy of workers' control makes sense only if we accept the principle that May 68 opened a revolutionary phase of a new type, analogous to the one that has existed for the past year in Italy. Mass struggle for workers' control, as it has been undertaken by the current movements since last spring, has the advantage over all other forms of struggle that it is homogenizing, that it gives a unity of perspective and an overall strategic view to conflicts which, in the short run, could only be sectoral or local. It is, in effect, utilizable in all situations in the advanced industries with a high level of profitability; it defeats the policy of profit sharing by first giving the workers other objectives than those of transforming their demands into money. In declining industries, it prevents the exploitation to the furthest limit of workers threatened by unemployment, and poses the problem of their re-employment.

One cannot insist too strongly on the alienating and alienated character taken on by the famous "quantitative" demands. One has only to recall that the struggle against unhealthy conditions or the dangerous character of certain jobs found its answer in the "bonus for high risks or unhealthy conditions." For a few pennies an hour more, the worker sometimes sacrifices fifteen to twenty years of life-expectancy.

The struggle for control once again gives the workers' demands a human dimension: by imposing a limitation on work speed, by eliminating certain kinds of dangerous or unhealthy work, by the authoritarian (I mean, by their own authority) shortening of the length of the working day, the workers learn to go beyond the psycho-sociological conditioning that the capitalist ideology has instilled in them for the greater profit of the employers: that "strange folly" which Paul Lafargue spoke of in his admirable pamphlet *The Right to Be Lazy*: "The moribund passion for work, pushed to the exahustion of the vital forces of the individual."[12] The myths of participation show themselves here to be powerless: the demand for control attacks the very heart of the system. Whereas the demand for higher wages accepts the mechanism of the appropriation of surplus-value, and helps only to push towards a development of productivity of which a very small part is given back to the worker, the demand for control raises the question of the determination and utilization of productivity in terms of the human needs of the workers: less work, less fatigue, less nervousness, better work schedules, etc. It rediscovers an enormous dimension of workers' demands, a dimension that was, just as much as wage demands, at the center of the action of the union movement of the nineteenth century—the struggle for better conditions of work—which had been abandoned and reified into bonuses, supplementary hours, profit-sharing points, and other lollipops.

The struggles for workers' control of the technical organization of production were born almost spontaneously from the new consciousness which was created in May-June 1968. The gigantic social movement of May-June 1968 made clear the will of large strata of workers in numerous sectors of production and services to stop putting up with negotiating bit by bit for wage increases which were almost immediately threatened by governmental economic policies, but instead to take control of the instruments of production and to put them to work in their service.

Though it became a popular expression during the general strike of May-June 1968, the demand for managerial control was quickly covered over by the general political situation. After long years of defensive, divided struggles fought under the servile slogan *"Charlot, des sous"* [Charlie, more money], the explosion of workers' anger led in a few days to the near collapse of a state power that everyone thought was much stronger. The struggle for control of the central power, political power, quickly went beyond the initial forms spontaneously adopted by the movement (in the universities as well as in the factories): the establishment of managerial power among the rank and file, denying bourgeois legality by the fact of effective control in the workplace. André Gorz is perfectly correct in saying that the sole correct position which would have permitted, in June 1968, the overthrow of the Gaullist power and the preparation of a transitional phase, was to "go forward:" "to undertake a double action: on the one hand, political and programmatic mediation

---

12.   Available in English from *Radical America* as a pamphlet, or along with other writings of Lafargue, from Charles H. Kerr & Co., Chicago, Illinois.

toward the reformist leaders without troops who would direct the provisional government; on the other hand, this same mediation toward the leaders of the movement...whom the Party could aid in elaborating and co-ordinating their own plans for reform and *in putting these plans into effect without waiting* [Gorz's italics]...by 'taking power' at the local or occupational level."[13]

This is—it is only honest to say it—the strategy the *PSU* (all its tendencies together) attempted to push at the time. But it was inevitable that it end in an impasse. The first reason for this is too well known: it is that the *PSU* had a correct strategic vision of what should have been done...by the Communist Party, a strategy for which it itself did not have the means at the time. But the second reason is perhaps deeper: if one excepts certain technologically advanced sectors—in which control orientations appeared beginning in 1958, but were slowed and dulled after 1963 because of the stagnation caused by the First Stabilization Plan[14]—the majority of the French, as well as of the world, working class had for a long time ceased to pose its social demands in terms of what had been the central theme of the development of the workers' movement: the reappropriation of the means of production by the producers. In rediscovering, with a new dimension, that the workers' condition could only be changed by restoring the managerial initiative of the working class, the movement of May-June 1968 in a few days profoundly upset the conditions in which union activity was carried on: but it did not, for all that, have the possibility of transforming a profound aspiration into a "unified praxis:" it scarcely dared formulate (I am speaking here, of course, of what took place in the factories) its will to abolish the essential taboo: the assimilation of the technological and organizational knowledge to the holding of power in the firm, whether the firm was of a classical capitalist or a technocratic type.[15]

---

13. *Réforme et Révolution*, Paris: Editions du Seuil, 1969, pp. 30-31. —SM
14. In *La nouvelle classe ouvrière* [Paris: *Editions du Seuil*, 1963]; I give certain examples of this phenomenon. —SM
15. An anecdote will illustrate this observation. At the time of the strike of the miners in 1963, the workers at the *SNPA* (natural gas at Lacq) undertook a three week strike. On the fourth day of the strike, the demands put forth at the beginning of the movement were attained. The unions never dared to formulate the real reasons for the movement: the rejection by the Minister in charge of the mines of their proposals for a radical reorganization of the work structures and the wage hierarchy. So for three weeks there was a "strike without goals." Having been there at the time, I was able to see, both among the union cadres and the rank and file, the reality of the aspiration to control which underlay that "gratuitous" strike. Some time thereafter, however, the investigators of the *ISST* [Institut des Sciences Sociales du Travail] obtained nearly unanimous replies from these workers justifying the strike by the necessity of

But as early as Spring, 1969, when the increase in the cost of living and the threats to the franc definitively dissipated the illusions born of the wage increases granted at Grenelle, one saw the development of quasi-wildcat strikes — that is, strikes started outside the initiatives of the union apparatus, even though they were then taken up by that apparatus — which stressed the objectives of workers' control. With the movements of *Usinor* and *Sollac* during the summer, the strike of the flight controllers at Orly, or of the semi-skilled metal workers at *CODER* in Marseilles, and that of the officers of the tugboats of the merchant marine and that of the operating personnel of the *SNCF*, and then with the disturbances in the automobile, aeronautical and electrical sectors, and even with the atomic energy workers at the *CEA* — one could see a continual gradation.[16] Although these movements were based, at the beginning, on situations specific to occupational categories (including those within the firm or the sector of production), although they were not linked to one another, and that on the contrary all sorts of means were used to make sure that they did not know about one another, they demonstrated from week to week a continually heightened level of the desire for control. At the beginning, they were centered around the control of the division of labor, the establishment of wage hierarchies, and the duration of work, but they rose, from one sector to another, from one strike to another, to the demand for control over the organization of production itself, even over the legal and societal status of the firm.

This is how the movement which was set off in the aeronautical industry, beginning with the defensive struggles against the liquidation of the research sectors of the *SNECMA*, led at *Hispano-Suiza*, then in the group *Sud-Nord Aviation*, to an opposition to the project for merging these companies, a project that had been planned outside the control of the workers. This is how the petroleum workers of *ANTAR* at Donges intervened in the struggle of the petroleum workers of *ELF* against their own bosses, etc.

It is giving too much credit to the company level groups of the *PSU* to say that they were responsible for this chain of movements. In proclaiming publicly the theme of workers' control as the center of its

---

"defending one's beefsteak." It was only after reminding them that the strike continued for two weeks after the wage demands were satisfied and without the formulation of new ones, that they got replies like: "We are not robots. We knew the work situation better than the Minister," etc. —SM

16. On this, see Mallet's discussion of these strikes in "Post-May, 1968: Strikes for Workers' Control," pp. 87-106 in this volume.

17. The extension of Mallet's analysis here to the LIP struggle which shot French social and political life in 1972 is obvious.

action during the next months, the *PSU* has only recognized the orientation that has imposed itself on strikes in France and Western Europe during the past year, and has drawn all the inferences from this on the level of theoretical and political practice, centering its principal *political* action in priority to the place of production.

Nevertheless, even if numerous activist sectors, influences by the May movement, today agree to place the struggle for workers' control at the center of their concerns, the nature of the initiative taken by the National Council of the *PSU* in November 1969 immediately raised serious political and theoretical questions. The first of these concerns *the slogan itself*. Though the demand for control is the fundamental basis of all political action of the working class, the slogan "workers' control" is not valid at all times and in all places, contrary to what certain licensed Talmudists of the workers' movement think. The campaign that the *PSU* is starting is situated in the *present* context of the class struggles in France and Western Europe; it is a response which sees itself as adapted to a situation of political crisis of the capitalist system. It is to this political question that the above analysis is a reply.

The second question concerns *the nature of the initiative*. Its impulse comes from a political organization which is trying, through this initiative, to structure itself at the very level of the productive forces, and thus at the level of the essential struggles. The decision of the National Council poses, once again, and in all its breadth, the famous problem of the Party-Union relation. The indirect intervention in the debates of the National Council of the *PSU*, which placed this on its order of business, by Georges Séguy [head of the *CGT*] and Edmond Maire (militant in the PSU and Secretary of the *CFDT*'s Chemical Union),   raised, especially in Maire's comments, complex problems of "jurisdiction" which must be dealt with in more detail.

II.

May-June 1968 was a severe object lesson for the unions—whether they were reticent throughout the movement, as with the *CGT*, or whether they quickly joined the movement and accepted its essential characteristics, as with the *CFDT*, or whether they were simply "forgotten" by the movement, as with *Force ouvrière*,[19] the national

---

18. These are published in full in *Tribune Socialiste*, no. 428 (November 6, 1969). —SM

19. I am speaking naturally of the Confederation [*i.e..*, the national level] and not of some of the minority-tendency federated branches, like those in Chemicals and those of the Technicians, nor of those departmental organizations in *FO* with an

offices had to take account of the fact that the mass movement didn't give a damn for the habits and legalisms of the unions. But the exceptional conditions in which the movement began, the fact that it developed from the initiatives of the student movement, could lead one to believe in a sort of "collective psychodrama," and many union leaders, in their heart of hearts, shared this analysis of Raymond Aron. The series of so-called wildcat strikes which developed, firm by firm and sector by sector, beginning in the summer of 1969 and continuing to the end of December, was probably much more revealing. This time, in fact, the movement clearly began from the working class itself—directly taking up the flame from a student movement broken and fragmented since the failure of May. It had objectives directly related to the lives of the workers and of the firms: it was no longer a contestation, as much verbal as general, of the "theoretical" structure of the relations of production, but of the precise, concrete, geographically and sectorially determined structure of the relations of production existing in such and such a firm or in a particular industrial branch. If for those who reduce it to only the student movement, the May movement seems to espouse in a caricatural manner the so-called Leninist schema of "consciousness brought to the workers from outside," then the movements of 1969 demonstrate on the contrary that in spite of the hesitations of its union and political organizations, the working class—or at least, its most advanced sectors—no longer would limit its demands to things which the capitalist system could digest without great difficulty. The traditional forms of action promoted by the union movement appeared just as inadequate as the timid demands (in the sphere of consumption) that it proposed.

This tendency was even more significant in that it was not limited, this time, to France alone. The wildcat strikes of the German workers, those of the Flemish miners at Limburg, the eruption of the "creeping May" in Italy—and finally, more spectacular because it broke out in the "model firm" of the "model country" of social integration, the iron mines of Kiruna—all these demonstrated the rebirth of revolutionary class activity throughout the developed capitalist countries of Western Europe.

One must admit that French unionism in general—and the strongest of the French organizations, the *CGT*, in particular—showed during this period a diabolical perseverance in their errors.

---

anarcho-syndicalist and Trotskyist (*O.C.I.*) majority, like the one in the Loire-Atlantique. —SM

Whereas the *CGIL* in Italy, outflanked by the wildcat strikes at Fiat, or the Social Democratic *DGB* in Germany, confronted with those in Schleswig, Bremen and Hamburg, were able, catching their second wind, to take over the direction of these struggles *by taking them up themselves*, the *CGT* limited itself to passing out insults and threats concerning the "ultra-leftist agitators," and often showed itself in practice to be impotent to check the movements it had first condemned: it thus lost on both sides, and appeared—the finishing touch—as a powerless force of *order!* One has only to recall, in October, the recantations of the *CGT* at the time of the lock-out at the *Renault* factory in Le Mans, or the demonstration of the workers of the *SNECMA*, denounced as "adventurist" by the *CGT* two days before it rallied to the strike.

But it has been too quickly inferred from this crisis that the workers are uninterested in the union movement *in general*. There was a real basis for the faction that appeared in the different revolutionary groups (including the *PSU*) which argued for the priority of the role of firm-level political organizations in directing their own struggles, leaving to the union movement what should be "its role:" defensive actions of a categorial or corporative sort. For, in places where the firm-level political groups existed (excluding cells of the *PCF*, which were more often back-up groups for the *CGT* than the opposite), the spontaneous movement of the workers could more easily find an expression that would not have gotten past the old habits of trade-unionism. But this admission—which signifies nothing but the *crisis of the union movement*—should not make us forget two basic characteristics of these movements: the first is that, in France as in Italy or in Sweden, it has been always and everywhere the union militants who were the animators and spokesmen of the strikes. Generally, these militants were able to carry their union sections with them (playing on the rivalry of the organizations, the *CFDT* putting the *CGT* in embarrassing situations, or sometimes the reverse). In the last analysis, even though they were not taken up at the top by the national headquarters or the branch unions, the strikes nevertheless certainly developed through *union channels*.

It may be true that the militant presence of firm-level political groups made this evolution of the unions possible; but it should be noted that in the rare cases where the political organization took the practical direction of the struggle, without bringing in the union as its partner, it was rapidly separated from the workers.

The second aspect is that all the struggles undertaken with the aim of control have also passed through union channels in order to arrive at "armistices." One must consolidate the territory that has been conquered, something that, whether one likes it or not, takes place through an "insitutionalization" of the armistice agreement. And there again, the union reappears as the designated spokesman, the negotiator of the armistice, and the guarantor of its terms. In a word, the movements of the fall of 1969 certainly put into question the branch and national level practices of the union movement. They also, in general, showed the strength and capacity for innovation of the firm-level union.

It is of course necessary to introduce here distinctions between sectors. That capacity for innovation and taking charge of the offensive will of the masses at the base showed itself in the large modern industries having a high level of technology (*Usinor, Sollac, Air France, SNECMA,* etc.): bottle-neck strikes, such as those prepared and organized by the highly skilled workers at *Renault* in Le Mans, at *Usinor* in Dunkerque, and with the operating personnel of the *SNCF*, as well as the spectacular actions directed at the general public (like the hunger strikes at Saclay) went through the firm-union, and thus outflanked the apathy or hostility of the higher spheres of the union movement.

On the other hand, it is evident that in a certain number of more traditional sectors, having a high percentage of somewhat older semi-skilled workers (that is to say, those trained "on the job" between 1960 and 1965), the firm-level organization, placed like a formal institutional skin on top of an unorganized mass, burst into little pieces in the face of the movements which began outside its control under the pressure of the younger workers. Here the action-groups are directly structured on the political level, assuring whether they like it or not the continuation of a faltering union action.

Thus, certain strike movements of the fall of 1969 presented an "inverted" image of the classical Party-Union relation: the political organization took on the launching of the action and the union concluded it. This inversion of roles weighed heavily in the impotence of the movements to enlarge themselves in coordinated actions. And one can ask oneself whether the political organization, playing in a way the role of a "union vanguard" does not condemn itself to give way to the union at the moment when the masses in struggle demand a respite, a breath—thus missing the possibility of truly playing its political role, of showing the workers the overall implications of their action and the necessity of developing it on a higher level.

We should not take that situation, whether we are politicals or unionists, as anything but the sanction of a double lack: the structural weakness of the union movement in the new context of struggle, and the fragility of the political revolutionary organization within the labor movement. In a word, and since this situation has forcefully reopened the old Party-Union debate, we have to ask ourselves the question: what union and what party do we need today? This is what this part of the article will try to do, starting from the postulate that, since May, 68, workers' struggles have changed in kind. Hence it is not useless to take up this old debate at its sources: the workers' movement is steeped with history, and the collective unconscious of the working class bears all its weight.

A. The Party-Union Debate in the Labor Movement

The tendency to give to unionism nothing but the "little demands" is not new. Already in a letter to August Bebel (March 28, 1875), Engels criticized the Gotha Program of the German Social Democracy on this point: "Fifthly, there is not a word about the organization of the working class *as a class* by means of the unions. And that is a very essential point, for this is the *real class organization* of the proletariat..."[20]

This properly political role of the unions had already constituted the major theme of the resolution on unions by the International Workingman's Association (the First International) at its Congress in Geneva in 1866: "In addition, without explicitly realizing it, the unions have become the centers of organization of the working class, as the municipalities and the communes of the Middle Ages were for the bourgeoisie. If the unions are indispensable for the daily skirmishes in the war between capital and labor, they are even more important as organized apparatuses for speeding up the abolition of the wage system."[21]

It was precisely this political capacity for action on the part of the unions that led Marx to oppose the purely economistic conceptions that were on the rise in English trade unionism. But it was also in terms of this conception that he fought Lassalle's position. Lassalle thought that "the Union, as a subordinate body, should strictly and absolutely subordinate itself to the Central Political Body."[22]

---

20. *Critique des programmes de Gotha et d'Erfurt*, Paris: Ed. Spartakus, 1947, p. 44. [English: *Critique of the Gotha Programme*, New York: International Publishers, 1938, p. 30.] —SM

21. Cited in the Appendix to *Salaires, Prix et Profits*, Paris: Editions Sociales, 1952, pp. 119-120.

22. Article by Lassalle's successor, J. Schweitzer, in *Der Sozial-Demokrat*, of

Replying to a question by the general treasurer of the German Metal Workers, in 1869, Karl Marx made clear that, contrary to Lassalle, his view was: "If they want to accomplish their task, the unions must never be attached to or dependent on a political group; to do so would be to strike a mortal blow against socialism... All political parties, no matter which they be, only catch the imagination of the mass of workers for a certain moment, for a short time. The unions on the contrary, hold the masses in an enduring manner; they alone are capable of representing a true workers' party and opposing a stone wall to the might of capital."[23]

This somewhat forgotten view, whose tactical implications have often been noted — "Marxists" and "Lassalleans" cohabited with difficulty at that time in an organization controlled by the disciples of Lassalle — was nevertheless constantly reaffirmed by the founder of scientific socialism. In a letter of 1871 to an American militant, he wrote: "...But on the other hand, each movement in which the working class as a class opposes the ruling classes, and attempts to make them give in to an external action, is a political movement...This is how a political movement arises everywhere from isolated economic movements."[24]

In this latter text, Marx prefigures the position that Rosa Luxemburg develops in her famous pamphlet, "Mass Strike, Party and Trade Unions." In the meanwhile, of course, the embryonic and divided Social-Democracy of Marx's time had become a strong mass party. It is from this point of view that Rosa Luxemburg notes that the "theory of the parallel action of Social Democracy and the trade unions, and of their 'equal authority'...is an expression of the well-known tendency of that opportunist wing of Social-Democracy which in fact reduces the political struggle of the working class to the parliamentary struggle, and wants to change Social Democracy from a revolutionary proletarian party into a petty-bourgeois reform party."[25]

But Luxemburg's analysis and conclusions are very far from those

----

September 14, 1869. French translation in appendix to *Salaires, Prix et Profits*, cited above. —SM

23. Article published in the journal *Volkstaat*, No. 17, 1869, reporting a discussion between Marx and J. Hamann. Karl Kautsky violently attacked this view later, in a 1909 article "Sect or Class Party," (*Neue Zeit*, no. 27, p. 8, 1909). French translation in appendix to *Salaires Prix et Profits* cited above. —SM

24. Letter to F. Bolte, February 23, 1871; French translation in *Salaires, Prix et Profits*, cited above.

25. Paris: Editions Maspèro, 1968, pp. 162-3. —SM [The English here is from Dick Howard's translations in *Selected Political Writings of Rosa Luxemburg*, New York: Monthly Review Press, 1971, pp. 253-254.]

which motivated the famous "Zinoviev letter" which posed the Twenty-one Conditions of the Communist International to the Socialist Party Congress at Tours, demanding the constitution of fractions in the unions. Analyzing the example of the mass strike of 1905 in Russia, Rosa Luxemburg notes in effect that the separation between "economic struggles" and "political struggles"—the former taken as the domain of the unions, the latter as that of the party—"is but an artificial, though also an historically conditioned product of the parliamentary period." "As soon as the period of revolutionary struggles begins. . . both the division of the economic struggle and the indirect parliamentary form of the political struggle cease. In a revolutionary mass action the political and economic struggles are one, and the artificial barriers between the unions and Social Democracy which make them two separate, totally independent forms of the labor movement will simply be washed away. . . There are not two different class struggles of the working class, an economic one and a social one. Rather there is only *one* class struggle which is directed at the same time at the limitation of capitalist exploitation within bourgeois society and at the abolition of exploitation together with bourgeois society." [26]

Rosa Luxemburg considers, in effect, that during the parliamentary period, union action is related to that of the party like "a part to the whole." But the same is true, she thinks for the parliamentary struggle. "Social Democracy is in itself the summation of both the parliamentary and the trade union struggles in a class struggle directed at the abolition of the bourgeois social order." [27]

The thousands of workers who belong to the union without belonging to the party do not for that reason feel themselves separated from the socialist party: "The Social-Democratically-minded worker from the masses who, as a simple man, can have no understanding of the complicated and refined two-souls theory [of the trade union leaders] feels himself Social-Democratically organized, even in the trade union." [28] "The appearance of 'neutrality' which exists for many trade union leaders does not exist for the mass of organized trade unionists." [29]

When noting the paradoxical situation of the German workers' movement ("the same trade union movement which below, in the broad proletarian mass, is completely one with Social Democracy,

26. *Ibid.* [p. 252] —SM
27. *Ibid.* [p. 254] —SM
28. *Ibid.* [p. 258] —SM
29. *Ibid.* [p. 259] —SM

parts abruptly with it above, in the administrative superstructure..."),[30] Rosa Luxemburg deduces from it that it is necessary once again to "subordinate the trade unions to the party,"[31] she makes clear immediately the nature of that subordination: "The guarantee of the true unity of the labor movement does not lie above, among the highest authorities of the leadership of the organization and their federative alliance, but below, in the organized proletarian masses."[32] In reality, one cannot separate the conception of the "subordination of the part to the whole," by which the founder of the Spartakus League seems to rejoin the conceptions preached by Lassalle and taken up by Lenin, from her general conception of workers' democracy and of the character of the party. We know that she violently attacked the "dictatorship" established by Lenin and Trotsky (in the pamphlet published by Paul Levi in 1922, *The Russian Revolution*)[33] which she called the "government of a clique," a "dictatorship of a handful of politicians, that is, a dictatorship in the bourgeois sense, in the sense of a Jacobin hegemony." She opposed the suppression of electoral freedom, freedom of the press and freedom of assembly; she denounced the dangers of a political monolithism imposed by the Bolsheviks. "Freedom only for those who support the government, only for members of a Party, no matter how numerous they are, is not freedom. Freedom is always at least the freedom of someone who has other ideas."[34] She demanded "democratic control by the masses;" "a broad democracy without the least limitation of public opinion" seemed to her the indispensable means for the construction of socialism. "The dictatorship [of the proletariat —SM] must be the work of *the class* and not of a small minority that rules in the name of the class..." Here we return, though not explicitly, to the aspiration formulated in "Mass Strike, Party and Trade Unions:" "theoretically, all the workers must be doubly organized."[35] The

---

30. *Ibid.* [p. 2767] —SM
31. *Ibid.* SM [p. 269. Note here that the term "subordinate" comes from the French version; the English in *ibid.* is more faithful to the German, using "rejoining" for the German "angliedern"—but since Mallet uses the term outside the quote it seemed better to leave "subordinate" in the text.]
32. *Ibid.* [p. 269] —SM
33. Rosa Luxemburg having been assassinated at the same time as K. Liebknecht at the tragic end of "The Bloody Week" of Berlin on January 15, 1919, this manuscript had been kept by Paul Levi and was published after her death. —SM
34. Rosa Luxemburg, *Ecrits Politiques*, tome 2, Paris: Editions Maspero, 1968, pp. 83-84. —SM
35. [English here from *Selected Political Writings of Rosa Luxemburg, op. cit.*, p. 257. Again, the French text differs from the German and the English; as the distinction is not important, we have used the English.]

reflection on the Party-Unions dichotomy with respect to the revolution of 1905 in Russia begins the exploration of a new path for socialist revolution, which Rosa Luxemburg elaborates in the speech that she gave at the first Congress of the German Communist Party [in 1919]: formed in the great German Social Democracy, discovering the rightist opportunism and its parliamentary temptations, then rejecting Lenin's "Blanquism," she found in the mass strike and its novel form of leadership, the workers' councils, the royal road to a social revolution which would begin, immediately on taking power, to radically transform the state. Referring to Engels famous statement concerning "the impossibility from now on of the proletariat's having recourse to street fighting," a statement that was taken up and amplified by the Bernsteinian Social Democratic rightists as meaning that the social struggle could only be parliamentary,[36] Rosa Luxemburg commented ironically: "history resolved this problem in its own way, which is at once more profound and more subtle: it led to the revolutionary mass strike which, certainly, does not replace or make superfluous direct and brutal confrontations in the streets, but reduces them to a simple moment in the long period of political struggles and at the same time ties to the revolution *a gigantic labor of civilization*...the material and intellectual elevation of the entirety of the working class, civilizing all the barbarous forms of capitalist exploitation."[37] The Party-Union dichotomy which Rosa Luxemburg analyzes and criticizes during the parliamentary period must therefore transcend itself, tending toward the *fusion* of the party and the union in the forge of revolutionary struggle, a fusion whose organizational expression is the Workers' Councils, that is, the organs of direct proletarian democracy. We should note that, on the whole, this Luxemburgian view was fairly widespread within the workers' movement. Through the experiences in Russia, Finland, Poland, Germany, Austria, Hungary and Italy, the Republic of Councils appeared to the majority of socialist theoreticians as the modern form of the seizure of power, at the same time that it makes manifest as the Austro-Marxist theoretician Max Adler remarked,[38] those forms of organization which announce the new order. Lenin, who combatted this view in "What Is to Be Done?"

---

36.   Preface to *La lutte de classes en France*, Paris: Ed. Sociales, 1950. —SM [On the circumstances of this statement by Engels, and its alteration by the Social Democrats, see *Selected Political Writings, op. cit.*, p. 383].

37.   *Ecrits Politiques, op. cit.*, p. 136. [In checking the French edition, we could not find this passage; Mallet thinks it may be from another edition—ed.]

38.   M. Adler, *Démocratie et Conseils Ouvriers*, Paris Ed. Maspéro, 1967, pp. 77. —SM

agreed to it at the time of his "April Theses." "If the workers' councils have that fascinating force of attraction that seizes all strata of the working population, it is precisely because of the hope that they awaken of being a real means of popular representation and thus of replacing a parliamentarism which is completely dated and devoid of prospects. The workers' councils reestablish the homogeneity of each basic economic unit and permit the formation of an effective general will, and the move beyond the deadness of the parliamentary system."[39]

As we can see, the Austro-Marxian theoretician's critique rejoins that of Rosa Luxemburg, basing itself like her on the evidence of the impotence of bourgeois parliaments to express workers' democracy. But Adler is less confident than Luxemburg of "the spontaneity of the working masses."[40] The revolutionary goal can only be attained by the councils system if this system is built in a socialist manner. Otherwise, it will soon degenerate into an "instrument of the petty and ridiculous interests of certain factories, plants and offices..."[41] And, after having remarked that to the extent that the workers' councils, "from the Central Council down to the local ones, did not just make decisions but immediately executed what they had decided"—that is, that they must place the bureaucracy under their vigilant control and thus eliminate it and transform it into a simple auxiliary organ in order to keep for themselves the power of organization and execution—he stresses that they can play this role only on two conditions: the first is that they make sure that they have the possibility of concerted and coordinated action, while the second is that "revolutionary education of the workers' councils, in the spirit of Marxism and the class struggle and of socialism, be considered as a

39. V. I. Lenin, *April Theses.*

40. The leader of the Hungarian revolution, Bela Kun, also seemed to share the spontaneist enthusiasm. (Cf. the article in *Pravda*, January 26, 1918.) He made his *autocritique* several times, analyzing especially the fact that in spite of moving rhetoric ("there were many people among the communists who held that any Party had become superfluous with the creation of the Republic of Councils, arguing that 'The Workers' Councils are everything, we must even do away with the unions' "), it was in fact "the unions that become the center of the labor movement because in the chaos of the first weeks of the revolution they had retained their old organizational forms." Having in fact aspired for some time to a return to the practice of "pure unionism" which they had utilized during the Austro-Hungarian empire, the union bureaucrats got rid of the Bolsheviks as soon as they could, and then immediately thereafter gave up their power without resistance in the face of Horthy's *coup d'état*. Cf. Bela Kun, *La République hongroise des Conseils* (French edition), Budapest: Ed. Kossuth, 1962, pp. 329-330. The Austro-Marxist Adler showed himself more "Leninist" than the Hungarian Bolsheviks when it came time for the Austrian experiment with Councils. —SM

41. M. Adler, *op.cit.* —SM

second critical and permanent task, along with those of administration."[42]

The reader of this article will understand, without my having to insist, why the *résumé* of the discussion within the labor movement leads here to an analysis of the experience of the councils' movement in Europe during the revolutionary phase of 1917-1920: the resurgence in May-June of the slogan "workers' power," the present development of "struggles for workers' control" obviously leads to the organizational notion of workers' councils, capable in a revolutionary phase like the one into which we have entered since 1966, though with forms and with a timing quite dissimilar, to be at once the "principal agents of the class struggle," and the embryo of the new form of popular power that will replace the bourgeois system of education.

The violent criticisms of these notions made by all the communist leaders during May-June, 1968 were directed, above all, at *this* form of workers' democracy which is just as insupportable to them as it was to the right wing Social Democrats (we have just seen that large fractions of the European Social Democrats had, from this point of view, a much more revolutionary conception than that of the present Communists), and this for the same reasons: having gotten to a certain level of bureaucratic development within the framework of bourgeois institutions, the party or union tends to function as the reflection of these institutions: the notion of the parliamentary conquest of power — even if it isn't utopian, and it isn't always — often masks the desire to insert oneself as one is within the existing structures and to utilize them to one's own profit. In a word, the Communist Party, like the German Social Democrats in 1914, *hasn't "given up" on the seizure of power, but it has given up on changing the nature of the state,* and its organizational structure is all ready to flow into that mold. The struggle for workers' control prepares the working class in practice to exercise power itself, and thus enters into conflict with the very nature of those bureaucratized institutions that the party and the union have become.

It is evident that the "root" of that fear of the world communist party (for the reaction of the *PCF* to the forms taken by the workers' initiatives in May-June 1968 is identical to that shown by the Russians in Czechoslovakia: as long as the Russians thought that the conflict concerned only themselves and the leaders of the Czech party, they didn't call in the tanks. The invasion was nothing but the laying down of the law concerning the workers' councils, whose rapid

42. *Ibid.,* p. 116. —SM

formation, coupled with the approach of the Party Congress, would have made them the fundamental law of the Czech Republic.)[43] is a practical one. But the theoretical basis of that attitude is founded in the authoritarian deviation of Marxism which, in the German and Austrian Social-Democratic Parties, was formulated in the theory of "consciousness brought from the outside to the working class." If we look at the most complete expression of that theory—that of Karl Kautsky—we can easily see its imprint on Lenin himself in "What Is To Be Done?"

Since 1968 all revolutionary organizations have included in their ritual the obligatory reference to Leninism. But to speak of the "construction of a Leninist party" avoids posing the concrete problems of the forms of revolutionary political organization which correspond to our real situation...and to our experience. The "Leninist conception of the party," whose canonization by Stalin encouraged the misunderstanding of Lenin's own ideas, is found almost entirely in Lenin's most outdated work, "What Is To Be Done?"—a book which, in the last analysis, is not even an original reflection: Lenin appears there as a completely orthodox disciple of Kautsky, whose article in the *Neue Zeit*[44] he cites at length. Kautsky's article was devoted to a critique of the Austrian Social Democratic Party program, dealing particularly with the famous notion of consciousness brought from outside to the working class. Kautsky criticized the following passage from that program: "The more the numbers of the proletariat increase due to capitalist development the more it is constrained to, and has the possibility of, struggling against capitalism. The proletariat thus becomes conscious of the possibility and the necessity of socialism." Thus, comments Kautsky, "socialist consciousness would be the necessary and direct result of the proletarian class struggle. And that is entirely false...Socialism and the class struggle spring forth parallel to one another; one does not cause the other...Socialist consciousness today can only be built on the basis of deep scientific knowledge...But the bearer of science is not the proletariat but *the bourgeois intellectuals* [K.K.'s emphasis]; it is in effect in the heads of certain individuals of that stratum that contemporary socialism was born, and it is through them that it has been communicated to the most intellectually advanced proletar-

___

43. The reader should consult my analysis of that situation in the article "Bureaucracy and Technocracy in the Socialist Countries," reprinted here. See also, in the journal *Autogestion*, no. 7, December 1968, the article by Rudolf Slansky (son of the ex-first secretary of the Czech CP shot in 1951), *"Les premiers pas de l'autogestion en Tchecoslovaquie."* —SM

44. Vol. XX, no. 3, p. 79. —SM

ians, who introduce it into the proletarian class struggle whenever conditions permit it. Thus socialist consciousness is an element imported from outside into the proletarian class struggle and not something that springs forth simultaneously." And Lenin comments on this: "From the moment that it is not a question of an independent ideology elaborated by the working masses themselves during their movement, the problem is posed *solely as follows* [Lenin's emphasis]; bourgeois ideology or socialist ideology... The spontaneous development of the working class movement results precisely in its subordination to bourgeois ideology, for in its spontaneous form the labor movement is trade unionism, *Nur-Gewerkschaftlerei*."[45] And in a footnote, Lenin refutes "in advance" those arguments founded on the existence of theorists of proletarian origins by saying that these theorists (Weitling or Proudhon) don't participate in the struggle as workers but as socialist theoreticians, that is, as intellectuals who have assimilated all of the "bourgeois" science of their time.

We needn't discuss here the theoretical "facileness" of these two texts—particularly, the quite idealist notion that makes socialism a creation of the heaven of university ideas which is then introduced into the proletarian struggle. That Kautsky never asks himself, contrary to Marx or Engels, whether the bourgeois intellectuals who come to a socialist position through a liberal humanism (as was the case of Marx and Engels) did not discover an unformulated socialist consciousness in the forms of action and organization adopted by the working class, and whether the "educators" were not themselves "educated" by the general historical conditions, among which the main one was precisely the existence of the working class. For Marx, "the proletarian party is spontaneously born from the historical soil of modern society"—and socialist theorists, whether they, as *individuals*, have proletarian origins or not, only become social theorists—by which I mean, having a direct influence on the historical process—to the extent that they *express* a collective historical consciousness, and that social groups *recognize themselves in that consciousness.*

The Marxist conception of the party-class relation, like its conception of the leaders-masses relation, is infinitely more complex, more dialectical than that quite academic notion of the "transmission of knowledge."

---

45. *Que faire?,* in *Marx-Engels-Lénine,* Moscow: Ed. en Langues étrangères, p. 149. —SM

Lenin's comparison between *"bourgeois* ideology" (which, in the proper sense of the term is not a particular theory but the ensemble of the theoretical, cultural and religious conceptions *needed* by the capitalist mode of production) and *socialist* (not proletarian) ideology is at once significant and theoretically disarming! Where does that socialist ideology, which does not at all seem to have class roots, come from?

The date at which Lenin wrote this article (Autumn, 1901) explains and justifies his position. Just like the present-day resurgence of that dogmatism of the "Party in itself" in groups essentially composed of young intellectuals of bourgeois origin, "What Is To Be Done?" appeared much more as the theory of the factual situation of the Russian Social Democrats at a time when a working class had only begun to be formed in Russia. His exile did not permit Lenin to draw all the lessons from the 1905 Revolution, which he hardly understood, and it took the "April Theses" and the generalized creation of Soviets for Lenin to definitively abandon that paternalistic conception of the party and the class. But he did abandon it totally, and this permitted him—in opposition to all the "Old Bolsheviks" that he had educated—to grasp the conditions of the socialist October Revolution. *State and Revolution* represents a decisive rupture with Kautskyism, with the conception of the Party-as-Guide: "The people can subdue the exploiters even with a very simple 'machine,' nearly 'without a machine,' without any special apparatus, by the simple organization of the armed masses, Soviets of workers and soldiers."[46] In this article, which leads immediately to the October Revolution, it is always the (armed) working masses who must directly "control," must organize production. "It is us, the workers, who will organize the production process, taking as a point of departure what has already been created by capitalism, and grounding ourselves in our experience as owrkers." (Lenin) Thus, it is in terms of their objective situation, their practical experience in the functioning of modern large-scale industry, that the workers directly acquire that famous "profound scientific consciousness."

Throughout the texts—unfortunately, always dealing with immediate problems of the moment—that Lenin wrote between 1917 and 1921, there runs like a red thread that: "...the living creative activity of the masses is the principal factor in the new public life... Socialism will not be constructed by orders coming from on

---

46. In *Marx-Engels-Lénine, op.cit.,* p. 149. —SM

high. Official and bureaucratic automatism is foreign to socialism. Living creative socialism is the work of the popular masses themselves."[47] "We must at all costs destroy that old, barbarous, base and odious prejudice according to which the supposed 'superior classes,' the rich or those who have gone to the schools of the rich, can administer the state, organize the edification of socialist society."[48] And at the Third All-Russian Congress of Soviets, he explained: "When we introduced workers' control...we wanted to show that we recognize only one path, that of transformations coming from below, where the workers themselves elaborate at the base the new principles of the economic system."[49]

Just as Marx learned from the Commune of Paris, and did not hesitate to question, in terms of that experience, his conception of the transitional from of the proletarian state, so Lenin, as soon as he returned to Russia, learned from the struggling masses of Petrograd, and *radically* altered his conception of the relation between "the leading role of the party" and "the revolutionary initiative of the masses." To want at all costs to discover a unilinear "Leninist conception," born in 1901, in "What Is To Be done?" on the basis of who knows what magical intuition and maintained without discontinuity throughout twenty years of extraordinary social turmoil, is to reduce the great Lenin, the revolutionary leader most attentive to the agitation of the masses, the theorist most deeply involved in action, to the sad image of a mummified professor repeating his doctoral thesis to the last stage of senescence.

But, unfortunately, it is not possible to ignore the fact that this conception of the party was, with the help of clandestinity and exile, the conception which created the Bolshevik Party. It was a conception that resisted all the warnings of its initiator. Having in fact lost control of the party after his illness, Lenin denounced with anguish in outraged letters what "the kernel of the vanguard of the proletariat," which had gotten used to thinking for the masses and in their place, had become with the exercise of power. The Testament that Lenin wrote in 1922, but which remained secret until 1966, is more clear-sighted concerning the real nature of the so-called vanguard party than anything the anti-authoritarians of the Luxemburgist or Pannekoek type were able to write. Speaking of the state apparatus, which was already confounded with the party which would totally take it over, he wrote: "We call our own an apparatus

---

47. *Oeuvres*, Vol. 26, p. 489. —SM
48. *Ibid.*, p. 432. —SM
49. *Ibid.*, pp. 491-495. —SM

which, in fact, is totally foreign to us, and which represents a hodge-podge of bourgeois and Tsarist remnants..."

Though it may not please those budding bureaucrats who abound in all the self-proclaimed vanguards, the Leninist conception of the party, that elitist, self-selected party practicing the rule of "secrecy" like all conspiratorial sects, does not have such a great record. Trotsky's *History of the Russian Revolution* shows, in spite of the author's attempts to save a conception which was not his own at the time of the Revolution but to which he rallied after the fact—and for a short time—shows eloquently that in February and in October the Bolshevik Party was "being towed along" by the action of the masses. In October, it was against the Party that Lenin and Trotsky (who had joined the Party in July) imposed the support of the revolutionary initiative of the masses. And a few years later, this party, heir to the statist tradition that the masses wanted to crush, reconstituted within itself all the characteristics of the old bureaucracy, "confiscating power from the masses."

That conditions specific to Russia in 1917 played an important role in the aborting of the revolutionary process, I would be the last to deny.[50] But these conditions weighed just as heavily on the conditions in which the conception of the party was elaborated.

We should thus stop rediscovering what seventy years of Social Democratic practice and fifty years of Stalinist practice have inexorably condemned.We need another type of organization, a party of a *truly* new type for which there exist no ready-made recipes.

*   *   *

The trouble that I have taken in this article to return to the history of the labor movement is not, my readers will know, habitual. But the historical context of this debate helps us in better posing today the concrete problem. In effect, two important lessons emerge from this historical reflection. (1) The first is that during the labor movement's gestation period, when it is confronted by the first historical phase of capitalist domination and attempts first of all to clearly understand its own situation, it is in the union organization, taken as the *organization of the entire class*, that the working class spontaneously becomes conscious of its specificity as a class. But this is also a phase in thich the workers' party as such does not yet exist; or, more exactly, led by writers and intellectuals who have come to it

---

50.   Cf. my article, "Bureaucracy and Technocracy in the Socialist Countries." —SM

directly from the liberal bourgeoisie, it can only formulate its opposition to capitalist reality by basing itself on the lived practice of the exploited working class. The formation of workers' class consciousness is first of all spontaneous; or rather, it elaborates itself through a subterranean culture, maintained since the Middle Ages within the closed strata of professional workers—a culture which has never been recognized by the bourgeoisie, and which in fact has never tried to get that recognition. Certain "omissions" in official history, even of the Marxist or left-leaning sort, are quite significant from this point of view—thus Marx and Engels praised the cooper Joseph Dietzgen for having, at the same time as they did, discovered the bases of historical materialism. Too, in spite of their differences, they considered the tailor Weitling as a "theoretical giant" of whom Marx wrote in 1844: "Without excepting its philosophers and intellectuals, where could the bourgeoisie find a work comparable to Weitling's *Guarantees of Harmony and Freedom.* Could one compare the timid and flat mediocrity of German political literature with this enormous and brilliant literary début of the German workers?"[51] The works of these worker-thinkers whose role was crucial in the foundation of the International never found favor in the University or the official publishing houses, whereas the most passionate works of Marx were nonetheless crowned by the doctorate.

Trotsky, the only one of the Bolshevik leaders to know the French labor movement well, did not deceive himself: "I am well aware of the aversion that certain sectors of the French working class who have been schooled in anarcho-syndicalism have for the 'Party' and 'politics.' I quite agree that it is not possible to abruptly counter that state of mind, which is perfectly explained by the past."[52] And contrary to the crude affirmations of Zinoviev, he explained that "it was not a question of subordinating the unions to the party, but of the unification of revolutionary communists and revolutionary unionists within the framework of a single party and a concerted, centralized effort of all the members of this unified party within the unions, which themselves remain autonomous." For Trotsky, "pre-war revolutionary syndicalism was the embryo of the Communist Party."

Here Trotsky touches a fundamental point in the history of the

---

51. In *Pariser Vorwärts*, 1844, cited by F. Engels. —SM [For the actual citation and the context, see Dick Howard, *The Development of the Marxian Dialectic,* Carbondale: Southern Illinois University Press, 1972, pp. 139 and 134-141.]

52. Letter to Pierre Monatte, July 13, 1921, in *Syndicalisme révolutionaire et Communisme,* Archives de P. Monatte, Paris: Maspero, 1968, pp. 296-97. —SM

labor movement in our country. The latent hostility of the best militants of the French—and European—labor movements concerning the political socialist parties, at all times and for all parties (the revolutionary minority of the *CGT* showed the same defiance towards the social-democratic politicians [Cachin, Frossard—SM] who had led the Communist Party as did the anarcho-syndicalists of pre-1914 towards the Socialist Party) is related to this fundamental dimension. It is not true that it was all that easy to effect the fusion between a spontaneous revolutionary practice of the working class and a revolutionary theory elaborated "outside" of that class by theorists who had deserted the bourgeois Alma Mater. The workers' political party was constituted as a party by detaching itself (in all the countries of the world) from the revolutionary petty-bourgeoisie at the moment when the latter had obviously come to the limit of its historical possibilities. The labor movement had its own history, passing through the *Compagnonnages*, the secret societies, the organizations of mutual aid (marked especially by the international character of their activities, whereas the revolutionary action of the petty-bourgeoisie, on the contrary, was always marked by its national character). The attitude towards parliamentarism was always a stumbling block between these two currents.

But that attitude has little to do with the problems of the tactics, or even the strategy, of taking power. Once again, in the context of the profound crisis of capitalism in Western Europe, nothing, at least theoretically, opposes the possibility of an electoral seizure of power by the parties claiming to be socialist—whether they are social-democratic (but still working class, as in Germany), or Communist (as in France or Italy). Though of course it would not be happy about it, for it knows that fundamental sacrifices would be required, but since it knows that armed insurrection is out of the question, the bourgeoisie can accept, tomorrow, the electoral seizure of power by these parties claiming to be socialist. The problem is that the seizure of power, in such conditions, would only change the identity of those who hold bourgeois power, and French history is rich with such changes of proprietors: the grandsons of inn-keepers and coopers who became army officers under the Empire, married the daughters of those whose heads their ancestors had cut off, and were mixed in the Who's Who and the boards of directors with the "blood aristocracy." The instinctive distrust of the working class concerning all the lesson givers, concerning all the self-proclaimed vanguards, all those who—masquerading in caps that the workers no longer wear—"bring" to the working class "consciousness" learned in the bourgeois university, is based on that intuitive knowledge of the mechanisms of social integration.

It is true that for a certain number of years, the working class, robotized in the production process, lost the confidence in its capacity to direct the society itself. It is true that the ruin of anarcho-syndicalism, such as that expressed in clear terms in the polemic between the Chemical branch of the *CFDT* and the *PSU* concerning the Party-Union relation,[53] also expresses the renaissance, in the conditions of modern capitalist production, of the objective basis of the demand for control in the new categories of work created by technical progress.

(2) But it is just as true that the insistence that the union have full political responsibilities, as the principal expression of the movement for the liberation of the working class, can today only be the act of the technological vanguard of the working class, which is the only part of the class capable of creating, through its concrete experience and scientific knowledge of the modern production process, those organs of social self-management that the struggle for workers' control is in the process of preparing. It is here that the center of the difficulty raised by the position of the *CFDT's* Chemical branch lies. In relation to its own organizational base, that union is in fact expressing a "possible consciousness," what a working class entirely integrated into the modern process of production could realize tomorrow. But this is only a partial reality, even in that advanced sector that is the Chemical industry. This is exactly the process that we saw developing in May-June 1968. While the technologically advanced part of the working class, in a quasi-spontaneous manner, based its action on demands for control, the majority of the class was not able, even in a "fully revolutionary" situation, to escape from the "trade-unionist consciousness" of which Lenin spoke, a consciousness which Séguy, who was promoted to "responsible interlocutor" by the bourgeoisie, fully incarnated in his prudent behavior. There never really existed, at any time, the possibility of making the desires for control in the advanced firms pass to the other sectors who could not effectively acquire such desires except by going beyond—indeed, by denying—their elementary trade-unionist consciousness based on wage demands. At no time did the Action Committees or the

---

53. One should consult the declaration of the executive commission of the *Comités Syndicalistes Révolutionnaires* of July 30, 1921, the basis of the future *CGTU*, which had an anarcho-syndicalist majority. "The Congress affirms that syndicalism represents the only force working on the level of the events that have been foreseen, and that in consequence, the great duty of taking in its hands the production, direction and administration of public and social life *belongs to it alone...*" —SM

workers' councils that were established have the possibility, by coordinating their action, of making evident the political alternative — other than some sort of ministerial replastering —, one that would be the embryo of a new type of power whose development would have assured the continuation of the revolutionary thrust.

Since I was one of the first to have analyzed in France the revolutionary possibilities of the working class in the advanced sectors, let me also note that, as a vanguard, it cannot let itself run the risk of isolation. Here we have to return to the schematic theory of Rosa Luxemburg, for whom the spontaneity of revolutionary working class consciousness was based on a lengthy theoretical analysis developed in *The Accumulation of Capital*. She believed in the exhaustion of the possibility of the growth of the productive forces within the world capitalist system. The whole theory of "under-consumption" has the tendency to disregard competition, and Ernest Mandel's critique of that theory shows perfectly, in my opinion, that it is "the inequality of the rhythm of development between different countries, different sectors and different enterprises that is the motor of the expansion of capitalist markets."[54] But the unequal rhythm of development that we noted earlier as explaining the structural weakness of French capitalism in general also applies to a country's internal production. It gives rise, therefore, to an unequal development within the working class itself. And that heterogeneity of the working class reflects first of all in union activity, which is by nature intimately tied to the different productive sectors.

Unifying factors can exist: the war of 1914-1918, which led to a collapse of the productive forces and a general crisis of underconsumption in all the belligerent capitalist countries except the U.S.A. is an example. But such situations are rare. The choice of strategic slogans always obeys precisely that fundamental unificatory necessity — and that is the role that the slogan of workers' control over the productive forces can play today.

But the unifying role that the struggle for workers' control can play in fact included two different procedures. In the modern sectors of production with a high rate of organic composition of capital, it can and often does effectively give rise to taking managerial control itself. The governmental counter-offensive in terms of the *accords de progrès* has precisely the goal of countering that tendency by detouring the demand for control towards profit-sharing — that old

---

54. E. Mandel, *Traité d'Economie Marxiste*, Vol. I, Paris: Julliard, 1962, pp. 450-456. [English translation by Monthly Review Press: New York]. —SM

slightly freshened carrot whose inanity the skilled workers and technicians of the advanced industries are well aware of. But the very fact of centering the determination of wages on the management of the firm—and here firm is to be understood on the level of the trust, or the holding company—directs the union itself, in a quasi-spontaneous manner, toward demands for control over management. The determination of production costs—and therefore control of equipment and raw materials, of fixed investments and marketing—the general orientation of the firm's activities and therefore of the determination of the goals of production, now become aspects of wage determination, thus linking in the consciousness of each worker the most elementary wage demands to the question of the capitalist management of the firm, making it clear to each that he has no control over the elements that determine his salary. This itself is not a great new insight; what is new is that this type of contractual relation dissipates the mystifying notion of a free labor market.

The objective integration of the workers into the firm thus facilitates the direct passage from trade union consciousness to political class consciousness, and it does so by means of the desire to gain control of the firm by and for the workers.

However, it is clear that all the traps of particiaption and of the particularism of each firm threaten the achievement of that consciousness. Not, as we have already seen, in that the workers in the advanced firms might seriously let themselves be "bought" by super-salaries: everything that we saw in May-June 1968 and since proves that on the contrary it is in these sectors that the essential thrust of contestation bears on the system of work organization, the hierarchy and the goals of production more than on demands which are stupidly called "economic." But, as in the case of the *CFDT*'s Chemical union, they risk, on the contrary, isolating themselves from the mass of workers whose contestation of the system can only be total because changing their lot implies first of all the total restructuring of the archaic apparatus of production in which they are still caught, and who, because they are conscious of their impotence to act through economic pressure, have a tendency either to give great weight—even though without much hope—to the electoral path, or to stress insurrectional practices which, as Rosa Luxemburg siad, can only be the secondary complement to the principal action: the mass general strike.

For the workers in the more traditional sectors of production and services, the struggle for workers' control has a more defensive character. The struggle against speed-up, for job security, for better work schedules, does not lead directly to managerial control; but it teaches the workers not to accept as a given the norms of capitalist exploitation, norms which are most oppressive precisely in these sectors.

Here it is still a question, in the strict sense of the term, of "economic" struggles which do not question the goals of production. And this is necessary. How could the workers in sub-contracting firms, for example, challenge within the framework of their firms, the general orientations of a production totally determined from outside; how can construction workers question, at the construction sites, the norms of a corporation which itself does not have decision-making autonomy; how can the workers in marginal industries, which are sooner or later condemned to close, be concerned with the direction of these industries?

In these cases, the struggle for workers' control only signifies a struggle in resistance to capitalist exploitation. But the terms themselves of that resistance are expressed in demands which are not cooptable: the struggle against productivity increases—that is, in this case, against physical super-exploitation—throws the system of competition in which the modern sector of production prospers into disequilibrium. By refusing to let their demands for a decent life be coopted into wage demands which can be integrated into the system at the price of a slight inflation; by refusing to accept a few *centimes* more per hour in exchange for working in conditions in which they risk their health or life (the so-called "risk and unhealthiness bonuses" which relieve the capitalists of the necessity of modernizing their equipment), the workers challenge the system of unequal development, the pact of "internal colonialism" that assures at once the proliferation of small and medium-sized Malthusian capitalists and the existence of hundreds of thousands of intermediaries tied to this system, and the excess profits of the big firms and the banking and commercial monopolies who pocket the "differential" margin that comes from this.

The struggle for workers' control in the retarded sector thus plays a direct role in the accentuation of the internal contradictions of French capitalism. Rather than associating itself with the anti-monopolist alliance, the working class in these sectors can and must, starting from the elementary conditions of the defense of their living conditions (and not simply their wages), precipitate the collapse of these parasitic sectors, and thereby attack the differential profit of the monopolies.

Let us take a specific example. At Sochaux-Montbéliard, *Peugeot* directly employs about 20,000 workers. They have either the possibility, because of their high technical ability, of blocking production at a time when it would hurt the bosses or, because they are integrated into assembly lines, of following the movements set off by the key sectors which paralyze production and make it easy for the semi-skilled workers to stop work. These workers can (and have done it, several times) impose agreements on their bosses ("armistices") which not only guarantee the increase of their wages and job security, but can also impose new productivity norms, improving working conditions and shortening work time. But each time that the *Peugeot* workers succeed in this manner in reducing the rate of exploitation to which they are subjected, the bosses recover at least a part of the losses imposed on them by worsening the terms of the contracts they sign with their sub-contractors—who recover their losses in turn from their workers.

The generalization of the phenomenon of sub-contracting— typified especially by the development of "slave labor" companies of the "Manpower" type—indicates clearly enough the interest in these new forms of the division of labor on the part of the large capitalist firms.

Thus, if it does not spread to the entirety of the *real* circuit of production of the firm, no matter what the juridical forms of interrelation, the struggle for workers' control in the big firms is threatened by the transfer of the appropriation of surplus-value from one part of the working class to the other. On the other hand, the struggle for workers' control in the secondary and dependent firms is inexorably doomed if it does not gain support from the workers in the mother-firm.

By the same token, the struggles for workers' control in the marginal sectors of industry can only in the long run *make the situation of these firms more difficult*. In themselves, these struggles can only lead to an enlargement of their context, either at the branch or regional level, if they raise the problem of regional reconversion—as we saw, for example, in the case of the workers at Saint-Etienne who supported the strikers of Manufrance whose jobs were threatened.

One must admit that, on the whole, the union movement is not adapted to this type of situation. And it is also certain that a transformation of the union movement like the one that has begun in federations such as the Chemical workers of the *CFDT* could permit it to play a more adapted role.

For A Mass Unionism

The transformation of the Union Movement [*Mouvement Syndical*] *is the first of the tasks for revolutionaries within the Labor Movement* [*Mouvement Ouvrier*]. They must understand that the present crisis of the union movement is not the crisis of unionism in general but rather that of the unionism of conflictual participation, that is, of a unionism living off the "institutionalization" of the struggle, of a unionism that agrees to put forward only demands that can be integrated into the system (wages, fringe benefits, possibly the length of the working day) but do not touch either the control of the work conditions (productivity, work rhythms, distribution and scale of pay for different jobs, hierarchical system in the firm, use of fixed capital) *or* the management of the firm (contorl of the books, markets, production costs, research contracts, goals of production). Since the Matignon Agreement in 1936 (ending the General Strike which came with the Popular Front), it is this type of union that dominates in France, as in all of Western Europe and the U.S.A. In different forms, this type of unionism, which transforms militant workers into *professional unionists* is also characterized by the *delegation of power from the masses to the union apparatus* (whether, in France, in the form of minoritary unionism, or as in the U.S.A. or Germany, in the complusory unionism of the closed shop).

The movements under way since May are characterized, on the contrary, by three fundamental traits:

a) *refusal to accept bourgeois labor legislation*: this is a reaction of the militants to fifteen years of conflictual participation and to the painful apprenticeship in managerial subterfuge, and takes forms like the refusal to give notice before striking, the refusal to accept firings, occupation of the factories, etc.;

b) *character of the demands*: control over the standards by which wages are assigned to different categories of workers, the division of jobs, work rhythms, length of the working day, and *the manner in which these demands are not just presented but first imposed* and *then* negotiated;

c) finally, the *constant exercise of union democracy at the base* (factory and shop assemblies, where the delegates explain their actions and where decisions are made in common).

The split between the workers' practice and the behavior of the unions comes principally from the fact that the unions, organized and conceived for defensive actions whose goal is to serve the immediate interests of the masses within the general framework of the unquestioned domination of capitalism over the production process, today have the greatest difficulty in understanding the offensive perspective in which the masses find themselves.

To adapt itself to the new role that it must play, unionism must almost completely renew its structures, its habits, and its practice.

Become a Mass Unionism: This does not come through the bureaucratic collection of dues, but by the permanent practice of workers' assemblies and the abolition of the distinction between unionized and non-unionized workers in decision-making. It also means the refusal of agreements made by the union staff (even if these are the staffs of the local union), but rather the frank discussion of diverging views in front of all the workers;

Be able to give the necessary information for putting workers' control into practice, and elaborate the simplification of all existing norms (from the viewpoint of wages as well as that of the technical organization of work);

Refuse central negotiation for the whole industry, and instead impose, factory by factory, branch by branch, armistices which ratify acquired positions of strength.

Assure the coordination of struggles and the victories won by following as closely as possible the real articulation of the integrated productive units (for example, extend victories won in the mother factory to the subcontracting ones) and organize the most intensive possible diffusion of successes won on issues of control.

The revision of the old union practice is already in progress. It is evident that it was at the center of the theoretical debates at the last Congress of the *CFDT*. More directly confronted with the new problems posed by the "wildcat strikes" in which its plant-level units actively participated, that union is attempting to formulate a broader conception of the union movement. The *CGT* will not be able to keep away from such an evolution for very long. The failure of conflictual negotiations of the Grenelle type leaves no other course to the *CGT* but to adapt itself to those wildcat strikes which, far from being "adventurist"—as some Communist militants who couldn't care less about precise scientific language repeat stupidly[55]—on the contrary enable the entirety of the working class, sector by sector, to progress without having to run the risk of an increased depression.

The old president of the *CGT* no doubt owes it to his anarcho-syndicalist origins to have been the first to formulate the true nature

---

55.   The pamphlet "Le contrôle ouvrier," published by the *PSU*, cites numerous examples of struggles that have used methods that are far more efficacious and "economical" for the workers than the traditional strike. The most recent and most significant of these was conducted by the technicians and workers at the *SNAP* at Lacq: "The strike without strikers," which reduced the production of natural gas to its technical minimum without losing a single day of work for the workers. —SM

of these strikes and their decisive importance for the future of the labor offensive. In a speech on February 10, 1970, before hundreds of *CGT* militants in the Michelin firm at Clermont-Ferrand, Benoit Frachon spoke of "what the bourgeois press calls wildcat strikes." These are in fact, he said, ". . . strikes whose character adapts itself to the new conditions of reinforced exploitation in the monopolist system. Industrial concentration, the strengthening of the monopolies and their domination not only bring changes in the system of capitalist exploitation; they also produce changes in the opposition of the classes in presence, and consequently lead the working class to modify its tactics and strategy in the struggle that it must undertake. The traditionalists who hold to the old methods and refuse to adapt themselves to the new conditions of class struggle can momentarily slow down the process; but they are impotent to stop it." "One can say," added the president of the *CGT*, "that these famous wildcat strikes constitute a sort of vanguard that opens up new hopes and new horizons for us."

But *in no case can such an evolution mean that the union, as an organization "of the whole class"*— and not its politicized vanguard— *has become useless.* More than ever, in a phase of capitalist evolution that is characterized by an ever greater integration of all the strata of the population in the capitalist mode of production, thus by a rapid proletarianization of tens of thousands of farmers, tradesmen and merchants, of cadres and bourgeois who formerly belonged to the "liberal" strata of the society, *the union is the necessary link between spontaneous class consciousness and political class consciousness*: but not at all in the sense of some sort of subordination of the part to the whole, or of a "transmission belt."

Enlarge the Areas of Union Struggle

On the contrary, to the extent that class contradictions within the whole social formation[56] worsen, unionism as the primary form of consciousness is no longer led to express only the viewpoint of the traditional working class, solidly fixed in the older industries and in its fixed political and union behavior, but of the new productive and semi-productive strata uprooted from the remains of pre-capitalist modes of production.

From this point of view, one can assert that in France—and in Italy or Spain—(that is, in those countries where the capitalist mode

---

56.   I use this term in the sense given it by N. Poulantzas in *Pouvoir politique et classes sociales,* Paris: Maspéro, 1968, pp. 72-75. Poulantzas writes that "A social formation consists in an overlapping of several modes of production one of which dominates. As a result, one confronts more classes than in the 'pure' mode of production." —SM

of production, although dominant for a century and a half, has left considerable fractions of the population in a marginal position) the last fifteen years have been marked by a considerable enlargement of the space in which the union movement functions. Unions of students, teachers, civil servants, cadres and farmers have developed as parasites of labor unionism, borrowing the essential mechanisms of conflictual participation which it developed (collective negotiations, constitution of pressure groups making their weight felt on the State).

The Fourth French Republic, and Christian Democracy in Italy, excelled for years in using the unions of the middle strata as instruments of stabilization. That practice has failed because of the needs of the growth process of the productive forces themselves. One after the other, these buffer-unions were led, with the integration of their masses into the capitalist mode of production, to enter into conflict with capitalism *at the same time liberating* the revolutionary potentialities of labor unionism. It is at its margins, through the revolt of the proletarianized and petit-bourgeois strata, that unionism has been forced to break with the quiet habits of conflictual participation: there is no longer a buffer between the capitalist class and the labor movement.

Since then, we are witnessing an evolution which has still barely begun of a unionism which is obliged to take into account not only the "immediate interests" of the *directly productive workers* but also, in the last analysis, those of *the majority of the population*. That evolution will exhaust the possibilities of compromise that the bourgeosie can accept. Unionism thus can no longer do without an "offensive" strategy, aiming directly at the nature of class power—a strategy whose broad lines the Seventh Congress of the *CGIL* at Livorno sketched when it proclaimed "the necessity of the transformation of every victorious demand into a conquest not merely unionist but society-wide through a displacement of the relation of forces in the firms and the country."[57]

A Differentiated and Articulated Strategy

Because of the heterogeneity of the social forces who are undertaking this offensive strategy by means of which all enter into conflict with the capitalist mode of production from totally different and divergent starting points and situations (including the level of consciousness), that strategy can only be a *differentiated* one. The active and direct participation of the workers in the struggle, the development of union democracy at the base, can only go in the

---

57. A. Novella, Closing address [at the Seventh Congress of the *CGIL*]. —SM

direction of specific actions that are suited to the organic reality of the sector of the capitalist mode of production where they work. The struggle for workers' control at the *SNPA* at Lacq, and that of the immigrant street cleaners in Paris are both exemplary struggles *whose complementarity is, however, only definable in terms of an overall strategy*, thus a political strategy, which tends to prevent the system from recovering on the one hand what it has lost on the other.

To arbitrarily unify these struggles by general slogans given from the top is to unify nothing. On the contrary, any attempt to homogenize the demands can only lead to their reduction to the lowest common denominator, that is, to abstract demands which are easily "cooptable" by the bourgeoisie and from which the workers no longer expect anything. *But the differentiated strategy must also be an "articulated" one*, otherwise it will run into the dead-end of demands limited to a single category; that is, it must insure *the communicativity of the demands for control of each group with the others*, permit the enlarging of successes won in one sector to another sector, maintain the conquests won by the workers in the face of the attempts to coopt them by management or the bourgeois state.

That strategy can thus only be political, that is, continually refer *to the overall situation of the class struggle* in the country, to the given relation of forces, to the analysis of the contradictions between the mode of production and the present social formation, thus to the social and political contradictions.

Two errors are born from the necessity for the union to have an overall political strategy as a necessary synthesis of broadly differentiated tactics: and those errors are what, in the new conditions, make the problem of the Party-Unions relation insoluble today.

Elite Theories and Modern Anarcho-Syndicalism

The first error is the one which developed following May 1968 in a certain number of "ultra-leftist" groups which organized themselves principally *outside* the working class, and based themselves on the experience of the student movement after May 68. The error consists in denying all revolutionary potentiality to the union organization itself, which is considered as inexorably "integrated" into capitalist society. The abusive use of this term "integration" is, incidentally, highly significant. The worker in industry has never, individually or collectively, asked whether he was or was not "integrated" into the capitalist mode of production: he knows by a wholly empirical experience that he is a constitutive part of this mode of production;

there can be no capitalist mode of production without the working class, and vice-versa. (In the scientific sense of the term, the notion of "working class" changes its content the day when the passage to socialism is realized. "The first act by which the working class establishes itself as the ruling class is also the act by which it negates itself as proletariat.") *It is precisely because it is integrated into the capitalist mode of production* by its physical being, by nature, *that the working class is revolutionary*: it has no other choice. The elements of the middle and petit bourgeoisie who are being proletarianized have an understandable, but not at all "Marxist" tendency to transcend the objective conditions that transform them into semi-proletarians by an ideological choice, an existential "act of freedom." It is more in conformity with the nature of intellectuals whose origins *and* education is petit-bourgeois to refuse nobly to be the "future cadres of the exploitative society" than to recognize modestly that four-fifths of them will go to reinforce the ranks of that "proletaroid intelligentsia" of which Max Weber spoke already, and which the workers of the time called more simply "proletarians in white collars."

Wanting to be radical, but misunderstanding the nature of the complex ties between the working class and its organizations—no matter how bureaucratic they are—this critique misses the real problem, that of aiding unionism in adapting itself to the new *conditions of struggle by means of a constant ideological struggle which enriches itself from the concrete experiences of the workers.* Blanquist urges or Leninist doctrinairism, in different forms, exhibit an identical content: they assert, through the critique of opportunist deviations of unions and other organizations, *the hegemony of a petit-bourgeois, self-proclaimed "revolutionary vanguard"* over an unconscious working class to whom the light can only be brought from the exterior (whether that light be given it by "exemplary action" or by bookish indoctrination).

But this external critique vitalized, in reaction to it, another conception, much more dangerous because it finds a favorable arena within the working class: that of *a union organization setting itself up as a political party.* This is a tendency which the particularities of the French situation, with the determining weight of the Communist Party committed by its international conceptions to the status quo, have only reinforced, and which appears as the expression of what today may be the central kernel of the working class—those employed in the advanced industries.

Conscious of the necessity of an overall union strategy, this conception tends to reject not only any notion of the union as a transmission belt, but even every political organization of the working class, tending to reduce the political party to a sort of particular sector of the union movement. Looking at the positions defended notably by Edmond Maire of the *CFDT* or by Maurice Labi of *Force ouvrière*, one sees the resurgence of a modern anarcho-syndicalism, founded like the old one on the hegemonic preeminence of the most advanced part of the skilled working class, those who hold the essential weight in the decisive sectors of production. Experience has shown the limits of that conception: it suffers from the same gaps as the theory of Rosa Luxemburg, in this case transposing the conditions of a fraction of the working class, be it strategically the most important, to the whole class, whereas the Polish theoretician saw a non-existent homogeneity of the class.

To the mechanistic conception of an intellectual vanguard bringing a political consciousness from the outside, by propagandistic action or revolutionary witness, to a homogeneous working class is opposed, in just as mechanistic a manner, that of an autonomous political expression of the vanguard kernel of the working class introducing its hegemony by means of the weapons it derives from its position in the relations of production themselves. *It is true that, in the last analysis, fifteen per cent of the French working class could block the mechanism of production. The confusion is not here, in the assertion of the decisive strategic and tactical role of the new working class in the revolutionary process*—it is not on this point, as one can imagine, that I would criticize the militants of the chemical or petroleum industries. *But it is in the underestimation of the internal antagonisms of the working class, as of those of the proletarianized strata among themselves and in relation to the working class.*

It is not sufficient to explain neo-anarcho-syndicalism by assiduously repeating the famous aphorism of Lenin: "The working class cannot spontaneously get to anything but trade unionism consciousness." The approach of the union organizations representing the new working classes—just like that of the old anarcho-syndicalism of the skilled workers—certainly rises to political consciousness. *But it does so through a theoretical schema which is "pure" and abstract: new working class vs. neo-capitalism. And in so doing, it isolates itself in relation to the real social formation* which is composed at once of advanced sectors and condemned branches, of new social strata inserted in the most developed processes of production and of vast populations who are so fearfully passing through the first phases of industrial accumulation —and these contradictions exist even within the same firm.

The direct passage from "trade union consciousness"—that is, the necessity of slowing down the process of exploitation—to political consciousness—that is, the necessity of abolishing the mode of production and its political system in order to stop the exploitation—is possible, and one can find numerous examples of it, in those firms with a high rate of organic composition of capital, where the anonymity of a management integrated into the productive ensemble facilitates the recognition of the relations of the system of exploitation to the state more than is the case in the "personalized firm."

But a homogeneity of conditions leading to a class consciousness does not exist. *There is not even—and there cannot directly be—a common consciousness of the society to be constructed. The revolt against the political power and the state by the proletarianized strata of the old middle classes,* that of the sub-proletarians of foreign origin or of the lowest strata of the national proletariat, *consists more in a pre-capitalist, agrarian nostalgia, reflecting itself faithfully enough in a neo-Christian ideology with Maoist tinges, than in a coherent vision of the socialist community of labor built on the basis of the enormous productive potential accumulated by the capitalist system.*

At the level of the union movement, *whose theoretical reflection cannot but formulate itself in terms of lived practice because of its structures and the nature of its insertion in society, the synthesis of the potential revolutionary factors cannot be achieved because it implies the theoretical transcendence of lived practice. It is at this level, that is at the level of the transcendence of the "contradictions within the people," that the irreplaceable role of the political, revolutionary party continues to be situated.*

But it is self-evident that *the capacity of the party to play this role of the collective intellectual which transforms into a vision of the future the consciousness of the lived alienations depends on its deep involvement in the social formation at the points where the contradictions express themselves.* The role of the party and that of the union do not fuse into one, but they must both be located in the same place! The initiative of the *PSU,* pushing the theme of workers' control in the firms, replied in part to an internal preoccupation: to involve the party in the field of real struggles.

A Party in the Firm

Since the month of May, 1968, the *PSU* has developed in a more spontaneous than organized manner inside the firms. In making this axis of development its issential preoccupation, the *PSU* is clearly seeking—and does not try to conceal it—to profoundly modify the social composition of a party more than fifty percent of whose troops, before May 68, were recruited among the ranks of the teaching corps, students, and civil servants.

But beyond that objective, it is also clear that it intends to carry out a radical transformation in its forms of organization. Already in 1960, the *PSU* had analyzed the process of formation of neo-capitalism, and had drawn two conclusions: the first was that, given the intervention of the state in the economy, there could no longer be economic struggles which were not at the same time political struggles—and vice-versa; the second was that the parliamentary system had become totally unsuited to perform the function of directing the society which the liberal bourgeoisie had assigned to it, and that it was an "empty shell" which nowhere had a real part in the important decisions.

However, the forms of organization of the *PSU* remained essentially unchanged in relation to those that it has inherited through the *PSA* and its Social Democratic heritage. Giving weight to the local section and the departmental Federation, permitting only a diminished party organization within the firm,[58] giving no political coordination to the struggles waged in different sectors or in a sector which was geographically dispersed, the organizational structures of the *PSU* in fact privileged the petty bourgeois elements in participation in political activity and in the assumption of positions of responsibility within the party. That social composition, in fact, was less that of the party strictly speaking—which always had had a certain number of workers as members—than that of its middle-ranking cadres. And one can only admit that this social composition played its role in the face that the party too often showed to the outside, which went caricaturally from opportunist practice to ultra-leftist phraseology. Forced to theoretically justify its autonomous existence—as a current—alongside of Social Democracy and the *PC*, the *PSU* little by little elaborated a new ideological platform and, on many points, was the first to deepen the analysis of the new contradictions of modern capitalist society. But like the good old Social Democratic parties, the tendency was too often to render formal homage to the theory "created in the sky" and not at all to take it into account in practical politics.

But, from this point of view, 1968 constituted a decisive rupture. Certainly, at the same time that it encouraged the return to a serious reading of the classics of Marxism—which is positive—the May Movement exacerbated, within the *PSU* as well as elsewhere, the dogmatic tendencies which are always the temptation of neophytes.

---

58.   The company-level groups that are recognized by the statues of the party did not have the fight of political deliberation in the official assemblies of the Party. —SM

But precisely these tendencies, on which the observers of the Congress of Dijon[59] particularly insisted, are not at all the attitudes of the workers in the party, whose representation at the rostrum of the Congress is always numerically small, but of the semi-intellectual elements who are at ease in the practice and style of such ritual conventions.

On the other hand, the May Movement also gave the *PSU* an important foothold in the firms for the first time in its history. The history of these groups, "born in May," is in fact very often significant: they were formed mainly by militants who did not belong previously to the *PSU* or who sometimes even only learned of its existence by the attacks of the adversary—I should say, the adversaries. Born in the struggle on the level of the firms, these groups intended to continue to make them their principal field of activity; and if they intervene on the local political scene, it is starting from the firm, and not the inverse as had been the rule in the past. The coordination and the extension of these groups, at the level of the sector of activity, the region, trust or industrial branch confronts the *PSU* today as an objective need posed by life itself. And it is evident that a reflection on the organizational structure of the Party flows naturally from this, a structure which will, in the end, radically transform the nature of the Party itself and give it a new face. This party structured on the basis of the arenas of struggle—enterprise sector, farm sector founded on the basis of the regrouping of integrated peasants and food industry workers, and university sector founded on the common practice of an activity which indirectly produces surplus-value—should be capable, and is alone capable of refracting the image of the diverse contradictions through which the old social formation is breaking up, and a new one is forming, modelled entirely by organization capitalism.

Union and Party in the Firm

But the foundation of the party on the basis of the arenas of struggle cannot without danger lead the party organizations to substitute themselves for the union organizations, to lead the struggles in their place, including times when these struggles are political—and the struggles for workers' control are always fundamentally political.

At this precise stage of social development in our country, marked at once by the rapid evolution of the process of concentration and by the resistances of the archaeo-capitalist structures, the union and the party have two *differentiated* and *complementary* functions: *it is through the union organization, if adapted to the new conditions*

---

59.   March, 1969; the Sixth Congress of the *PSU*. [Since Mallet wrote this article a major and several minor splits have occurred in the *PSU*, the major one costing it a large number of intellectuals and workers who went over to Trotskyism.]

that we have analyzed above, that the masses will act, that the resistance to capitalist oppression of the diverse parts of the exploited strata will express itself in its specificity. From this point of view, to subordinate the union, which is the organization of the entire class, to the decisions of the party, which is only a part of the class, would be a monumental stupidity which would isolate the party not only from the "masses," as the saying goes, but quite simply from the reality of the class struggle.

But, for the moment, and until the working class is recomposed and homogenized—a process which in fact already implies the changing of the mode of production—*it is only through the party, that is, through the organization which is freely adopted by the fraction of workers who have understood the necessity of inserting their critical challenge of the capitalist mode of production into the perspective of a radical change of the socio-economic model, that the synthesis of the diverse attacks carried on by the masses from different angles can be elaborated.*

To give this role to the union would be to force it to renounce its supple strategy, to lead it to reduce the diverse struggles to one unifying model which implies total success, whereas in fact it is necessary to have an organization to wage not only *defensive struggles* (the role in which the present unionism in fact shuts itself up), but also partial offensive struggles, struggles which must be terminated by armistices.

It is vain to try to trace rigid frontiers between the action of a party that is organized in the firms and sectors of production and a union organization whose offensive struggles will have a marked political character. It is probable that in many circumstances the party will be tempted to take the place of the faltering union—that is what happened in Northern Italy, where the political groups animated union struggles of a new type which the union organization later took over and conducted to their conclusion. On the other hand, in a firm where there is no political organization, the union will be tempted to take on its functions. The essential thing is that the two functions— that of the organization of the masses through which their action is structured, and that of the party, which informs the masses and resituates the partial struggles within the overall conjuncture which gives the offensive actions their ultimate goals—operate effectively, *at the same time and the same place.*

The distinction between the party and the union thus appears simply as the form taken by the division of labor in the class struggle. A division of labor which cannot be transcended overnight.

This conception of the Party-Union relation, based on a new

practice of union organization and a new type of party, obviously entails some consequences with reference to the present situation: the most important[60] is obviously the passage from the *elite, minority* union to the mass union; and this in turn implies the realization of *one union* [in place of the several presently competing in France]. The resolution of the Seventh Congress of the Italian *CGIL* quite correctly concluded its elaboration of a new union policy with that demand. Their analysis and their conclusion could be taken over in France nearly word for word: "The impetuous development of the movement, the positive and generalized experience of the unity of action among the unions, the new forms of direct participation of the workers in the elaboration of the objectives, in the definition of the forms of struggle, and in conducting the negotiations, the entry into action of important new masses of workers in the South and in the North; the construction and the conquest of sophisticated instruments to be used by a united union power; the perspective of asserting a more advanced and specific political role of the union — all this has opened a new phase in the relations among union organizations. The recent development of experiences in unity creates the need to attain, in concrete and immediate terms, the objective of organic unity. All future action, in particular the big contractual struggles, should lead us also to effect a resolute leap ahead concerning the content of our unitary relations, creating those unitary instruments of organization and direction of the struggle on different levels, from the factory to the policy within the locality, from the "Chambres du Travail" to organizations of each specific category of workers. All of these instruments must express the creative capacity of the workers. The struggles of these past years, and the experiences in unity that have developed, have inaugurated a process renewing all the components of the Italian union situation, and have affirmed the class line which characterizes the new phase of the united process. That need for union unity corresponds to the deepest aspirations of the workers, and becomes more and more the common patrimony of the diverse union forces."

The realization of a united mass unionism, and the existence of a permanent political discussion at the level of the firm — because there will be political pluralism in the majority of the factories — are today, in the concrete conditions of the class struggle in Western Europe, the two arms that the workers' movement must give itself in order to move towards victory.

---

60. The French text is incomplete on the "lessons." On a letter to D.H., Mallet notes that "the second [lesson] is the existence of a permanent political discussion in the enterprise. . .as indicated in the discussion of 'a party in the enterprise' above."

Glossary

ACCORDS DE PROGRES: See Contrats de Progrés.

ALLIANCE DES JEUNES POUR LE SOCIALISME (AJS): Formerly the FER (Fédération d'Etudiants Révolutionnaires), established by the CLER (Committée de Liaison d'Etudiants Révolutionnaires), itself born in 1961 from the Lambertist group of the Trotskyists. Critical of the stance of the NLF in Vietnam. Opposed participation in the barricades struggle of May 10-11, 1968.

ARGUMENTS: Journal in which many ex-communist party left-intellectuals published during the late 1950s and early 1960s. Its chief editors were Axelos, Degar, Duvignaud and Morin. The issue of January-March, 1959 (Vol. III, Nos. 12-13) was partially devoted to the problem of the nature of the New Working Class, and contained articles by Mottez, Touraine, Mallet, Mothé, Le Brun, Barjonet, Detraz, Collinet, Dofny and Crozier.

BARJONET, André: Former secretary of the Centre D'Etudes Economiques et Sociales of the CGT, and the best known theorist of the PCF in industrial sociology. In May 68, he quit his post with the CGT and quit the PCF, publishing a pamphlet justifying this action by a critique of the PCF's unwillingness to move forward to seize power. Joined the PSU, and is presently in charge of its section dealing with the Comités d'enterprise.

BASLY, the Indomitable Miner: A well known leader of the miner's union at the turn of the century. Remembered because of an anarcho-syndicalist song, "Le grand meetingue de grand Métropolitain," which has since been made into a commercial record.

BEDAUX, Charles: French engineer who developed a more modernized form of Taylorism still much used today.

BETHEL SCHOOL: The National Training Laboratories at Bethel, Maine, which have been influential in the spread of sensitivity training.

BORINAGE STRIKES: Belgian mining region which in 1959 and 1961 witnessed a series of strikes of an insurrectional character with occupation of the centers of power, barricades, etc. The movement spread to the iron and steel factories of Liège, but after 3-4 months, due to the weakness of Belgian socialism and its incapacity to pick up the ball, it gradually dissolved.

BULL: Compagnie des Machines Bull. The leading French entry in the race to develop computers. In 1964, due to lack of funds, it had to sell a large part of its stock to General Electric, despite De Gaulle's purported desire to keep French companies French. One of the three studies in *La nouvelle classe ouvrière* is devoted to Bull. A new French entry into the computer market was later founded, only to be fused with Bull in 1975 when its small size proved too great an obstacle to further development.

CEA: Commission de l'Enérgie Atomique (Atomic Energy Commission).

CFDT (Confédération Française Démocratique du Travail): Emerged from a split in the CFTC (Confédération Française des Travailleurs Chrétiens) due to its recognition of the need for class struggle. Open to many different tendencies, it is the national union in which the PSU and other radical groups tend to work.

CGIL (Confederazione generale italiana del Lavoro): equivalent to the French CGT, though not so thoroughly dominated by the Communist Party.

CGT (Confédération Générale du Travail): Largest French union, communist dominated, though open to non-communists. Its history predates the founding of the Communist Party, which split from it in 1921 forming the CGTU, and reunited with it in 1936.

CGTU (Confédération Générale du Travail Unitaire): the minority (community) element in the split of 1921, which rejoined the CGT in 1936.

CHABAN-DELMAS, Jacques: Prime Minister under Pompidou until June, 1972. His regime was marked by numerous scandals within the ruling Gaullist party (including the revelation that he had paid no income taxes). Candidate for President of the Republic after Pompidou's death, but severely defeated.

FORT CHABROL: At the defense of Verdun, 1916, French troops resisted here to the last man, despite their encirclement.

CHARBONNERIE: French equivalent of the Italian Carbonari. Clandestine Republican groups at the time of the Restoration, composed mainly of petit-bourgeois.

CHARLETY: Stadium where, on May 27, a large meeting of the non-communist left was held, despite a ban on public meetings. The order and organization of the crowd, and the slogans for a new student-worker-peasant power created great fear in the government, as did the crowd's recognition of Mendés-France, who did not speak publicly but was being considered as an interim leader of the revolutionary government.

CLAUSEWITZ, Carl von: Prussian general whose posthumous work, *On War* (1832), was profoundly influential during the 19th and 20th centuries partly due to statements like the famous "war is the continuation of diplomacy by other means."

COLBERTISM: French form of Mercantilism developed by Colbert, finance minister under Louis XIV, who was responsible for development of an economic system based on state intervention through state spending and bookkeeping.

COMPAGNONS: workers of a syndicalist and a-political bent whom the petit-bourgeoisie attempted to integrate in the 19th century.

CONTRATS DE PROGRES: Procedure developed in 1969 by Jacques Delors, then the "social counselor" to the cabinet of Chaban-Delmas. A regular increase in wages based on the increase of productivity is built into the contract. Consequently, strikes during the period of the contract were to be eliminated. The first such contract was at the Gaz de France, the second at Berliet in Lyon. But in both cases, the procedure was quickly questioned, and the form has not developed.

CRS: Companies Républicaines de Sécurité. Created by the (socialist) Minister of the Interior in 1945, the CRS are a kind of national police force whose role includes a variety of civil tasks (life-guards, etc.), but whose main political function is indicated by the slogan from May 1968: CRS equals SS.

DEBRE, Michel: De Gaulle's first Prime Minister, replaced by Pompidou after the Algerian War, he went to the Ministry of Finance, then to that of Foreign Affairs.

DEWENDEL: A large steel producer in Eastern France.

DGB: Deutsche Gewerkschaftsbund. The umbrella organization of the German Trade Unions functioning similarly to the AFL-CIO in the U.S.

DIETZGEN, Josef: A German worker and social-democrat who in the 1870s and 1880s arrived independently at some principles common to Marxist theory.

DRU, Jean: Leader of the so-called "Jean-Dru revisionist group" in the PCF which, under this collective pseudonym published in 1962 *Le Pari démocratique* and in 1965, *L'Etat socialiste*. Their views were close to those of the Italian leader Giorgo Amendola, insisting on the necessity of going beyond both reformism and Leninism.

EDF: Eléctricité de France (sometimes referred to by Mallet as the EDF-gdf), a state-owned monopoly.

EUROPE 1: Radio station located outside France but broadcasting in it; privately run, and hence often more lively and critical than the state-owned ORTF. Played an important role in May 1968 by virtue of the reports of its roving reporters whose activity permitted those demonstrating, as well as their audience, to know what was happening in different locations. Hence, the government refused to let the reporters use the air-waves, though the station stayed on the air by using telephoned reports instead.

FEN: Fédération de l'éducation nationale. Brings together the unions of the primary (SNI), secondary (SNES), technical (SNET) and university (SNESup) teachers. Not affiliated with any of the national unions, it includes most teaching personnel except those belonging to the Christian union (SGEN) which is affiliated with the CFDT.

FGDS: Fédération de la Gauche démocrate socialiste. non-communist socialist reunification under the direction of François Mitterand which pretended to be the true opposition force to the Gaullists by attempting unity with the PCF. Its irrelevance was shown in May 1968, though since that time the attempt at united action with the Communists has gone further and been more (electorally) successful, as witnessed by Mitterand's near-victory in the 1974 elections.

FO: Force Ouvrière. Originally founded after a split in the CGT (with the aid of the CIA) to represent a "democratic" alternative, it is still the most conservative and craft-oriented, business-unionist, and non-political of the three major Franch unions. However, since it is small and somewhat open, militants of Trotskyist, Maoist and Anarchist leanings often join it, and even control some of its Federations. Cf. the activity of M. Labi.

FOCILLON, Henri: French aesthetician at the Collège de France, published *La vie des forms* (1947), containing a "praise of the hand."

FOUCHET, Christian: Minister of the Interior at the time of May 1968, after having been Minister of Education from 1964-67, and elaborating the famous Fouchet Plan for "rationalizing" the University through processes of selection, etc. The coincidence of his holding these posts successively could not be unremarked by the students in May 1968.

LA GAUCHE PROLETARIENNE: Maoist group emerging from May 1968 after the banning of the UJC-ML. Active in some factories, their form of Maoism (not recognized by the Chinese) is called "Mao-spontex." Their best known leader, A. Geismar, played a key role in May 1968 befor joining them, was later jailed for incendiary remarks; their newspaper, *La cause du peuple* had two of its editors jailed before Sartre took over its direction (legally, not politically). They were for a time the largest Maoist group in France.

GDF: Gaz de France. Cf. EDF.

GRENELLE ACCORDS: Signed May 27 between the striking unions (CGT, CFDT) and the Patronat, after the mediation of the government. They granted large wage hikes but little else. When Séguy, the leader of the CGT, brought the accords back to the Renault workers at Billancourt, he was jeered and the strike continued. The historical parallel of the Grenelle agreements is the Matignon Agreements of 1936, which ended the General Strike of that year.

GRIFFEULHES, Victor: 1874-1923. Revolutionary syndicalist, Secretary of the CGT from 1902-1909.

L'HUMANITE: daily newspaper of the PCF.

ISST: Institut des Sciences Sociales du Travail. A sociological research group run by the government and directed by Jean-Daniel Raynaud.

KAUTSKY, Karl: Leader of the German Social Democratic Party and the voice of socialist theory and orthodoxy after Engels' death. His orthodoxy implied a radical rhetoric, though his politics were centrist, ultimately reflecting back into his theory as well.

KUN, Bela: Hungarian Communist leader of the Councils Republic of 1919. Later international militant for the Third International in Germany, Spain, etc.

LAFARGUE, Paul: French Socialist leader, best known for his pamphlet, "The Right to be Lazy," and as one of the leaders of the Second International explicitly excluded from the Third International in the "21 Conditions" because of his stance during the War.

LASALLE, Ferdinand: Philosopher, lawyer, politician. Friend of Marx's in the 1848 "League of Communists." 1862-64, a popular labor organizer, founding the General Association of German Workers (ADAV) which was united with the Marxian Eisenach group at Gotha in 1875. Differed from Marx on the role of the state and the function of cooperative societies; believed that socialism could be introduced by parliamentary reforms.

MATIGNON accords (1936): After the victory of the Popular Front in the elections of 1936, a general strike broke out with factory occupations. Negotiations at the residence of the Prime Minister (Matignon) conducted by the victorious socialist L. Blum, ended the strikes with pay increases, increased union recognition, and the principle of the 40 hour week. Still discontented, workers wanted more; and were greeted by the famous reply of M. Thorez (PCF leader): "Il faut savoir terminer une grève."

MENDES-FRANCE, Pierre: Former Prime Minister under the IVth Republic who concluded French involvement in Vietnam. Respected for his honesty and his technical abilities. Member of the right wing of the PSU in May 1968, he was suggested as a temporary leader for a provisional government because of his wide acceptibility. He has since quit the PSU and functions as part of a technocratic element within the socialist party (PS).

MOTHE, Daniel: Pseudonym. A self-educated worker at the Renault factory, a Trotskyist during the Resistance, and later active in the group "Socialisme ou Barbarie." Presently works with the CFDT and, having been injured in the factory, as a sociologist. Author of many articles as well as two important books: *Militant chez Renault* and *Journal d'un ouvrier*.

PANNEKOEK, Anton: Dutch left-communist, active in Germany before World War I; critical of the Bolshevik politics and those of the Third

International for their suppression of the workers' councils, Pannekoek was viciously attacked by Lenin in "Left-Wing Communism: An Infantile Disorder." Pannekoek remained theoretically active in the Council Communist movement through his death in 1960.

POTTIER, Eugène: Worker and poet. Author of the poem from which the "Internationale," the song of the workers' movement, was created.

PSA: Parti Socialiste Autonme, constituted by a split in the SFIO in 1958, led by Dupreux, Verdier, Tanguy-Prigent, Mayer, etc. Joined by Mendés-France in 1959. Joined with the UGS (Union de la Gauche Socialiste), itself a formation of several currents (left socialists like G. Martinet and C. Bourdet; a part of the Heune République; and Left Catholics). The latter were the larger group. They united to form the PSU in 1960.

PSI: Partito Socialista Italiano. One of the Italian socialist parties.

PSU: Parti socialiste unifié. Emerged from the "New Left" which grew out of opposition to the Algerian War and to the PCF's incapacity to pose an alternative to Gaullism. Known particularly for the intellectual perspicacity of its analyses and programs, it was of little importance until May 1968 when it was able to use its close contacts with the UNEF (whose officers were members) to take an advanced position during the struggle. Was and remains divided between left-technocrats, leftists trying the parliamentary road, and other factions, though it recently (1973) purged its Trotskyist and Maoist elements.

PTT: Postes, Télégraphs et Téléphones, a state monopoly directed by a minister.

POUJADISME: Movement of small shopkeepers reacting to the interference of the state in their affairs, and the competition of big business, named for its leader in the 1950s, Pierre Poujade. Perceived by some to represent a strong "fascist" threat during the period of the Algerian War. A similar movement re-emerged in the 1960s, and continues (under the leadership of G. Nicoud), though without the Algerian situation it is less of a threat.

SEGUY, Georges: Member of the Central Committee of the PCF, and Secretary-General of the CGT. Had only just come to office in the CGT in May 1968. His baptism of fire came with the Grenelle Accords and their rejection.

SGEN: Syndicat Général de l'Education Nationale. Affiliated with the CFDT. Cf. FEN.

SIK, Ota: Czechoslovak economist and reformer whose ideas played a key role in the "Prague Spring" of 1968.

SNECMA: Société Nationale d'Etudes et de Construction de Moteurs d'Avions, formerly the firm Gnôme et Rhône, nationalized in 1945.

THOREZ, Maurice: Leader of the PCF from the 1930s through his death in 1964. Spent the war years in Moscow. Built the party from a small quarrelsome sect to a major and disciplined social force. Of strict Stalinist obedience.

TOURS CONGRESS (and Split), 1920: Meeting of the French Socialist Party (SFIO) which had to decide whether to adhere to the Third International and accept the 21 Conditions (among which were demands for the exclusion of pre-war leaders who had supported the war, demands for obedience to Moscow, clandestinity, etc.; in short, Bolshevisation). Frossard and Cachin led the pro-Third International forces, Blum and Longuet the anti's. After the Zinoviev Telegram and a clandestine appearance by Clara Zetkin, the vote for adherence was 3-1, creating a split in the Left.

UDR: Union Démocratique Républicain, the Gaullist Party after 1958.

UNEF: Union Nationale des Etudiants de France. Student union which took the lead in organizing opposition to the Algerian War. Its strength was eaten away after the war by quarreling of sects, government interference with its subsidies, and the contradictions of being a left student movement. Though there existed right wing student movements (both political and corporativist, like the FNEF), the UNEF's claim to represent all students permitted it to play an important role in May 1968.

URSSAF: Union de Recovrement de Sécurite Sociale et Caisse de Sécurité Sociale et Allocations Familiales.

VIERZON STRIKES: Famous strikes in the early 20th century which, finally beaten, left one worker as a holdout, refusing to go back to work until the union told him so. That one worker became a symbol and slogan for those engaged in strike support.

WALDECK-ROCHET: Secretary-General of the PCF after the death of Thorez. Ill during May 1968, he played little role then or thereafter; and has since given up his position to Georges Marchais.

WEITLING, Wilhelm: German artisan and autodidact. Author of several works cited by Marx as marking the beginning of the self-emancipation of the working class. Quarrelled with Marx in 1846 after he had turned to an apocalyptic vision of the future emancipation tinged with Christian overtones. Emigrated to the U.S. in 1848.

ZINOVIEV TELEGRAM: Sent by Zinoviev, Lenin, Trotsky, Bukharin and Rosmer to the Tours Congress, it was referred to by those who opposed the Third International and its Bolshevisation as a "ukase," telling the French Communists to split or else.